☞ **W9-CQZ-890**

DISCARDED

The Vietnam War

Other Books in the Turning Points Series:

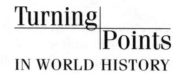

Turning Points

IN WORLD HISTORY

The Vietnam War

Diane Yancey, *Book Editor*

David L. Bender, *Publisher*
Bruno Leone, *Executive Editor*
Bonnie Szumski, *Editorial Director*
Stuart B. Miller, *Managing Editor*

Greenhaven Press, Inc., San Diego, California

Every effort has been made to trace the owners of copyrighted material. The articles in this volume may have been edited for content, length, and/or reading level. The titles have been changed to enhance the editorial purpose.

Library of Congress Cataloging-in-Publication Data

The Vietnam War/Diane Yancey, book editor.
    p. cm.—(Turning points in world history)
  Includes bibliographical references and index.
  ISBN 0-7377-0613-9 (pbk.: alk. paper)—
  ISBN 0-7377-0614-7 (lib. bdg.: alk. paper)
    1. Vietnamese conflict, 1961–1975—United States. I. Yancey, Diane. II. Turning points in world history (Greenhaven Press).

DS558 .V557 2001
959.704'3373—dc21   00-042169
                                                          CIP

Cover photo: © Bettmann/Corbis

Library of Congress, 143
U.S. Army/Harry S. Truman Library, 50

©2001 by Greenhaven Press, Inc.
P.O. Box 289009, San Diego, CA 92198-9009

Printed in the U.S.A.

Contents

Chapter 1: The First Vietnam War

One of the most important figures in Vietnamese history,
Ho Chi Minh embraced communism early in his turbulent lifetime. By 1941, he was determined to wrest control of Vietnam from the hands of outside oppressors.

In the late 1940s and early 1950s, France waged a long
and bitter war to retain control of Vietnam. Unable to
comprehend the motivations and covert fighting prac-
tices of the Vietnamese, it was eventually defeated.

The emergence of global communism gave rise to the
domino theory, the belief that a chain reaction would
occur if free nations fell to the Communists. Allegiance
to the domino theory motivated American policymakers
to become involved in the fight against communism in
South Vietnam.

Chapter 2: America Steps In

The United States provided significant support to the
South Vietnamese as they fought North Vietnamese
Communists in the early 1960s. Greater American involvement seemed inevitable, and predictions were that
the conflict would be long and frustrating.

In the early 1960s, America's dissatisfaction with South
Vietnam's president Ngo Dinh Diem and his anti-
Communist regime grew. The Kennedy administration's

tacit support of a military coup led to Diem's assassination and the subsequent instability of the government of South Vietnam.

Chapter 3: America Fights a Losing War

years of war. The quick collapse of the Army of the Republic of Vietnam emphasized its essential weakness and the important role the U.S. military played during its tenure in Southeast Asia.

Foreword

Certain past events stand out as pivotal, as having effects and outcomes that change the course of history. These events are often referred to as turning points. Historian Louis L. Snyder provides this useful definition:

> A turning point in history is an event, happening, or stage which thrusts the course of historical development into a different direction. By definition a turning point is a great event, but it is even more—a great event with the explosive impact of altering the trend of man's life on the planet.

History's turning points have taken many forms. Some were single, brief, and shattering events with immediate and obvious impact. The invasion of Britain by William the Conqueror in 1066, for example, swiftly transformed that land's political and social institutions and paved the way for the rise of the modern English nation. By contrast, other single events were deemed of minor significance when they occurred, only later recognized as turning points. The assassination of a little-known European nobleman, Archduke Franz Ferdinand, on June 28, 1914, in the Bosnian town of Sarajevo was such an event; only after it touched off a chain reaction of political-military crises that escalated into the global conflict known as World War I did the murder's true significance become evident.

Other crucial turning points occurred not in terms of a few hours, days, months, or even years, but instead as evolutionary developments spanning decades or even centuries. One of the most pivotal turning points in human history, for instance—the development of agriculture, which replaced nomadic hunter-gatherer societies with more permanent settlements—occurred over the course of many generations. Still other great turning points were neither events nor developments, but rather revolutionary new inventions and innovations that significantly altered social customs and ideas, military tactics, home life, the spread of knowledge, and the human condition in general. The developments of writing, gunpowder, the printing press, antibiotics, the electric light, atomic energy, television, and the computer, the last two of which have recently ushered in the world-altering information age, represent only some of these innovative turning points.

Each anthology in the Greenhaven Turning Points in World History series presents a group of essays chosen for their accessibility. The anthology's structure also enhances this accessibility. First, an introductory essay provides a general overview of the principal events and figures involved, placing the topic in its historical context. The essays that follow explore various aspects in more detail, some targeting political trends and consequences, others social, literary, cultural, and/or technological ramifications, and still others pivotal leaders and other influential figures. To aid the reader in choosing the material of immediate interest or need, each essay is introduced by a concise summary of the contributing writer's main themes and insights.

In addition, each volume contains extensive research tools, including a collection of excerpts from primary source documents pertaining to the historical events and figures under discussion. In the anthology on the French Revolution, for example, readers can examine the works of Rousseau, Voltaire, and other writers and thinkers whose championing of human rights helped fuel the French people's growing desire for liberty; the French *Declaration of the Rights of Man and Citizen*, presented to King Louis XVI by the French National Assembly on October 2, 1789; and eyewitness accounts of the attack on the royal palace and the horrors of the Reign of Terror. To guide students interested in pursuing further research on the subject, each volume features an extensive bibliography, which for easy access has been divided into separate sections by topic. Finally, a comprehensive index allows readers to scan and locate content efficiently. Each of the anthologies in the Greenhaven Turning Points in World History series provides students with a complete, detailed, and enlightening examination of a crucial historical watershed.

Introduction

More than thirty years after its conclusion, the Vietnam War is remembered as one of the most complex and controversial events in U.S. history. Motivated by a fear of the spread of communism, the nation's leaders based foreign policy decisions on the assumption that weak governments throughout the world needed to be protected from conquest. In Vietnam, their efforts escalated from advice and monetary aid to full-scale combat with American troops doing the bulk of the fighting. Yet the United States never officially declared war in Vietnam and never adopted a winning strategy. Opposed by Vietnamese Communists who were willing to fight indefinitely to achieve their goals, the American government became bogged down in a conflict that came to be perceived as a colossal blunder, an impossible mess. "The [Johnson] administration vastly underestimated the enemy's capacity to resist . . . and did not confront the crucial question of what would be required to achieve its goals until it was bogged down in a bloody stalemate," observes historian George C. Herring.

The Vietnam War occurred because America believed it had a duty to fight communism during the Cold War. As the conflict progressed, and that conviction became lost in a tangle of arguments over what the war was, how it should be fought, and whether the United States was justified in being involved, it had to face the painful fact that its involvement in Southeast Asia was neither moral nor effectual. That realization sparked much pain and anguish. Nevertheless, important lessons were gleaned from the new awareness.

Turning Points in World History: The Vietnam War delineates those lessons as it traces the course of the war. It begins with Vietnam's struggle for independence and its eight-year conflict with France that foreshadowed America's involvement. It details Lyndon Johnson's war policies that produced division and disillusionment both at home and in the military. It focuses on Nixon's efforts to end the war, and the after-effects of the conflict on the United States. The articles, selected for readability and content, analyze the motivations of the leaders of the war as well as the historical ramifications of the conflict.

Like other titles in the Turning Point Series, this book has many features helpful to the student of history. Each volume begins with a historical overview of the subject, and each selection opens with an introduction that summarizes the arguments of the author and explains the historical context of the article. A detailed chronology lists the most significant events, and a selection of primary source documents provides additional observations, statements, and relevant excerpts.

Young readers have no direct memory of the Vietnam War and the turmoil it generated in the United States but a parent or family member who lived through the era may have shared personal reminiscences. The readings presented here are intended to give added insight into a turbulent time that helped define the twentieth century.

A Brief History of the Vietnam War

In 1947, President Harry Truman announced a policy of resistance to Communist aggression worldwide that became known as the Truman Doctrine. "I believe that it must be the policy of the United States to support free peoples who are resisting attempted subjugation by armed minorities or by outside pressures. I believe that we must assist free peoples to work out their own destinies in their own way," he stated in a speech before Congress on March 12th of that year.

Truman had no inkling that his policy would propel America into one of the longest and most devastating wars of the country's history. From 1947 through the 1980s, however, the fear of communism and a desire to contain its spread dominated U.S. foreign policy and motivated policymakers to support anti-Communist regimes throughout the world. In Vietnam, that support gradually escalated from financial aid and advice to full-scale military intervention between 1954 and 1973.

Communism and the Cold War

Communism, advanced by Karl Marx in the mid-1800s, was conceived as an economic system based on collective ownership and the organization of labor for the common good of all citizens. In the early 1900s the philosophy gained a significant following in Russia where an exploited working class dreamed of social improvement, but it soon evolved into a system of government wherein an authoritarian state wielded power and controlled the economy.

The Communist philosophy was not inherently violent, but it became identified with revolution, and its followers seemed ready to use force if necessary to expand their influence over non-Communist governments throughout the world. The Russian Empire (renamed the Union of Soviet Socialist Republics or USSR) came under Communist control during the Revolution of 1917. Eastern Europe fell to Soviet Communists shortly after World War II. At about the

13

same time Korean Communists gained power in North Korea, they attempted to seize South Korea in 1950. Mainland China fell to Communist revolutionaries in 1949. Communist dictator Fidel Castro gained control of Cuba in 1959, and threatened the United States with Soviet missiles in 1962.

The relationship between Communist and free countries was constantly tense and troubled between the end of World War II and the 1980s, a period called the Cold War. Communist governments and movements were seen as threats to democracy, and the United States believed that if one nation fell to communism, neighboring free nations were in danger of toppling "like a row of dominos." The Domino Theory seemed to explain Communist aggression and the unstable state of world affairs, at least to American policymakers such as Truman and his successors Presidents Dwight Eisenhower, John F. Kennedy, and Lyndon Johnson. The possibility of world war, perhaps worldwide Communist domination, looked very real, and containment was an imperative that could not be shirked or ignored.

America and Ho Chi Minh

When Vietnamese revolutionary Ho Chi Minh and his political organization, the Vietminh, seized control of parts of Vietnam and declared the nation's independence from France in 1945, policymakers in Washington, D.C., saw the move as another Communist takeover. In fact, Ho was as much a nationalist as he was a Communist. Vietnam had a long history of foreign rule, having been conquered and controlled by the Chinese, the French, and the Japanese (for a time during World War II). An adherent of Communist doctrines, Ho longed above all else for Vietnamese unity and freedom from outside invaders, and he was willing to accept aid from any country who would help further his nationalist objectives.

Ho looked to the United States as an ally for a time prior to the Cold War. He and the Vietminh rescued downed American pilots, located Japanese prison camps, and provided valuable intelligence information to the United States during World War II. In an effort to gain validation for his cause, Ho wrote several letters to President Truman, requesting that the United States recognize Vietnam's independence from the French.

Truman feared that Ho was a puppet of the Soviet Union and Communist China, so he ignored the revolutionary's pleas. Instead, determined that Vietnam should not fall under Communist rule, the president offered aid to the French who had controlled Indochina—Vietnam, Laos, and Cambodia—for almost a century before World War II, and were fighting to regain control in the postwar era. U.S. involvement in France's Indochina War from 1946 to 1954 was limited to supplying military equipment. After the French defeat at the Battle of Dien Bien Phu in 1954, however, President Dwight Eisenhower's administration determined that the United States should take greater responsibility for opposing Communist aggression in Vietnam.

The Geneva Accords

In the face of defeat in Indochina, France asked world powers to help devise a plan for its withdrawal from the region. Representatives from France, Great Britain, the USSR, China, the United States, Vietnam, Laos, and Cambodia met in Geneva, Switzerland, from May 8 to July 21, 1954, and drafted a set of agreements called the Geneva Accords. These provided for the removal of French forces, a temporary division of Vietnam at the 17th Parallel, the establishment of the Communist-led Democratic Republic of Vietnam in northern Vietnam, and the establishment of a French-sponsored regime headed by the last emperor of the Nguyen dynasty, Bao Dai, in the southern half of the country.

The Accords called for elections to be held throughout all of Vietnam by 1956. At that time, the country would unite under one government which would be elected by popular vote. Fearful that Ho Chi Minh's Communists might win that election, the United States refused to sign the Accords in 1954. Two months later, Secretary of State John Foster Dulles initiated the formation of the Southeast Asia Treaty Organization (SEATO), an alliance of nations (Australia,

France, Great Britain, New Zealand, Pakistan, the Philippines, Thailand, and the United States) dedicated to economic cooperation and the prevention of the spread of communism in Southeast Asia. SEATO was the doctrine by which the United States justified its involvement in South Vietnam in coming years.

The Truman administration encouraged South Vietnamese president Ngo Dinh Diem, who replaced Bao Dai as head of the anti-Communist regime in southern Vietnam in 1955, to refuse to participate in Geneva-sanctioned elections. Instead, Diem held elections only in southern Vietnam and won, although rumors of fraud abounded. With American support, Diem declared South Vietnam an independent nation, the Republic of Vietnam (RVN). Many Vietnamese saw the establishment of Diem and the RVN as unwarrantable interference by the United States.

Interim

Diem was a strong anti-Communist, but he was a far from perfect leader, and became increasingly repressive toward his people as time passed. A Catholic and an aristocrat, he made such unpopular moves as putting Catholics in positions of power, persecuting Buddhists (who made up 90 percent of the population), and taking land away from peasant farmers. He forcibly moved many villagers from their ancestral land into controlled communities (in an attempt to limit Communist activity) and drafted their sons into the Army of the Republic of Vietnam (ARVN). His policies caused many Vietnamese to turn to the Communist Party who promised them land and a greater say in government.

For a time Vietnamese Communists resisted initiating a full-scale armed struggle in South Vietnam, since they believed doing so would invite greater U.S. military involvement. By 1960, however, anti-Diem feelings were so powerful that Communist sympathizers in South Vietnam formed the National Liberation Front (NLF), a political organization sanctioned and supported by the North Vietnamese government. The NLF began training and equipping many South Vietnamese to take part in guerrilla warfare against

Diem and his supporters. Diem derogatorily called these South Vietnamese irregular forces "Viet Cong," a term similar to "Commies."

Increased Communist aggression had a predictable effect in South Vietnam. Conflict between the NLF and the ARVN increased, as did the number of U.S. military advisers sent to supervise the escalating violence. The Communists called their own activities "a war of national liberation," and emphasized their efforts to drive out a foreign power rather than their aim of bringing the entire country under Communist domination.

Coup D'Etat

Despite Diem's shortcomings, the United States supported him as an anti-Communist ally from 1955 to 1963. During John F. Kennedy's presidency, thousands of military advisers were sent to South Vietnam to help train the ARVN and to win back the loyalties of the South Vietnamese. When Kennedy took office in January 1961, only eight hundred advisers were in Vietnam; by November 1963 there were 16,700. Enormous American efforts built up the South Vietnamese military, but it remained relatively ineffective in combating Communist aggression, and the republic grew increasingly unstable.

By 1963, dissatisfaction with Diem reached a new high. His efforts to combat Communist rebel guerrillas were largely unsuccessful, and his policies toward his people were increasingly brutal. When Buddhists staged a protest demonstration, police were ordered to fire on the crowd. When Buddhist monks publicly protested by setting themselves on fire, Diem downplayed the suicides as publicity stunts. When grade school and high school children rallied against the government, Diem had over one thousand of them arrested. Both the United States and many of Diem's own military leaders viewed the South Vietnamese president as an embarrassment. Some of the latter believed the country would benefit from his removal.

In October 1963, South Vietnamese general Duong Van Minh informed United States ambassador Henry Cabot

Vietnam

Lodge of an impending coup d'etat—an overthrow of the Diem regime. Kennedy and his advisers, among them Secretary of State Dean Rusk and Secretary of Defense Robert S. McNamara, let it be understood that they could not condone but would not oppose such a move. They believed Diem's removal might stabilize and strengthen the South Vietnamese government.

Diem was assassinated on November 2, 1963, as he attempted to flee Saigon, capital of South Vietnam. (Kennedy himself was assassinated on November 22, leaving Vice President Lyndon B. Johnson to carry on the war in Vietnam.) Contrary to all expectations, Diem's overthrow did not stabilize the Republic of South Vietnam. A series of ten successive governments came and went within the course of the eighteen months after his death. (The final regime, headed by Nguyen Van Thieu, endured from 1965 until just before the Communist overthrow in April 1975.) During those eighteen months, the NLF continued to gain power and popularity and the North Vietnamese government sent more war materiel and units of its own army into the South. By late 1964, the Viet Cong controlled and influenced almost 75 percent of South Vietnam's population.

Escalating Involvement

Like Truman, Eisenhower, and Kennedy, President Johnson was determined that South Vietnam should not fall to the Communists. He believed that the key to stopping Communist aggression was to intimidate Ho Chi Minh with the threat of full-scale U.S. military intervention. Johnson had retained Secretary of State Rusk, Secretary of Defense McNamara and other staff and cabinet members from the Kennedy administration and they championed his pro-war position.

Johnson increased the number of United States advisers in South Vietnam to twenty-seven thousand by mid-1964. He also approved top-secret air attacks against North Vietnamese and Laotian targets that same year. When U.S. warships became involved in a controversial attack by the North Vietnamese in the Tonkin Gulf in early August 1964, Johnson used the incident to gain almost unanimous approval from Congress and the American public to expand the war even further. No formal declaration of war was ever made against North Vietnam, but the Gulf of Tonkin Resolution gave Johnson the authority he needed to conduct the war for the next four years.

In early 1965, Johnson further escalated the war in Vietnam with Operation Rolling Thunder—the sustained bombing of North Vietnam. Because he feared drawing the Soviet Union and Communist China into the conflict, however, he limited targets that could be bombed, never contemplated the overthrow of the North Vietnamese government, and ruled out the use of atomic weapons.

That left the deployment of ground forces, a step that Kennedy had also considered during his administration. In March 1965, the first U.S. Marines landed near Da Nang in South Vietnam. The buildup of ground forces continued until, by 1969, the number of American combat troops in Vietnam reached a peak of 540,000. (They were joined by about 800,000 South Vietnamese soldiers and 69,000 men from Australia, New Zealand, the Philippines, South Korea, and Thailand. North Vietnam and the Viet Cong had over 300,000 troops.)

The movement of thousands of foreign soldiers onto Vietnamese soil gave the Communists reason to claim that the South Vietnamese government was nothing more than a puppet in the hands of the United States. Both the North Vietnamese and members of the NLF successfully appealed to the nationalism of ordinary Vietnamese citizens and urged them to work to help drive the foreign army out, just as they had driven the French from the land in 1954.

Character of the War

General William C. Westmoreland, head of the Military Assistance Command, Vietnam (MACV) directed the U.S. military effort in Vietnam for four years beginning in 1964. He was succeeded by General Creighton Abrams in 1968. Westmoreland was convinced that, with superior military firepower and manpower, the United States could destroy the Communists' will to fight.

Vietnamese Communists, recognizing that they were no match for America's military superiority, adopted a different strategy. For the most part they fought a defensive war, avoiding major battles in the open where U.S. firepower could destroy them. Instead, small groups of irregular forces chose the time and place for fighting, hitting the enemy hard and unexpectedly before withdrawing.

This guerrilla technique, combined with determination to outlast the enemy no matter what the cost, had proven effective against the French in the 1950s, and it effectively thwarted Westmoreland in the 1960s. "Today the locust [grasshopper] fights the elephant, but tomorrow the elephant will be disemboweled," Ho proclaimed in a message to the Vietnam Workers' Party in February 1951. American troops were given no front or battle lines from which to operate; they were reduced to going out on "search and destroy" missions to attempt to flush out the enemy. Often that enemy was difficult to identify, since he could masquerade as an innocent Vietnamese civilian when he was not fighting the war. Even women and children could be dangerous since they were capable of tossing grenades and setting booby traps that maimed and killed unwary soldiers.

American troops grew frustrated and demoralized as they repeatedly "cleansed" a region of the country, knowing that the enemy would return as soon as they left the area. The knowledge that they often killed innocent Vietnamese civilians made their assignments even more disturbing. During the course of the war, millions of young Americans grimly served a one year term in Vietnam. The earliest forces were eager volunteers. Later in the war, draftees reluctantly answered their country's call to fight in Southeast Asia.

Soldiers vented their anger and frustration with the war in a variety of deleterious ways. Racism was a particular problem, both against minority soldiers and against the South Vietnamese, who were seen by many Americans as untrustworthy and less than human. Drug abuse reached crisis proportions, as did rebellion expressed by deliberate disobedience of orders, avoiding combat, going AWOL (absent without leave), or fragging (killing or injuring) an unpopular superior. While the majority of soldiers refrained from violent actions, most suffered from low morale and yearned to be through with their term of service so they could get back to "the World" and get on with their lives.

Course of the War

By the end of 1967, the war had reached a stalemate despite massive U.S. military efforts. Military leaders' optimistic predictions were shattered by the unexpectedness of the Tet Offensive of January 1968, which proved that the enemy was not demoralized, the war not close to being won. The U.S. Embassy in Saigon, thought to be invulnerable to enemy attack, was captured by the NLF for eight hours and U.S. troops worked for three weeks to oust NLF fighters from the capital. Tet went down in history as a U.S. victory, but it emphasized the strength of Communist resistance and the high cost of continuing the war effort in Vietnam.

Americans felt defeated and disillusioned after the Tet Offensive, and even members of the president's cabinet, once staunch supporters of the war, began to express doubts of its validity. In response to pressure from his advisers, Johnson changed the course of the conflict in March 1968 by announcing a cutback in the bombing in North Vietnam. The move was designed to bring warring parties to the peace table. An American delegation headed by Averell Harriman began meeting with North Vietnamese representatives in Paris in mid-May.

Johnson also announced that he would not seek reelection in the presidential elections of that year. His decision was a token of how deeply the war had influenced and undermined his administration. "There is division in the American house now. There is divisiveness among us all tonight. And holding the trust that is mine, as President of all the people, I cannot disregard the peril to the progress of the American people and the hope and the prospect of peace for all peoples," he stated in a televised address to the nation on March 31, 1968.

Protest Movement

Opposition to the Vietnam War began shortly after the Gulf of Tonkin incident in 1964. That opposition centered around traditional pacifist groups such as the Society of Friends (Quakers) and the intellectual elite. As early as 1965, students and professors organized "teach-ins" on university campuses, and eventually an antiwar organization existed on every campus. Some students joined the Students for a Democratic Society (SDS) and other organizations opposed to the draft and military service.

As time passed, rising casualties, lack of progress, and controversial events such as the Tet Offensive, the invasion of Cambodia, and the My Lai massacre added to antiwar sentiment. America became divided into two camps—"hawks" who supported the war but believed it should be fought more aggressively, and "doves," who wanted peace, opposed U.S. involvement, and took part in demonstrations and protests to express their feelings.

Increasing numbers of ordinary citizens began participating in opposition activities as the war went on, and antiwar demonstrations became almost commonplace. In October 1967, fifty thousand protesters marched on Washington, D.C. During The Moratorium, a one-day demonstration against the war in October 1969, millions of people stayed home from work while students staged demonstrations on campuses across America. Newly elected President Richard M. Nixon claimed that a "great silent majority" of Americans supported involvement in the war, but polls indicated that half believed it to be "morally indefensible," while 60 percent stated it was a mistake. Some opposed the conflict because of the high cost involved. Others were outraged because the draft imposed an unfair burden on working-class youth who did most of the fighting and dying in Vietnam.

On June 13, 1971, the Pentagon Papers, secret Department of Defense documents, were published by the *New York Times* newspaper, and support for the war dropped even more dramatically. Officially titled "The History of the U.S. Decision Making Process in Vietnam," the papers showed a pattern of deliberate deception by the government regarding the war dating back to the Truman administration. For instance, documents revealed that Lyndon Johnson had committed ground troops to Vietnam while reassuring the public that he did not plan to change the character of the war.

As a result of the Pentagon Papers, public distrust of the government deepened, and 70 percent of Americans demanded a withdrawal from the conflict.

Vietnamization

On September 3, 1969, Ho Chi Minh died of heart failure in Hanoi at the age of seventy-nine. Despite his death, the Communists continued fighting with unabated determination under the joint leadership of Prime Minister Pham Van

Dong, Minister of Defense General Vo Nguyen Giap, Secretary General of the Vietnamese Communist Party Le Duan, scholar-theorist Truong Chinh, and peace negotiator Le Duc Tho.

They were now dealing with Richard M. Nixon who assumed office as the thirty-seventh president of the United States in January 1969. Nixon declared that he would bring his nation "peace with honor" and expanded the peace talks in Paris to include representatives of the Republic of Vietnam and the Viet Cong. He also initiated a policy called Vietnamization, under which the United States would gradually withdraw from Vietnam as it turned responsibility for fighting the war over to the ARVN. Training programs for the ARVN were stepped up so they could take over the bulk of the fighting. In July the first U.S. troops were withdrawn from Vietnam. Nixon also assigned National Security Adviser Henry Kissinger the task of meeting secretly with North Vietnamese negotiators in Paris, a process that would continue until a successful peace treaty was agreed upon in 1973.

Peace talks and troop withdrawals did not stop Nixon from pursuing a hard-line policy against the Communists, however. In March 1969, he ordered the secret bombing of Cambodia to destroy North Vietnamese army and NLF base camps along the border. In April 1970, he announced that he was sending U.S. troops into Cambodia. The move was necessary, he argued, for the security of the South Vietnamese government and to protect American units as they withdrew from Vietnam. U.S. college campuses exploded with protests at this expansion of the fighting. About five hundred campuses closed due to student walkouts. In a tragic incident at Kent State University in Ohio, four students were killed when panic-stricken National Guardsmen shot into a crowd of protesters.

Nixon recalled American troops from Cambodia at the end of June. At the same time, an unsupportive Congress terminated the Tonkin Gulf Resolution. In December 1970, Congress also passed the Cooper-Church Amendment which specifically forbade U.S. troops to be used outside of South Vietnam. The measure did not forbid bombing, however, and Nixon supported secret B-52 bombing missions into Laos to support an ARVN invasion on February 8, 1971. He also continued to order air strikes in Cambodia until 1973.

America Pushes for Peace

Despite American skepticism that the war would ever end, troop withdrawals continued and by the spring of 1972, combat strength was down to six thousand. With the American military presence fading, North Vietnamese leadership determined that another offensive against the South was in order. On March 30, 1972, over thirty thousand North Vietnamese troops crossed the demilitarized zone that divided the country at the 17th Parallel and attacked South Vietnam in the Easter Offensive. The United States was taken by surprise but quickly rallied. Nixon authorized sustained bombing attacks on North Vietnam, and later ordered a blockade to cut off war supplies coming into North Vietnam from the Soviet Union and China. The blockade involved mining ports and bombing railroads and highways that linked Vietnam to China. Nixon believed that such tough action would shorten the war, but many Americans felt he risked expanding and lengthening the conflict.

Nixon again sanctioned the bombardment of North Vietnam in late 1972 in an effort to break the will of the Communists and advance peace negotiations in Paris. The Christmas bombing of Hanoi, capital of North Vietnam, and the port city of Haiphong earned him worldwide condemnation and angered the North Vietnamese. Tensions rose in Paris, but in early 1973, a breakthrough occurred at the peace table. Kissinger was finally able to broker a treaty that all sides reluctantly accepted. Cease-fire agreements were finally signed on January 27, 1973. The last American troops left Vietnam at the end of March of that year.

The War Continues

Peace accords did not bring peace to Vietnam, however. North Vietnam still wanted unification of the country under a Communist government, while South Vietnam struggled to survive as a free nation. Both sides violated the terms of the treaty, while Nixon continued to assure the South Vietnamese that the United States would back them with military force in case of overwhelming Communist aggression.

Nixon's presidential influence was on the decline, however, as revelations about Watergate gradually brought down his administration. The political scandal involved burglary of the Democratic national headquarters and other illegal activities designed to help Nixon win re-election in 1972. Investigations eventually uncovered a White House–sponsored plan of espionage against political opponents that involved many of the highest officials in the land, including White House Chief of Staff H.R. Haldeman, White House Special Assistant on Domestic Affairs John Ehrlichman, and Nixon himself.

The president's ability to lead the United States back into the war was further weakened when, in July 1973, Congress voted to prohibit further U.S. involvement in Southeast Asia. Conflict between North and South Vietnam continued until 1975, when another Communist offensive quickly toppled the South Vietnamese government and sent more than 1 million people fleeing the country. The war ended on April 30, 1975, when General Duong Van Minh, acting president, surrendered to the North Vietnamese army in Saigon.

Despite its earlier investment of time, money, and human suffering in Southeast Asia, the United States did nothing to prevent the overthrow. Divided and cynical Americans had had enough of war. The fall of South Vietnam to the Communists only served to emphasize what a wasted effort the years of fighting had been.

Aftermath of War

When all was said and done, the cost of fighting the war in Vietnam proved immense. About fifty-eight thousand Americans died in the war, and over three hundred thousand were wounded. The United States spent over $150 billion supporting the conflict.

Four times the tonnage of American bombs were dropped on Vietnam as the Allies dropped on Germany during World War II. Portions of North Vietnam were devastated during American bombing raids, but ironically South Vietnam sustained the greatest damage, since most of the fighting occurred there. Use of bombs and defoliants scarred the landscape and killed crops and animals. Up to 10 million South Vietnamese (about one half of the country's population) became refugees because of the war.

Americans at home were spared bomb and rocket attacks, but thousands of veterans coped with a myriad of physical challenges on their return. Emotional suffering was widespread and intense throughout the United States as well. Vietnam was the first war that the nation had failed to win, and many Americans were left with shame, bitterness, and painful memories. Philosophical differences based on whether one supported or opposed the conflict led to divisions in government, among families and friends, and throughout society as a whole that took years to bridge.

Many of the almost 3 million veterans who served in Vietnam were seriously traumatized by their service there. Angry, disillusioned, and troubled, they came home not as heroes, but to face hostility from those who opposed the war. Such hostility drove many vets to depression and despair. While a majority managed to adjust smoothly to civilian life, others struggled for decades with post-traumatic stress disorder, drug abuse, violence, joblessness, and divorce. High rates of suicide were common.

Their pain was intensified as the government who had sent them to fight the war proved unsympathetic to their plight. Traditional veterans groups such as the Veterans of Foreign Wars and the American Legion ignored their emotional and physical needs as well. Vietnam vets achieved some satisfaction after some veteran-activists established self-help groups that collectively forced the Veterans Administration (VA) to take notice of their problems. For instance, the VA established storefront counseling centers throughout the United States beginning in the late 1970s. Increased medical benefits were provided to veterans and their families who suffered from the after-effects of Agent Orange, a defoliant widely used in Vietnam.

Despite such action, many veterans remained bitter and withdrawn from society as they continued to believe that their country and their fellow citizens did not recognize or appreciate their sacrifice.

The War in Perspective

With time, America has come to terms with its disastrous involvement in Vietnam. Articles, books, and movies have explored and examined the war's complexities and shone a light on its most controversial aspects. The dedication of a national Vietnam Veterans' Memorial, "The Wall," in Washington, D.C., in 1982 helped promote healing by publicly honoring those who served. Today the memorial provides a place of reflection and reconciliation for those who struggle with painful memories of Vietnam.

Despite time and perspective, many Americans still disagree on the main issues and lessons to be learned from the Vietnam War. Some maintain that the conflict was a civil contest which the United States should have avoided. Some insist that participation was just and correct, but should have been carried out more aggressively. Many find consensus in asserting that the nation should avoid wars it does not intend to win, particularly those that do not threaten its safety or vital interests.

As a result of the war, more Americans are skeptical of their government, more willing to challenge it on foreign policy decisions, more cautious about assuming that the United States has a right to interfere in the affairs of other nations. Although America has successfully taken part in foreign conflicts in recent years, Vietnam remains a specter of what can happen when good intentions go awry, when well-meaning people become entangled in a conflict for which there is no "peace with honor."

Chapter 1

The First Vietnam War

Turning|Points

IN WORLD HISTORY

Ho Chi Minh Champions Vietnam's Independence

Stanley Karnow

Vietnamese revolutionary Ho Chi Minh was one of the most significant figures in both France's and America's Vietnam wars, leading the Vietnamese Communist Party from 1954 until his death in 1969. A frail and gentle man, Ho did not appear to be the leader whose tenacity and ruthless determination would bring about the defeat of two major world powers. Yet such was the case.

In the following selection, Pulitzer Prize–winning journalist Stanley Karnow relates the complex and sometimes mysterious details of Ho Chi Minh's life and development as a revolutionary, including his entrance into world politics in 1919 and his unsuccessful efforts to garner Western support for Vietnamese independence. Karnow reported from Southeast Asia for *Time* and *Life* magazines in the 1960s. He has also written *In Our Image: America's Empire in the Philippines* and *Paris in the Fifties*.

Ho [Chi Minh], originally named Nguyen Sinh Cung, was born in 1890 in a village of Nghe An province in central Vietnam, where shimmering green rice fields stretch from the sea to a hazy horizon of blue mountains. His father, Nguyen Sinh Sac, a concubine's son relegated to menial farm work, had risen to the rank of mandarin [a high-ranking official] through assiduous study. But he quit the imperial court in Hué and, abandoning his wife and three children, roamed the country for the rest of his life as an itinerant teacher and medicine man. Ho inherited his father's wanderlust on a grander scale; he traveled the world in solitude for decades, never married, and rarely contacted his kin. The fate of Vietnam was his obsession, as he revealed in 1950 when, failing to attend his older brother's funeral, he telegraphed relatives to beg forgiveness for having "sacrificed family feelings to state affairs." . . .

Learning from the West

Ho Chi Minh started his real education at nineteen, when he went south. He taught for a few months at a village school. Then, in Saigon in 1911, he signed on as stoker and galley boy aboard a French freighter, the *Amiral Latouche Tréville*. He called himself Van Ba, *ba* being the Vietnamese term for third child. Thirty years passed before he saw Vietnam again.

Though a prolific pamphleteer, Ho never kept diaries, wrote memoirs, or related his experiences to a biographer. His life is therefore filled with mysteries, among them his motives for going to Europe rather than to Japan, then a beacon for Asian nationalists. Perhaps he foresaw then that to count on the Japanese against the French would be, as he warned later, to "drive the tiger out the front door while letting the wolf in through the back." Or perhaps, as a comrade explained, he hoped to learn from the West how to fight against the West.

He spent nearly three years at sea, stopping at ports like Bombay [India], Oran [Algeria], and Le Havre [France], where he worked briefly as a gardener for his ship's captain. In 1913, employed aboard another French vessel, he crossed the Atlantic, visiting Boston and San Francisco before settling in Brooklyn as an itinerant laborer. The skyscrapers of Manhattan dazzled him as emblems of Western industrial progress. He ventured into Harlem, and he was impressed by the fact that Chinese immigrants to the New World, with whom he chatted in Cantonese, enjoyed the legal rights of American citizens. When he proclaimed Vietnam's independence from France in 1945, his speech would feature an excerpt from the American Declaration of Independence.

Politics and Patriotism

After almost a year in the United States, he sailed to London, where he found a job in the kitchen of the elegant Carlton Hotel, whose renowned chef, Georges Auguste Escoffier, promoted him to assistant pastry cook. Now known as Nguyen Tat Thanh, he began to flirt with politics, meeting Irish nationalists, Fabian [antirevolutionary] socialists, and Chinese and Indian workers. He improved his English, and eventually spoke it fluently, along with Russian and at least three Chinese dialects besides French and Vietnamese.

But Paris beckoned. A hundred thousand Vietnamese had arrived in France during World War I as soldiers and laborers, and they were ripe for conversion. Ho adopted a militant new name, Nguyen Ai Quoc, or Nguyen the Patriot. He was to remain in Paris for six years, combining his conspiratorial activities with extraordinarily eclectic cultural pursuits. . . .

In 1919, when President Woodrow Wilson arrived at Versailles [France] for the conference that formally ended World War I, Ho drafted a statement to hand him. Inspired by Wilson's famous doctrine of self-determination, Ho had written that "all subject peoples are filled with hope by the prospect that an era of right and justice is opening to them . . . in the struggle of civilization against barbarism." His appeal to Wilson modestly requested constitutional government, democratic freedoms, and other reforms for Vietnam—conspicuously omitting any reference to independence. Ho never saw Wilson, whose principles presumably applied only to Europe, but his gesture attracted the attention of French socialists like Jean Longuet and Léon Blum, later prime minister. Critics of colonialism, they invited Ho to join them, and, as "representative from Indochina," he attended their congress held in December 1920 at Tours, a charming town in the Loire River valley. It was a decisive moment in his career.

A superb photograph taken at the meeting shows Ho, thin and intense, addressing a collection of corpulent Frenchmen with walrus mustaches. Speaking without notes, he rebuked the delegates who interrupted him as his speech rose to an impassioned plea: "In the name of all mankind, in the name of all socialists, right wing or left wing, we appeal to you, comrades. Save us!"

The decision that faced Ho at the Tours congress transcended Vietnam. A majority of socialists, enthused by the Russian Revolution, had broken away to form the Communist party. Ho might have preferred to stick with socialists like Longuet and Blum, whose gentle temperament he shared. But he opted for the Communists, figuring that their Soviet patrons had the potential power to spark the global revolution that would liberate Vietnam. As Ho explained years afterward, "it was patriotism and not Communism that originally inspired me."

Professional Revolutionary

Ho Chi Minh became a prodigious polemicist [skilled in disputation] during the Paris years. His diatribes contained flashes of acerbic wit, like the remark in his pamphlet, *French Colonialism on Trial*, that "the figure of Justice has had such a rough voyage from France to Indochina that she has lost everything but her sword." He wrote for the French Communist daily, *L'Humanité*, and he edited *Le Paria*, a journal put out by a group of Asian and African nationalists. Smuggled back to Vietnam and circulated secretly, his writings exposed many Vietnamese for the first time to Lenin's thesis that revolution and anticolonial resistance were inseparable. "It opened a new world to us," recalled Tran Van Giau, a veteran Vietnamese Communist. . . .

In 1924, Ho moved to Moscow. Now known as Linh, he met [Joseph] Stalin, Leon Trotsky, and the other Soviet leaders, but decried their lack of sufficient interest in Vietnam. They were busy squabbling over the succession to [Vladimir] Lenin, who had just died. Besides, as a Bolshevik analysis put it, Vietnam's nationalists were "disorganized" and its masses "politically inert," and scarcely worth an investment. Still, Ho used his time in the Soviet Union to attend the so-called University of Oriental Workers, an academy for Asian insurgents, where he learned Lenin's key dictum: revolution must be launched under favorable conditions. He was to wait another twenty years before staging his revolution, and even then he may have acted prematurely.

The sojourn in Moscow transformed Ho from a propagandist into a practical organizer, a role that he would begin to play when he traveled to Canton later in 1924. There the Chinese Nationalist Generalissimo Chiang Kai-shek, then allied with the Chinese Communists, had a Soviet adviser, Mikhail Borodin. . . . Ho, now using the alias Ly Thuy, became Borodin's part-time interpreter while peddling cigarettes and newspapers to supplement his income. . . .

During this period, Ho started to mobilize Vietnamese students in southern China, creating . . . the Revolutionary Youth League. Following classic Communist precepts, he taught his pupils to form small cells to avoid detection and to write tracts for specific audiences, and he inculcated them with the boy scout virtues of thrift, generosity, and perseverance. Above all, he urged them to be concrete. "Peasants," he cautioned, "believe in facts, not theories."

But Ho's prospects suddenly dimmed in 1927, when Chiang Kai-shek slaughtered his Communist associates in a surprise betrayal. Ho fled back to Moscow and then, with little else to do, toured Europe to gaze at castles and cathedrals. He secretly slipped into Paris under the name of Duong, and nostalgia for the city welled up in him. A French Communist friend of the time recalled . . . how he met Ho standing on a bridge overlooking the Seine. Ho said to him wistfully, "I always thought I would become a scholar or a writer, but I've become a professional revolutionary. I travel through many countries, but I see nothing. I'm on strict orders, and my itinerary is carefully prescribed, and you cannot deviate from the route, can you?"

A year later, Ho turned up in Bangkok, now a center of Vietnamese dissidence. He shaved his head and donned the saffron robes of a Buddhist monk to proselytize in the temples. Then he went to northeast Siam, the site of a large expatriate Vietnamese community, where he opened a school and published a newspaper. He concealed his identity under a collection of pseudonyms, such as Nguyen Lai, Nam Son, and Thau Chin, which means Old Man Chin in Siamese— another language he mastered. Even after becoming North Vietnam's president in 1954, Ho continued to hide behind aliases, perhaps a holdover from his clandestine past. He wrote articles under such names as Tran Luc, Tuyet Lan, Le Thanh Long, and Dan Viet, the last of them signifying Citizen of Vietnam.

Advocate for Vietnamese Independence

Inside Vietnam in the late 1920s, the revolutionary climate was bleak, as some impatient and impulsive nationalists provoked fierce French repression. . . .

The disorder was aggravated by the economic depression of the 1930s. World rice and rubber prices plummeted and production was cut. Unemployed workers staged strikes, and hungry peasants in many areas seized estates and took over village councils. In Ho's native Nghe An province, they even set up a "soviet" [Communist legislative council]. Ho Chi Minh realized that the moment had come to form a cohesive Communist party. . . . He went from Bangkok to Hong Kong. There, in June 1929, he assembled different factional leaders at a local football stadium during a match to avoid detection by the British colonial police, and persuaded them to close ranks. They labeled the new movement the Indochinese Communist party, its name reflecting the ambition of the dynamic Vietnamese to extend their reach over Cambodia and Laos. Its program called for Vietnamese independence and a proletarian government—a far cry from Ho's moderate requests in 1919 of Woodrow Wilson.

At that stage, Ho went through another one of the adventures that make his life seem like the subject of a movie thriller. The Hong Kong police, on a periodic sweep of political troublemakers, arrested him. But a local British lawyer, Frank Loseby, obtained his release on a writ of habeas corpus [legal protection against unlawful imprisonment]. . . . A British doctor had diagnosed Ho as tubercular and now generously sent him to a sanatorium in Britain. The persistent Hong Kong police, however, charged him with illegal departure and had him extradited from Singapore, where his ship had stopped, to Hong Kong, where they put him in a prison infirmary. This time he escaped to China, having persuaded a hospital employee to report him dead. His obituary appeared in the Soviet press and elsewhere, and the French authorities closed his file with the notation: "Died in a Hong Kong jail." . . .

Ho, the wanderer, meanwhile continued to wander through the 1930s, leaving a trail of legends behind him. One year he would be in Moscow, then China, then in the Soviet Union again—a traveler for weeks aboard cramped freighters that stopped at Asian, African, and Mediterranean ports, or jammed into a squalid compartment of the Trans-Siberian Railway, the temperatures either freezing or torrid, the food inedible and the air polluted by the alcoholic breaths of drunken Russians. On one occasion, he trekked for five days across the mountains of central China to the Chinese Communist stronghold in the caves of Yenan. He was no longer the young seaman of the *Amiral Latouche Tréville*, but a man approaching fifty, tubercular and un-doubtedly plagued as well by amebic dysentery and recurrent malaria. A French Communist agent who worked with him then recalled: "He was taut and quivering, with only one thought in his head, his country, Vietnam."

Ho cultivated a reputation for ascetic celibacy during those years, but reality may have been different. One old comrade has claimed that the Russians had furnished him with a "wife" in Moscow. A Communist official in Hanoi in 1981 told me that Ho had loved a Chinese woman, a doctor, who died before they could marry. And yet another story has it that General Lung Yun, the warlord of Yunnan province, who frequently lodged Ho on his estate in Kunming, arranged a liaison for him with a Chinese woman. Whatever the truth, Ho cultivated the image of himself as Uncle Ho, his passions devoted solely to his national family.

Bringer of Light

In 1940, a tidal wave swept over Southeast Asia. The Japanese, pouring down from China, their offensive timed to Germany's conquest of France, crushed the French administration in Vietnam. They pushed on, driving the British from Malaya, the Dutch from Indonesia, the United States from the Philippines. An Asian nation had destroyed European colonialism.

Native nationalists throughout Southeast Asia rallied to Japan, but Ho feared the Japanese wolf as much as he opposed the French tiger. He aligned himself instead with the Allies, expecting them to defeat Japan, oust the discredited French from Japan, and reward his country with independence. The strategy strained his allegiance to the Soviet Union, which had signed a self-serving pact with Germany and forbade Communists everywhere to resist the Axis powers. But Ho's sole concern was Vietnam.

In early 1941, disguised as a Chinese journalist, he went by foot and sampan into southern China, then slipped across the border back into Vietnam—his first return in thirty years. A comrade had found a cave near Pac Bo, a village nestled amid the strange northern landscape of limestone hills. There Ho met confederates like Pham Van Dong and Vo Nguyen Giap. They called him Uncle, their attitude reverent yet familiar. In the Confucian spirit, he was the respected elder.

The time had come, Ho told them, to form a broad front of "patriots of all ages and all types, peasants, workers, merchants and soldiers," to fight both the Japanese and the French then collaborating with Japan, just as the Vichy regime in France obeyed Germany's dictates. The new organization, led by Communists, appealed to Vietnamese nationalist sentiment. They called it the Viet Nam Doc Lap Dong Minh, the Vietnam Independence League—soon to be simply the Vietminh. Ho borrowed from the movement his official pseudonym, Ho Chi Minh—roughly, Bringer of Light. But decades of dark violence lay ahead.

France's Vietnam War

David Halberstam

On September 2, 1945, Vietnamese Communist Ho Chi Minh declared Vietnam's independence, and his followers, members of the Revolutionary League for the Independence of Vietnam (the Vietminh), moved quickly to gain control of many parts of the north. Western powers were unwilling to recognize Ho's declaration, however, and the French, who had ruled Vietnam before World War II, seized control of the southern part of the country. War between France and the Vietminh broke out on December 19, 1946.

During the Indochina War, also known as the first Vietnam War, the French possessed military superiority, but the Vietnamese had a strategic advantage since they fought as guerrillas, irregular forces that appeared out of nowhere to strike before slipping away into the jungle. In the following selection, author David Halberstam describes the war as a revolution and maintains that the odds were with the Communists from the start because they controlled the minds and loyalties of the people. Vietnamese tenacity eventually defeated the French, just as it defeated the United States two decades later.

Halberstam is a Pulitzer Prize–winning journalist who wrote for the *New York Times* in Vietnam from 1962 to 1964. His books include *The Making of a Quagmire*, based on his own experiences in Vietnam; *The Unfinished Odyssey of Robert Kennedy*, a political memoir; and *The Best and Brightest*, a portrait of the men who conceived and executed the Vietnam War.

Excerpted from David Halberstam, *Ho*. Copyright © 1971 David Halberstam. Reprinted with permission from International Creative Management, Inc.

It was a revolutionary war, that is, it was at once warfare and revolution. It was brilliantly conceived and brilliantly executed. Political considerations were always of the essence. The Vietminh leaders considered that reaching the mind of the guerrilla was their most important object. He must know who he was fighting and why, as must the simple peasants around him. Even as the war continued it seemed to strengthen the Vietminh politically at home. The French did his recruiting for him. Each day the war went on, the job for Ho [Chi Minh] and [General Vo Nguyen] Giap [head of the North Vietnamese Army] became easier—less the minority Communist party against the French nation, and more the Vietnamese nation against the colonial oppressor. His opponents thus were being swept aside: to be Ho's political opponent now was to be an enemy of the Vietnamese people.

The French and the rest of the Western world read the daily dispatches telling of the noble struggle of the West against the Communists, and noted approvingly what seemed to be an endless stream of French victories. But for the Vietnamese it was another war; it was the struggle not for Communism, but to throw the white colonialist out. The most restless and patriotic men of a generation signed up with the Vietminh, for *this* was the great cause. This was the heroic war for freedom. All those long-submerged and powerful Vietnamese aspirations were unleashed—and the Vietminh harnessed them to their revolution.

Creating a Military Force

The Vietminh were always sensitive to local nuance, always sensitive to Vietnamese tradition. A captured soldier was once asked by interrogators: "When you joined the [National Liberation] Front did you tell your family?" This, after all, was the critical question; the greatest loyalty is to the family. "No, I did not," he said, "I felt it was my filial duty, but I talked to the Front and they said to me, 'Comrade, your words show that you are a fine son filled with filial piety and we admire that very much, but in the face of the loss and destruction of your country you have to choose between filial duty and duty toward your country. In this war the people are your family too, and you have to suffer. If you do your duty toward your parents—tell them of your decision—then you fail your country. But if you fulfill your duty toward your country, then by the same act you will have completed your duty toward your family, because they will be free and no longer exploited.' "

For a Vietnamese of that generation there was only one question: Which side are you on, the Vietnamese side or the colonialist side? And from this passion, the Vietminh over a period of eight years welded an extraordinary political and military force. To the peasant, consigned by birth to a life of misery, poverty, ignorance, the Vietminh showed a way out. A man could be as good as his innate talent permitted; lack of privilege was for the first time in centuries not a handicap—if anything, it was an asset. One could fight and die serving the nation, liberating both the nation and oneself. Nepotism and privilege, which had dominated the feudal society of the past, were wiped away. One rose only by ability. . . . And in putting all this extraordinary human machinery together, the Vietminh gave a sense of nation to this formerly suspicious and fragmented society, until at last that which united the Vietnamese was more powerful than that which divided them—until they were in fact a nation, just as Ho had claimed. . . .

Illusory French Superiority

The French never really understood the war; as the Americans would, they thought of it in terms of terrain controlled, bodies counted; they heard of supply problems and shortages among the Vietminh and were sure that collapse was imminent. From time to time they met with Vietminh units face to face, and on those occasions killed more of the enemy than they lost themselves. This they would claim as a victory. It would be extensively reported in the French press. They never considered that perhaps the battle had taken place precisely because the Vietminh had wanted it, that despite the apparent imbalance in casualties, the Vietminh might well be the winner because the Vietnamese people would find the greater casualties somehow more bearable than would the French people thousands of miles away. For to the French it was a distant war, a war of vanity and pride, whereas to the Vietnamese it was a war of survival; they would pay any price. "It is the duty of my generation to die for our country," one Vietminh soldier told an American at the time. The casualty lists might be heavy but they were acceptable—anything as precious as independence could not come cheap.

The French never understood that the fact that they had absolute military superiority was illusory because the Vietminh had absolute political superiority. And since this was a political war, it meant that in the long run the Vietminh had the absolute superiority. The French, like the Americans after them, would fight limited war against a smaller nation that, in contrast, fought *total* war, a war of survival. For time was on the Vietminh side. Though the French might win a single battle, battles meant nothing; it was not a war for control of land, but for control of people and their minds, and here the Vietminh was unchallenged. Indeed, the very victories of the French came back to haunt them—there would inevitably be dead civilians left behind, and their relatives would see the corpses. That night Vietminh agents would slip into the village, and sign more recruits.

Even the white skin of the French troops was a symbol of their alien role. Enemies seemed everywhere. Every Vietnamese servant, houseboy or clerk was a potential Vietminh agent; every woman in every village, a potential spy, telling the Vietminh exactly where a French patrol had gone, how many men were in it, what kind of weapons they carried, but telling the French nothing. The ambush was the key to Vietminh tactics; it was perfectly designed for their kind of war. Aided by the warnings of the population, the Viets could blend into the scenery the way the French could not. The very fear of an ambush eventually became a deterrent, making the French wary of going into the interior. This allowed the Vietminh more time to propagandize, to recruit among the population. Again and again it would happen: the French convoy moving slowly, ponderously ahead, watching for mines, when suddenly thousands of Vietminh would attack. It was, said one young French officer recounting a typical ambush, "an execution."

> For a few minutes the column fought back furiously, weaving to and fro and breaking into thousands of separate personal battles . . . But there were too many Viets; the ones who were killed didn't count—there were always more, coming from behind every bush and every rock. Each of us had to go through those appalling seconds when you feel there is no possibility of resistance any more and that now you are merely something to be killed off. And with some of us this was mixed up with a realization of an impossible state of affairs—that Europeans could be wiped out in this way by Asians. . . .

The Vietminh Control the War

The Vietminh could be everywhere and nowhere; they did not have to be in a village to control it. They found it easy to introduce an excellent, completely indigenous political organization to run the village and keep it in line. Such an organization intimidated any possibly pro-French elements. Often these [pro-French] sympathizers were publicly assassinated—a symbol of what might happen to friends of the colonialist, a reminder that the French could not protect their own. The French were weak in the villages; they had to be there physically to dominate them. In order to control terrain, the French had to stand on it, and the terrain absorbed them, sucked them down; it was a quagmire, first to the French and then to the Americans [in the 1960s]. Five hundred thousand men sounded like a lot, but they would be tied to fixed points, bogged down, the Vietminh always knowing exactly where they were, they never knowing where the Vietminh were, the Vietminh shifting, regrouping. The terrain was the friend of the Vietminh. They could do very few things, but they did them well: the ambush, camouflage, and finally the assault. To the French the jungle was an enemy, the night was an enemy; danger was everywhere. To the Vietminh the night and the jungle were

Philosopher-Warriors

The second most important figure in the history of Communist Vietnam was General Vo Nguyen Giap, commander-in-chief of the Viet Minh forces against the French and chief military leader in North Vietnam's war with the United States. A master of guerrilla war tactics, Giap understood the subtleties of fighting a superior enemy. He details some of them in an interview for the CNN special "The Cold War," a portion of which can be found on the Internet at CNN Cold War—Interviews: Vo Nguyen Giap.

We had to resort to different measures, some of which are quite simple, like hiding in man-holes and evacuating to the countryside. And we fought back with all our forces and with every kind of weapon. We fought with anti-aircraft artilleries and with small guns, even though (it was) sometimes solely with the strength of our local force. An 18-year-old girl once said that she followed routes every day and studied the patterns of American flights and when they would attack. I told her that she is a philosopher to understand that, because only philosophers talk about principles. Later she used [a] small gun to shoot down an aircraft from a mountainside. That is an example of the military force of the common people. . . . We had ingenuity and the determination to fight to the end.

Vo Nguyen Giap, "On Fighting Technologically Superior U.S. Forces," *The Cold War*, Cable News Network, 1998. http://cnn.com/SPECIALS/ cold.war/episodes/11/interviews/giap.

friends, offering protection against airplanes and tanks. And they taught this to the peasants, destroying his fear of the night and the jungle.

And always the revolution went on—the indoctrination against the French and the wealthy class, and the dividing up of land which they had taken. The Vietminh took the young peasants who had been beaten down by the system and told them that they were as good as the French and the mandarins [upper class], that they were as strong and as talented as the upper class, and that, yes, they could rise up. Above all the Vietminh gave the peasant a sense of being a person. Those who had been shown again and again their lack of value now found that they had their rights too—even if only the right to die for an idea, that smallest right. And in doing this the Vietminh finally produced an extraordinary revolutionary force, whose bravery was stunning, which believed in itself and its cause.

The Vietminh leadership understood exactly both its own strengths and limitations, and using its strengths, it created a new form of modern revolutionary warfare—political, psychological, and of course military. The Vietminh had decided regretfully that human life was a small price to pay for freedom. Yes, use terror, but use it discriminately. Terrorize the right person, one already despised in the village, showing the villagers that you have the capacity to strike audaciously, and that you are on their side against the hated officials. Whatever grievances existed against the old order, and there were many, the Vietminh took over and exploited politically. . . .

French Demoralization

For eight years the war dragged on. To the French it was always victories, always heavier Vietminh casualties, always winning the war. But always there were more Viets, until slowly it began to dawn on some French officials that this was a war of attrition and that despite the heavier Vietminh casualty rolls, it was finally the French who were being worn down and exhausted.

It was as Giap and Ho had predicted: the colonial power was tiring of a war which among other things was turning out to be poor economics; Indochina was costing France far more than it was worth. Thirty years earlier in Comintern [international communist] circles, where others had presented grandiose schemes for toppling Western powers, Ho had written that the way to do it was through long and punishing colonial wars which would sap the very fiber and vitality of the colonial country until both colony and country came apart. He was not far from wrong. That the French could not defeat the Vietminh, the little yellow ones, was a frustrating lesson. Front-line French officers cabled back their reports of losses and of growing Vietminh strength. But the French high command steadfastly refused to listen; it was sure it could win the war. At home, the opposition to the war steadily mounted. To the French command in Hanoi it was those politicians back home who were causing problems, aiding a cowardly enemy who refused to come out and fight.

Final Defeat

Finally, as the war dragged on, as the French casualty lists grew longer, the French command decided to set a major trap for the Vietminh. They would position a French garrison in a distant outpost as bait. The Vietminh, who were new to modern warfare, simple people, really, would gather to attack, and as they did, the French would destroy them with artillery and air power. This was the set-piece battle the French wanted so badly.

The name of the outpost was Dienbienphu. The planning was done by men who had underestimated their enemy from the start, who understood neither his talent, his objectives, nor his thinking.

A friend of mine visited the outpost shortly before the battle began. It was in a valley, he noted, surrounded by high peaks in the distance. It gave him a somewhat uneasy feeling—the first rule of warfare is to take the high ground. "Who has the high peaks?" he asked a French officer.

"Who knows?" said the Frenchman, shrugging his shoulders, implicitly indicating that if anyone had them, it was the Vietminh.

"But what if they are there and they have artillery?" my friend insisted.

"They do not have artillery, and even if they did, they would not know how to use it," the Frenchman said.

But they did have artillery. They had carried the pieces up and down mountains, through the monsoons, at night—hundreds of peasants, crawling over the mountain trails like ants, carrying one part after another. . . . And not only did they have the artillery pieces, they knew how to use them. They had created extraordinary bunkers, perfectly camouflaged, almost impossible to detect from the air.

On March 13, 1954, the battle began. It was, in fact, over before it started. The Vietminh held the high ground and they had the French badly outgunned. The French artillery commander, shouting, "It is my fault! it is my fault!" committed suicide the first night. Day after day the battle wore on as the Vietminh cut the French up. The French garrison made a legendary stand, substituting its own gallantry for the incompetence of its superiors, but all in vain. Fifty-six days later the fort fell. General [Henri] Navarre, the French commander, told his other troops: "The defenders of Dienbienphu have written an epic. They have given you a new pride and a new reason to fight. For the struggle of free peoples against slavery does not end today. The fight continues." His men, of course, knew better, as did the rest of the world. The French had been fighting against a revolution and had never realized it until the end.

Anti-Communist Fears Trigger U.S. Aid to South Vietnam

James S. Olson and Randy Roberts

Authors James S. Olson and Randy Roberts explain in the following viewpoint that America's foreign policy in the 1950s and 1960s reflected the country's fear of the spread of communism. Eastern Europe had fallen to the Communist-led Soviets after World War II, and Communists took over China in 1949. Motivated by that fear and the "domino theory"—the belief that if one country fell to communism, neighboring nations would soon topple like a row of dominoes—the United States became increasingly involved in Southeast Asia. Olson and Roberts point out that American policy makers condemned Vietnamese Communist revolutionary Ho Chi Minh's fight for independence, labeled him an emissary of international communism, and backed French attempts to gain control of the country.

Olson is the chair of the Department of History at Sam Houston State University in Huntsville, Texas. Roberts is an associate professor of history at Purdue University in West Lafayette, Indiana.

In 1949 [France's] war [in Vietnam] became part of a much larger global struggle between the United States and the Soviet Union. From 1945 to 1948, anticommunist rhetoric had grown shrill in Washington. President [Harry] Truman announced the Truman Doctrine in 1947 to provide $400 million in military and economic assistance to Greece and Turkey in the fight against leftist-backed guerrillas. The fall of Greece and Turkey, Truman argued, would threaten all

Excerpted from James S. Olson and Randy Roberts, *Where the Domino Fell: America and Vietnam, 1945 to 1990.* Copyright © 1991 St. Martin's Press, Inc. Reprinted with permission from James S. Olson.

the eastern Mediterranean and the Mideast. To save Western Europe, Truman announced the Marshall Plan in 1948—a $12.6-billion program of American economic assistance. Unemployment and inflation gave communists fertile ground for political growth in Italy, France, the Netherlands, Spain, Portugal, and Belgium.

Three events in 1949, however, elevated anticommunism in the United States from fear to paranoia. In 1948, hoping to starve West Berlin into surrender, the Soviets blocked the highway from West Germany to West Berlin. Truman responded with the Berlin Airlift, an unprecedented daily resupply of a city of 2 million people. Most Americans viewed the blockade as raw Soviet aggression, and tension escalated well into 1949 until the Soviets backed down. When the Soviet Union detonated an atomic bomb in 1949, a wave of fear swept throughout the United States. Finally, at the end of 1949, Mao Zedong and the Chinese communists drove Chiang Kai-shek and the Chinese nationalists off the mainland out to the island of Taiwan. The most populous country in the world, an ally of the United States just four years earlier, had fallen to communism.

Communist Fears

Americans accepted at face value the idea of monolithic communism. Because of Soviet support for communist groups throughout the world, as well as Soviet control of much of Eastern Europe following World War II, many Americans were convinced that an international communist conspiracy was set to take over the world from Moscow. Whenever communists caused any trouble anywhere, the Truman administration blamed Moscow. Late in 1948 Republican Congressman Richard M. Nixon of California accused Alger Hiss, a Democrat and former State Department official, of being a communist. The trial, which resulted in Hiss's conviction for perjury, generated headlines throughout much of 1949. Early in 1950 Senator Joseph McCarthy, a Republican from Wisconsin, charged that 205 communists were working in the State Department. Congress passed the Internal Security Act in September 1950 requiring registration of communist and communist-front organizations. Communist subversives seemed to be everywhere.

American policymakers began seeing the war in Indochina from another perspective. Ever since President Franklin D. Roosevelt's pronouncements on the inherent problems of French imperialism, prominent Americans had at least been able to recognize the existence of Vietnamese nationalism. But as the fear of communism increased, most prominent Americans lost sight of Vietnamese nationalism. All they could see through their new ideological glasses was Ho Chi Minh's communism, which they believed tied him inextricably to Josef Stalin and the Soviet conspiracy. They had no idea of the extent of Ho's political independence.

A few people expressed a different point of view. In Paris, General [Jacques Philippe] Leclerc repeated his conviction that "anti-communism will be a useless tool unless the problem of nationalism is resolved." Raymond Fosdick, a State Department expert on Asia, claimed that whether "the French like it or not, independence is coming to Indochina. Why, therefore, do we tie ourselves to the tail of their battered kite?" But Leclerc and Fosdick were lonely voices. Far more typical was Dean Acheson, Truman's secretary of state. To Acheson, Ho Chi Minh was simply a communist bent on aggression. The world should not make the same mistake with him that it had made with Hitler. In 1949 Acheson remarked that whether "Ho Chi Minh is as much nationalist as Commie is irrelevant. . . . All Stalinists in colonial areas are nationalists."

The Domino Theory

Out of that fear of Indochinese communism emerged a new foreign policy for Asia. Although Truman used the logic—if not the analogy—of dominoes to describe the disaster that would befall the eastern Mediterranean if communists seized Greece and Turkey, the "domino theory" grew to full maturity in its application to Southeast Asia. As Soviet-American relations deteriorated in the late 1940s and early 1950s, the domino theory became a mainstay of United States foreign policy. For a time in the 1950s and early

1960s, it was central to the way Americans interpreted the world, rivaling the Monroe Doctrine and the Open Door in importance. It appeared as if the whole free world depended upon the survival of French Indochina. If Ho Chi Minh succeeded in conquering Tonkin, Annam, and Cochinchina [French divisions of Vietnam], it would only be a matter of time before Laos and Cambodia fell. With Indochina in communist hands, dominoes would fall in two directions: Thailand and Burma would go under, then Pakistan and India. Afghanistan, Iran, and the rest of the Middle East would follow. Then communism would infect North Africa and the entire Mediterranean.

As recent historians like Andrew Rotter and Gabriel Kolko have pointed out, there was more to the domino theory than anti-Soviet rhetoric and anticommunist paranoia. Communist expansion was no idle threat in the region. The Philippines were already dealing with communist guerrillas, and in Malaya and Burma the British government faced similar threats. Radical insurgents in Indonesia were undermining the Dutch colonial regime. Political leaders in Australia and New Zealand were genuinely concerned about the prospects of a communist victory in Vietnam. The fall of Vietnam might topple Malaya, the Philippines, and Indonesia, and once Indonesia fell, so would Australia and New Zealand.

Harry S. Truman

In strategic and economic terms, Southeast Asia was also critical to American interests. The fall of Southeast Asia would threaten the island chain stretching from Japan to the Philippines, cutting off American air routes to India and South Asia and eliminating the first line of defense in the Pacific. Australia and New

Zealand would be isolated. The region was loaded with important natural and strategic resources, including tin, rubber, rice, copra, iron ore, copper, tungsten, and oil. Not only would the United States be cut off from those resources, but huge potential markets for American products would be threatened. Communist victories in Indochina, Malaya, and Indonesia would also place a geopolitical noose around the Philippines. In 1940 the United States had faced a similar threat when Japanese expansion threatened Indochina, Malaya, and Indonesia, and the outcome had been World War II. How long could the Philippines stay free of communism if its neighbors fell?

The United States was also particularly concerned about the relationship between Southeast Asia and Japan. The Japanese economy was notoriously resource poor, and with China now in communist hands, one reliable source of raw materials for the Japanese economy was gone. If the Japanese economy stagnated, the possibility of Japanese communists gaining power was very real. One way to preserve the economic integrity of Japan was to effect an economic integration of Japan and Southeast Asia. But if Southeast Asia fell to communism, such an integration would be impossible. A 1952 National Security Council (NSC) memo specifically stated that concern: "In the long run the loss of Southeast Asia, especially Malaya and Indonesia, could result in such economic and political pressures in Japan as to make it extremely difficult to prevent Japan's eventual accommodation to the Soviet Bloc."

There also seemed to be a connection between Southeast Asia and the survival of Western Europe. In 1949 Great Britain was still in the economic doldrums and dangerously low in dollar reserves. The recovery of the British economy required huge capital investments, and the entire British empire needed to increase its exports to the United States. Southeast Asia was critical to that process. Before World War II a vigorous triangular trade existed between Great Britain, the United States, and British Malaya, which had valuable rubber and tin assets. That trade needed to be revived. Nor could the French economy be restored to health as long as the war in Indochina was such a financial drain. American policymakers looked carefully at all these issues. The United States abandoned nationalism in Southeast Asia because the survival of Great Britain, France, and Japan as noncommunist allies seemed more important. Historian George Herring has argued that "America's Indochina policy continued to be a hostage of its policy in Europe."

Justification for U.S. Involvement

The domino theory became the foreign policy expression of these political, economic, and ideological needs, and as McCarthyism fanned the flames of anticommunism, the image of falling dominoes captured the public imagination. On September 20, 1951, during a visit to Washington, General Jean de Lattre de Tassigny, the commander in chief of French Indochina, described a chain of dominoes reaching from Tonkin to Europe: "Once Tonkging [sic] is lost, there is really no barrier before Suez. . . . The loss of Asia would mean the end of Islam, which has two-thirds of its faithful in Asia. The fall of Islam would mean upheavals in North Africa jeopardizing strategic defense bases situated there."

American leaders preferred to describe a row of dominoes in the other direction, from Asia across the Pacific to the United States. Secretary of State John Foster Dulles said in 1953 that if "Indo-China should be lost, there would be a chain reaction throughout the Far East and South Asia," posing a "grave threat to Malaya, Thailand, Indonesia, the Philippines, Australia and New Zealand." Thomas Dewey, the Republican governor of New York, went even further, claiming that the "French are holding Indo-China, without which we would lose Japan and the Pacific." In 1965 Senator Thomas J. Dodd of Connecticut carried the domino theory to its extreme: "If we fail to draw the line in Vietnam we may find ourselves compelled to draw a defense line as far back as Seattle and Alaska, with Hawaii as a solitary outpost."

Throughout 1950 political events in Asia seemed to confirm American fears. Early in 1950, the Soviet Union and China extended diplomatic recognition to Hanoi, which for Dean Acheson revealed "Ho in his true colors as the mortal enemy of native independence in Indochina." The United States responded quickly, confirming the Elysée Agreement by recognizing Bao Dai's State of Vietnam as an "independent part of the French Union." In February the National Security Council provided formal justification for United States involvement in Vietnam by recognizing "that the threat of Communist aggression against Indochina is only one phase of anticipated Communist plans to seize all of Southeast Asia." On May 15, 1950, President Harry Truman announced his decision to supply $15 million in military assistance to France to fight the Vietminh.

A few weeks later the strategic atmosphere in Asia changed dramatically. When North Korea invaded South Korea in June [1950], the Truman administration became convinced that the Soviet Union wanted all of Asia. Truman increased the American commitment to France, sending more than $133 million in Indochina aid at the end of the year. Truman committed another $50 million for economic and technical assistance—food, clothing, health care, and agricultural development programs. A contingent of DC-3 Dakota aircraft landed in Saigon in June. . . . Late in November, Chinese troops joined the Korean War, killing thousands of United States soldiers. To most Americans, the international communist conspiracy was well under way.

Chapter 2

America Steps In

U.S. Military Buildup in Vietnam

Homer Bigart

In the following viewpoint written prior to the Vietnam War, journalist Homer Bigart reports that America was deeply involved in fighting Communist aggression in Vietnam by 1962. U.S. military advisers, pilots, and others trained the South Vietnamese army and took part in bombing missions against the Communists. Even at this early date, Bigart states, the Kennedy administration was contemplating sending ground troops to Southeast Asia to help strengthen President Ngo Dinh Diem's controversial leadership of South Vietnam.

Bigart gives background on Diem and his regime and points out that the United States appeared fully committed to fighting a war in Vietnam. A Pulitzer Prize–winning journalist, Bigart served as a correspondent in both the Korean and Vietnam Wars and wrote for the *New York Times* for many years. He died in 1991.

The United States is involved in a war in Vietnam. American troops will stay until victory.

That is what Attorney General Robert Kennedy said here [Saigon] last week [February 1962]. He called it "war . . . in a very real sense of the word." He said that President Kennedy had pledged that the United States would stand by South Vietnam's President Ngo Dinh Diem "until we win."

At the moment the war isn't going badly for "our" side. There is a lull in Viet Cong activities, and the South Vietnamese forces are both expanding and shaping up better as a fighting force. But all that is needed to precipitate a major

Excerpted from Homer Bigart, "A 'Very Real War' in Vietnam—and the Deep U.S. Commitment," *The New York Times*, February 25, 1962. Reprinted with permission from *The New York Times*.

war is for the Chinese Communists and Communist North Vietnam to react to a build-up of American forces.

American support to Vietnam has always been based on the fear that Communist control of this country would jeopardize all Southeast Asia. And it continues despite the fact that Diem's American critics—especially liberals repelled by the dictatorial aspects of his regime—have been predicting his imminent downfall.

Diem remains firmly in charge and Washington's support for his regime today seems more passionate and inflexible than ever.

U.S. Involvement

Actually the United States has been deeply involved in the fate of Vietnam since 1949 when the decision was made to subsidize the continuation of French rule against the Communist Viet Minh rebellion [established and led by the revolutionary Ho Chi Minh]. The first United States Military Assistance Advisory Group (M.A.A.G.) arrived in 1951 to supervise the distribution of supplies. Thereafter the United States played an increasingly important role. To use a favorite Washington term, aid was "escalated" until today [1962] $2 billion has been sunk into Vietnam with no end to the outlay in sight. . . .

The battle in Vietnam currently involves some 300,000 armed South Vietnamese and 3,000 American servicemen on one side, against 18,000 to 25,000 Viet Cong Communist regulars operating as guerrillas.

The battle that is being fought is complex—in the nature of the fighting, in the internal political background and in its international implications.

The United States does not have any combat infantry troops in Vietnam as of now, but we are getting ready for that possibility. Marine Corps officers have completed ground reconnaissance in the central Vietnam highlands, a potential theater of large-scale action between American troops and Communist forces coming down from the north.

American combat troops are not likely to be thrown into Vietnam unless Communist North Vietnam moves across the seventeenth parallel or pushes large forces down through Laos into South Vietnam. . . .

The situation right now is far more stable than it was last September [1961],when the Communists were attacking in battalion strength and were even able to seize and hold a provincial capital, Phuoc Vinh, for a few hours. The September action seemed a prelude to an all-out Communist drive to overturn the Diem Government. It precipitated the present flood of American military advisors and service troops.

Today American warships are helping the embryonic Vietnamese Navy to guard the sea frontier against infiltration from North Vietnam, and U.S. Navy servicemen presently will arrive to help clean out guerrillas from the maze of tidal waterways in the Mekong River delta. The U.S. Army helicopter crews have come under fire taking Vietnamese combat troops into guerrilla zones or carrying pigs and other livestock to hungry outposts surrounded by hostile country. U.S. Air Force pilots have flown with Vietnamese pilots on bombing missions against reported enemy concentrations and against two frontier forts recently evacuated by the Vietnamese Army.

So far our contribution in blood has been small. One American sergeant has been killed by enemy action and another is missing and presumed captured. Inevitably our casualties will grow. . . .

President Diem

The man who is at the center of the Vietnamese effort and who is also a center of controversy—President Diem—is something of an enigma. He is a mandarin (an aristocrat) and a devout Catholic. So there are two strikes against him at the start, for mandarins were regarded by the masses as greedy and corrupt, and Catholics as an unpopular minority.

Diem, however, has proved incorruptible. Rumors of personal enrichment of members of his family have never been proved. . . . He is a man of great personal courage, but he is suspicious and mistrustful. The creation of a central intelligence agency here was delayed for months until Diem found a director he could trust.

Diem, a 66-year-old bachelor, often has been accused of withdrawing inside his narrow family clique and divorcing himself from reality. Critics say he distrusts everyone except the family and takes advice only from his brothers, particularly Ngo Dinh Nhu, his political advisor. His brother Nhu and his attractive, influential wife, are leaders, according to critics, of a palace camarilla [group of scheming advisors] which tries to isolate the President from the people.

As commander-in-chief of the armed forces, Diem keeps close tabs on military operations. His personal representative on the General Staff is Brig. Gen. Nguyen Khanh who has appalled Americans by taking general reserve troops on quick one-shot operations without coordinating with the area commander. Khanh is young, vigorous and driving but, according to his critics, lacking balance and experience.

Lieut. Gen. Le Ven Ty is Chief of the General Staff but he is in his sixties and lacks vigor. Consequently much of the military direction comes from the President through Khanh.

Underrated Force

It is well to remember that Diem has been right and the United States wrong on some crucial issues. In 1955, for example, Diem wanted to crush the powerful Binh Xuyen gangster sect that controlled both the police and the gambling dens and brothels and made a mockery of government authority. President Eisenhower's special ambassador, Gen. Lawton Collins, opposed Diem's plan, fearing civil war. Diem coolly proceeded to assert his power and used loyal troops to crush the Binh Xuyen in sharp fighting in Saigon's streets.

More recently the United States resisted Diem's urgent requests for aid in the creation of the civil guard and self-defense corps. The United States insisted that a 190,000-man regular army was all Diem needed for national defense. Diem went ahead and organized the two forces, arming them with antiquated French rifles. Finally, after alarm bells were ringing to the widespread revival of Communist guerrilla activity and vast sections of the countryside were lost to the Viet Cong, the Americans conceded Diem's point. Last year the United States started training and equipping the civil guard.

It is now generally agreed that the civil guard and the self-defense corps are absolutely vital. For until these reserve forces are ready to take over the defense of villages, railroads, harbors, airports, provincial capitals and so on, the army will be so tied down to static defense duties that it will not have the manpower to chase guerrillas.

Last week, in another apparent concession to Diem's wisdom, the United States agreed that any relaxation of tight political controls would be dangerous now. In a speech cleared with the State Department, Ambassador Frederick E. Nolting Jr. urged Diem's critics to cease carping and try to improve the government from within.

Government Advantage

Just how serious the criticism is is not clear and there seems to be no agreement among observers whether the President's popularity is rising or falling. One former Diem adviser said he was shocked by the loss of support among the people in the past two years. He blamed this on the fact that Government seemed to grope from crisis to crisis without a clear policy: "It's just anti-Communist and not pro anything."

But another qualified observer, perhaps less biased, cautioned against underrating Diem. Increased guerrilla activity had not been matched, he said, by a corresponding rise in popular discontent and this failure to respond must have depressed the Communists.

Most villages, he added, were like a leaf in the wind: "When the Viet Cong enters, the population turns pro-Communist; when the Government troops arrive, sentiment shifts to the Government." But generally the village people would settle for the Government side, he said, not because they admired the Government but because they wanted peace.

Consequently the Government has a great advantage. He estimated that of the 30 per cent tending to the Viet Cong, only a third were hard-core, another third would adhere to the Communists under adversity, while the remaining third would break off under pressure.

Freedom from dictatorship and freedom from foreign domination are major propaganda lines for the Viet Cong. Americans in uniform have now been seen by the peasants in virtually all sections of the country. This has given the Communists a chance to raise the bogey of foreign military domination.

Problems and Prospects

The lack of trained troops to keep the Viet Cong under relentless pressure probably will continue to handicap the [South Vietnamese] military command throughout 1962, because at least a year must elapse before the self-defense units will be really capable of defending their villages.

Whether because the [South Vietnamese] Army is beginning to take the initiative and is penetrating secret areas of Viet Cong concentrations or because the Viet Cong has abated its activities in order to recruit and train, the fact remains that security seems better in most parts of Vietnam.

In peaceful, booming Saigon there is much speculation on how the Viet Cong will react to an American buildup. Senior American officers have been studying an enemy guide book to guerrilla warfare searching avidly for clues, as though this modest work were the Viet Cong's "Mein Kampf."

There will never be enough troops to seal off the frontiers. There aren't even enough troops to ring Viet Cong enclaves near Saigon. Not before summer, when the civil guard and self-defense units are slated to take over the burden of defending their villages will enough troops be freed for a counter-guerrilla offensive. Then, instead of a conventional setpiece offensive of limited duration, a counter-guerrilla drive will seek to keep Viet Cong units on the run at all times, tire them out by constant pressure and force them into less hospitable country where food supplies are scarce.

The offensive cannot succeed unless the Government is able to mobilize positive popular support. This will be difficult, for the Government is just beginning to develop grass roots political cadres. . . .

The struggle will go on at least ten years, in the opinion of some observers, and severely test American patience.

The United States seems inextricably committed to a long, inconclusive war. The Communists can prolong it for years. Even without large-scale intervention from the north, which would lead to "another Korea," what may be achieved at best is only restoration of a tolerable security similar to that achieved in Malaya after years of fighting. But it is too late to disengage; our prestige has been committed. Washington says we will stay until the finish.

The Kennedy Administration Supports a Military Coup

Dean Rusk

By 1960, the United States was strongly committed to preventing the fall of South Vietnam to communism. To accomplish that goal, President John F. Kennedy and his advisers lent support and aid to South Vietnam's anti-Communist government, headed by President Ngo Dinh Diem, who was also head of the country's armed forces.

A Catholic and an aristocrat, Diem had become highly unpopular with his own people, who were predominantly Buddhist peasants. By 1963, some leading members of the South Vietnamese army had turned against the president, and rumors of an impending coup d'état (government overthrow) made their way to Washington, D.C.

In this excerpt, Kennedy's former Secretary of State Dean Rusk provides an eyewitness account of the Kennedy administration's reaction to that news, as well as the extent of American involvement in Diem's overthrow. Contrary to expectations, Diem's fall ushered in a period of instability that weakened rather than strengthened the South Vietnamese government.

Rusk, a soldier, statesman, and diplomat, was appointed by Kennedy in 1960 and continued in office under Lyndon B. Johnson until 1968. He was one of the key players in forming American policy on the war in Vietnam. He died in 1994.

As President Kennedy increased our advisory role from 685 administrative and logistical personnel to 18,000 military advisers between 1961 and 1963, the United States gradually committed itself to the security of South Vietnam. We undertook this buildup in stages, and I agreed with and supported the early decisions and the later ones as well.

To be sure, the situation in South Vietnam in the early 1960's was grim, but to some extent my views were affected by my own experiences and memories of other dark situations that worked out for the better. Ten years before, American and South Korean forces had been driven into a tiny perimeter around Pusan. The situation looked extremely grim. General MacArthur at one stage recommended that we withdraw from the Korean peninsula. In World War II, three months after the Japanese attack on Pearl Harbor, Allied resistance was collapsing all over the globe. German armies had attacked Russia, Rommel was driving through North Africa toward Cairo, and the Japanese had destroyed our fleet at Pearl Harbor.

Having lived through dark times before, I was not willing to yield to pessimism in Vietnam just because the outlook was bleak. And I discouraged that kind of thinking by my colleagues, except at the very highest levels, believing that those kinds of policy reappraisals would inevitably leak to the press and cast doubt on the sincerity of the American commitment. Had this happened, pessimism could easily have become a self-fulfilling prophecy.

President Kennedy hoped that economic aid and advisory support would enable the South Vietnamese to handle North Vietnamese aggression themselves, without the direct involvement of American combat troops. He did not want to Americanize the war or send large numbers of U.S. forces to help South Vietnam deal with what was then a relatively low level of infiltration from North Vietnam. When this infiltration increased and conditions in South Vietnam continued to deteriorate, we still hoped to limit our role to an advisory nature. Throughout the Kennedy years and the first year of the Johnson administration, we tried to help the South Vietnamese do this job themselves. This approach had worked in combating Communist guerrillas in Greece.

Honoring a Commitment

For me, the issue at stake in Vietnam was collective security. In 1961 the United States had a treaty commitment to South Vietnam and forty-two other allies. The integrity of the American commitment to collective security involves the life and death of our nation. When an American president makes a commitment, what he says must be believed. If those opposing us think that the word of the United States is not worth very much, then those treaties lose their deterrent effect and the structure of peace dissolves rapidly. If the president cannot be believed, we will face dangers we've never dreamed of.

By 1962, when we were considering whether to build up American forces in Vietnam, the United States had just come through two dangerous crises. We had in our minds this question: What might have happened had Nikita Khrushchev not believed John Kennedy during the Berlin crisis of 1961–62 or the Cuban missile crisis of October 1962? There could easily have been general war.

The credibility of an American president at a time of crisis and the fidelity of the United States to its security treaties are not just empty matters of face and prestige. They are pillars of peace in a dangerous world. When John Kennedy took office in January 1961, the SEATO [Southeast Asia Treaty Organization, a mutual security pact between the United States, Britain, France, and free nations of Southeast Asia as protection against Communist aggression] Treaty was part of the law of the land. That treaty linked South Vietnam to the entire structure of collective security, created at such painful cost in the postwar period. In Vietnam I felt our honor as a nation was at stake. Honor is not an empty eighteenth-century concept or a question of one prince's being offended by a neighboring prince. This word, "honor," is a matter of the deepest concern to the life and death of our nation. When the president of the United States makes a commitment, it is vitally important that what he says is believed. When both my presidents said, "Gentlemen, you are not going to take over South

Vietnam by force," I felt we had to make good on that pledge.

The Problem of Ngo Dinh Diem

As we gradually stepped up our presence in South Vietnam during 1962 and early 1963, my concern about the political situation there continued to rise. I saw no way to help improve South Vietnam's military position unless President Diem began governing more effectively.

I had met Ngo Dinh Diem once before in 1957, when I was president of the Rockefeller Foundation. Diem had inquired about agricultural assistance. We did not fund his project, but I was impressed with him. He seemed to be a genuine nationalist, an experienced and successful leader, and dedicated to his country. Diem helped reconcile dissident sects within South Vietnam and presided over growing economic prosperity. He impressed me as being a doughty [courageous] fighter, committed to the independence and security of South Vietnam. We appreciated his staunchness.

But in the early 1960's President Diem lost touch with his own people. For reasons we never quite understood, Diem came to rely upon his brother Ngo Dinh Nhu and his wife, Madame Nhu, rather unsavory characters who appealed to Diem's darker instincts. Also, Diem was very suspicious of anyone who did not support his views, so he permitted no "loyal opposition" in South Vietnam; political opponents were treated harshly. His regime became increasingly repressive, and he alienated Buddhists, students, and elements of the armed forces. Much of this may have been due to the activities of his brother Nhu and Madame Nhu, but clearly Diem lost the support of his people. I hoped that Diem would get rid of his brother, ameliorate his repressive policies, and get on with the job of governing South Vietnam. We tried unsuccessfully to persuade Diem to remove the Nhus from government and at one point urged Diem to send his brother as the South Vietnamese ambassador to Washington, where we could keep an eye on him.

Failing to convince Diem to end his repressions of the Buddhists and broaden his base of political support, we held up economic assistance, protested through diplomatic channels, and had our ambassador, Henry Cabot Lodge, pursue a policy of aloofness in his relationship with Diem as a sign of our displeasure. But our actions had little effect. We didn't want to be positioned as supporting Diem's repressions of the Buddhists, and yet cutting back on American aid may have encouraged those contemplating a coup d'état. We were on the horns of a dilemma.

In the summer of 1963, as the Nhus' private army brutally crushed Buddhist opposition, a lively debate broke out within the administration over whether the defense of South Vietnam could succeed with Diem in power. Some elements within the administration—including the CIA, United States Information Agency (USIA), State Department, our Saigon embassy—and some *New York Times* reporters felt we ought to nudge Diem into retirement or even conspire with other elements in South Vietnam to bring about a coup d'état. I was personally repelled by Diem's repressive rule but uncomfortable with talk about trying to replace him, thinking this was not a decision for Americans to make. In any event, coup d'états don't always produce better leadership.

But it was clear in the wake of the Nhus' brutal suppression of the Buddhists that the Nhus would have to go if Diem's government were to survive. What to do if Diem refused to part with his brother was less clear.

General Confusion

On August 24, 1963, on a Saturday when President Kennedy, [Secretary of Defense] Robert McNamara, and I were all out of town, Undersecretary of State George Ball, Assistant Secretary of State for Far Eastern Affairs Roger Hilsman, Undersecretary of State for Political Affairs Averell Harriman, and White House specialist for Vietnamese affairs Michael Forrestal drafted a cable to be sent to our ambassador in Saigon, Henry Cabot Lodge, that said in part: "U.S. Government cannot tolerate situation in which power lies in Nhu's hands. Diem must be given chance to rid himself of Nhu and his coterie and replace them with best military and political personalities available.

"If in spite of all of our efforts, Diem remains obdurate and refuses, then we must face the possibility that Diem himself cannot be preserved."

George Ball called me on an open phone and in rather guarded tones read me the cable. I thought George told me Kennedy agreed with this cable. I later learned that Kennedy had said, "I will approve it if Rusk and McNamara approve it." But at the time, thinking Kennedy's approval restricted my own freedom of action, especially in dealing with such a sensitive matter on an unclassified phone, I gave my concurrence. I added one provision: that we continue to furnish assistance to the South Vietnamese even if the Saigon command structure broke down.

When Kennedy, McNamara, and I returned to Washington that Monday—August 26—we looked at this cable and realized that it went further than we wanted to go. At that time the United States had only a small presence in South Vietnam. We did not have the power to sustain Diem if the Buddhists, students, the armed forces, and his own people were determined to get rid of him. Nor did we have the power to unseat him if he had the support of his people. In any event, I felt that it was not up to Americans to decide whether Diem should stay in office; that was a matter for the people of South Vietnam.

We had a rather stormy meeting at the White House that Monday. I more or less summed up the general confusion by observing that if the situation in Vietnam didn't change, we would be heading toward a disaster, but at the same time we couldn't encourage a coup. After some reflection we realized that our Saturday cable was precipitous, and we took steps to pull back on it, in effect withdrawing our authorizing Lodge to encourage a coup. We did not want to be a prime mover in any coup d'état.

The cable was not entirely a bolt from the blue, as the issue that prompted it—political turmoil in Saigon—was under lively discussion in Washington. But the Saturday cable was a snafu to which we all contributed. We should never have sent so important a cable without meeting separately on it and all of us flyspecking the text.

No Turning Back

Three days later Ambassador Lodge cabled back his objections to withdrawing American support for a coup: "We are launched on a course from which there is no respectable turning back, the overthrow of the Diem government. There is no turning back because U.S. prestige is already committed to this end in large measure and will become more so as the facts leak out. In a more fundamental sense there is no turning back, because there is no possibility in my view that the war can be won under a Diem administration."

Lodge proposed that aid to Diem be halted, that this was the signal awaited by the generals to launch the coup, and that its outcome would depend "at least as much on us as on them."

My own position remained what it had always been: that the real problem was the Nhus more than Diem and that they had to go. I sent a cable back to Lodge asking for his views about whether the Nhus could be somehow removed from office with Diem staying on, and Lodge said it couldn't be done. Even after I got Lodge's response, it seemed to me that the situation was not that clear-cut, nor would a coup likely improve it. But I strongly believed that Diem had to reconcile with the Buddhists, who amounted to 95 percent of the population. And if he did not, the end of his regime was in sight, however the end came. I didn't feel that the United States could acquiesce in Diem's repressions of the Buddhists.

With my thinking that our support for a coup had been withdrawn, the situation in Saigon continued to percolate through September and on into October. A flurry of cable activity in early October stressed that the United States did not want to encourage a coup. But then, on October 6, President Kennedy cabled Lodge that "the United States will not thwart a coup." Lodge later claimed that was his green light to move ahead.

While I don't remember all the details of this cable traffic or any effort by Washington to encourage a coup, we definitely wanted to follow the coup planning to know what was going on. There were lots of cables between Washington and Saigon during this period, routed through the State Department. I believe I read them all. I doubt there was back-channel communication between Lodge and Kennedy that I didn't know about. My impression remains that after the August 24 [1963] cable we took steps to withdraw authorization for encouraging a coup d'état, that we wanted to keep tabs on developments but not actively promote or be involved in a coup.

Obviously there were discrepancies between how I saw the situation in Saigon from where I sat in Washington and what various Americans were doing on the streets in Saigon. Some of our people may have encouraged the generals to undertake a coup d'état. I have some doubts as to the precise role which President Kennedy played. I talked often with Kennedy during these weeks, and I wanted the United States to keep a distance from this turmoil in Saigon because our commitment to South Vietnam would require us to pick up the pieces and try to work with whatever leader and government emerged. It may be that Ambassador Lodge at times pumped up the generals or otherwise fudged on our desire not to commit the United States to a coup. I can only recall my own participation, and even this is sketchy.

I cannot vouch for what various Americans in our mission might have said to various South Vietnamese in the weeks preceding the November coup. If they pledged American support in overthrowing Diem, they did so without authorization from the president and secretary of state. I am convinced that when the South Vietnamese generals moved to overthrow Diem, it was their show—their judgment that he could no longer run the country and their decision to remove him. I personally believe that opposition forces generated by President Diem himself and his repressive policies led to his downfall. In situations involving personal jeopardy, when plotters make what John Locke called the "appeal to God" and put their own lives on the line, the United States is a long way off.

Clearly, Henry Cabot Lodge was more supportive of a coup than we were in Washington. Lodge was a man of great stature, a take-charge type accustomed to exercising authority. That was why we sent him to South Vietnam. He was on the scene, and I encouraged my colleagues to delegate heavily to him. And necessarily so—during political confusion in foreign capitals, Washington cannot call the shots. Accounts that Lodge may have played a more active role in the coup than we wanted don't surprise me. But even if this happened, his ability to influence events was limited because the real decisions were in the hands of the South Vietnamese generals.

We did tell Cabot Lodge to try to insure Diem's safety in the event of a coup. When Lodge heard the coup was under way, he telephoned Diem and offered to make arrangements for his safe departure from the country. But in hopes of finding military units that would support him, Diem rebuffed this offer, was captured and killed. Had we been as actively involved in the coup as others suggest, we could at least have prevented Diem's death.

Increased Instability

We all were shocked by the news of President Diem's assassination. President Kennedy had a grudging appreciation for Diem and realized that he faced massive difficulties in trying to rule his country. Vice President Johnson was especially disturbed by the assassination, having met with Diem personally in Asia. He thought Diem's overthrow was a great mistake. I myself was deeply distressed but hoped that his successors would bring greater unity to the country.

The immediate result of Diem's downfall was positive since South Vietnam no longer had public demonstrations in the streets and civil chaos in Saigon. General Duong Van Minh's ascension to power led to widespread rejoicing in Saigon and much of South Vietnam; he had become a national hero by resisting the Japanese occupation during World War II and was popular with the people.

But the bloom soon wore off; one coup followed another in rapid succession. South Vietnam had repeated changes of government after the Diem assassination. Almost every political leader had his own party, and the military itself broke up into small cliques that were unable to act as a cohesive group. The generals were unable to subordinate their personal ambitions to the war effort, and I resented this enormously. I sometimes wondered if this reflected the French political tradition where every politician has his own party. This lack of social cohesion that most Western democracies enjoy gave reality to the question I raised in 1961, What is there to support? That problem continued to plague our efforts.

Constant turmoil in Saigon adversely affected American aid; each change of government narrowed the base of officials available for administrative duty. When the generals moved against Diem, officials who worked for Diem were considered ineligible for posts in the new government. That pattern repeated itself with each coup. We pressed all kinds of programs upon the South Vietnamese to improve agriculture, public health, and education and to help broaden the base of political support. We strongly encouraged the regime to implement these programs—I remember one count of forty-two—but this profusion was simply beyond the administrative capability of the South Vietnamese government. It didn't have the muscle to put them into effect.

An Unanswered Question

Three weeks after Diem was killed, President Kennedy was assassinated in Dallas. As American involvement in Vietnam continued to escalate in subsequent years, the question inevitably arose about whether John Kennedy would have followed the same policy course that Lyndon Johnson did. This question became all the more important when, sometime after Kennedy's death, his appointments secretary, Kenneth O'Donnell, and Senator Mike Mansfield both commented that Kennedy had told them that he was planning to withdraw American troops from South Vietnam in 1965, following the elections of 1964.

Despite his frustration over Vietnam, I do not believe John Kennedy came to any such decision. I say this for two reasons, one unimportant reason and one critical. First, I talked with John Kennedy on hundreds of occasions about Southeast Asia, and not once did he ever suggest or even hint at withdrawal. This by itself is not conclusive, since for reasons of his own, Kennedy possibly didn't want to confide in me his future plans for Vietnam.

The important reason is that had he decided in 1963 on a 1965 withdrawal, he would have left Americans in a combat zone for domestic political purposes, and no president can do that. Neither Kennedy nor any other American president could live with himself or look his senior colleagues in the eye under those conditions. Had Kennedy said that to Bob McNamara or me in 1963, we would have told him, "If that is your decision, Mr. President, you must take them out now." John F. Kennedy was the kind of man who would have seen that point immediately. Kennedy liked to bat the breeze and toss ideas around, and it is entirely possible that he left the impression with some that he planned on getting out of Vietnam in 1965. But that does not mean that he made a decision in 1963 to withdraw in 1965. Had he done so, I think I would have known about it. . . .

Had Kennedy lived to witness the future in Southeast Asia, he might well have decided to withdraw from Vietnam. Kennedy's statements suggest that he might have stayed the course as well. In 1956, then senator from Massachusetts, Kennedy said that South Vietnam's independence was "crucial to the free world." In a news conference in September 1963, two months before his death, he summed up what he called "a very simple policy" in regard to Vietnam: "We want the war to be won, the Communists to be contained, and the Americans to go home. That is our policy. I am sure it is the policy of the people of Vietnam. We are not there to see a war lost."

The Tonkin Gulf Resolution: Justification for War

Robert S. McNamara

In the following viewpoint, Robert S. McNamara provides a detailed account of the Tonkin Gulf Incident, an episode that involved two North Vietnamese attacks on U.S. destroyers stationed in the Gulf of Tonkin in August 1964. The attacks came in response to covert operations—the bombardment of two islands off the coast of North Vietnam—carried out by South Vietnamese naval vessels and supported by the CIA. America retaliated with air strikes against North Vietnam.

McNamara attempts to clear up the controversy surrounding the incident, as well as clarify Congress's intentions in passing the Tonkin Gulf Resolution on August 7, 1964. Congress understood the power the Resolution gave President Lyndon B. Johnson, McNamara argues, but did not intend for that resolution to be used as a justification for an expanded war in Vietnam.

McNamara, who served as secretary of defense under both John F. Kennedy and Johnson, eventually became a critic of the war in Vietnam. He went on to become president of the World Bank after his term as secretary of defense. He is the recipient of numerous awards, including the Presidential Medal of Freedom and the Albert Einstein Peace Prize.

The closest the United States came to a declaration of war in Vietnam was the Tonkin Gulf Resolution of August 1964. The events surrounding the resolution generated intense controversy that continues to this day.

Excerpted from Robert S. McNamara, *In Retrospect: The Tragedy and Lessons of Vietnam.* Copyright © 1995 Robert S. McNamara. Reprinted with permission from Random House, Inc.

Before August 1964, the American people had followed developments in Vietnam sporadically and with limited concern. The war seemed far off. Tonkin Gulf changed that. In the short run, attacks on U.S. warships in the gulf and the congressional resolution that followed brought home the possibility of U.S. involvement in the war as never before. More important, in the long run, the Johnson administration invoked the resolution to justify the constitutionality of the military actions it took in Vietnam from 1965 on.

Congress recognized the vast power the resolution granted to President Johnson, but it did not conceive of it as a declaration of war and did not intend it to be used, as it was, as authorization for an enormous expansion of U.S. forces in Vietnam—from 16,000 military advisers to 550,000 combat troops. Securing a declaration of war and specific authorization for the introduction of combat forces in subsequent years might well have been impossible; not seeking it was certainly wrong. . . .

Covert Operations in the Gulf

The events in the Tonkin Gulf involved two separate U.S. operations: the Plan 34A activities and what were known as DESOTO patrols. . . .

In January 1964 the National Security Council had approved CIA support for South Vietnamese covert operations against North Vietnam, code-named Plan 34A. Plan 34A comprised two types of operations: in one, boats and aircraft dropped South Vietnamese agents equipped with radios into North Vietnam to conduct sabotage and to gather intelligence; in the other, high-speed patrol boats manned by South Vietnamese or foreign mercenary crews launched hit-and-run attacks against North Vietnamese shore and island installations. The CIA supported the South Vietnamese 34A operations, and MACV [Military Assistance Command Vietnam] maintained close contact with them, as did General Krulak of the Joint Staff in Washington. . . .

DESOTO patrols differed substantially in purpose and procedure from 34A operations. They were part of a system of global electronic reconnaissance carried out by specially equipped U.S. naval vessels. Operating in international waters, these vessels collected radio and radar signals emanating from shore-based stations on the periphery of Communist countries such as the Soviet Union, China, North Korea, and, more to the point here, North Vietnam. . . . The information collected could be used in the event U.S. military operations ever became necessary against these countries. Fleet naval commanders—in this case, Pacific Fleet Commander Adm. Thomas Moorer—determined the frequency and course of DESOTO patrols and reviewed them with the Joint Staff in Washington.

Although some individuals knew of both 34A operations and DESOTO patrols, the approval process for each was compartmentalized, and few, if any, senior officials either planned or followed in detail the operational schedules of both. We should have.

Long before the August events in the Tonkin Gulf, many of us who knew about the 34A operations had concluded they were essentially worthless. Most of the South Vietnamese agents sent into North Vietnam were either captured or killed, and the seaborne attacks amounted to little more than pinpricks. One might well ask, "If so, then why were the operations continued?" The answer is that the South Vietnamese government saw them as a relatively low-cost means of harassing North Vietnam in retaliation for Hanoi's support of the Vietcong.

North Vietnamese Strike the *Maddox*

On the night of July 30, 1964, a 34A mission carried out by South Vietnamese patrol boats attacked two North Vietnamese islands in the Tonkin Gulf thought to support infiltration operations against the South. The next morning, the U.S. destroyer *Maddox* on a DESOTO patrol steamed into the gulf well away from the islands. Two and a half days later, at 3:40 P.M. (3:40 A.M. Washington time) on August 2, the *Maddox* reported it was being approached by high-speed boats. Within a few minutes it was attacked by torpedoes and automatic weapons fire. The *Maddox* reported no injuries or damage. No doubt existed that the vessel had been fired upon: crew members retrieved a North Vietnamese shell fragment from the deck, which I insisted be sent to my office to verify the attack; furthermore, North Vietnam, in its official history of the war, confirmed that it ordered the *Maddox* attacked. At the time of the incident, the *Maddox* lay in international waters, more than twenty-five miles off the North Vietnamese coast.

At 11:30 A.M. on August 2, the president met with his senior advisers to study the latest reports and consider a U.S. response. [Deputy Secretary of Defense] Cy Vance represented my office. The group believed it was possible that a local North Vietnamese commander—rather than a senior official—had taken the initiative, and the president therefore decided not to retaliate. He agreed instead to send a stiff protest note to Hanoi and to continue the patrol, adding another destroyer, the *C. Turner Joy*. . . .

At 3:00 P.M. the next day, [Secretary of State] Dean Rusk and I briefed members of the Senate Foreign Relations and Armed Services committees in closed session on the events of July 30 and August 2. We described the 34A operations, the attack on the DESOTO patrol, and why the president had decided not to retaliate. Although I have been unable to locate any record of the meeting, I believe we also stressed that we had no intention of provoking a North Vietnamese attack on the DESOTO patrol. We informed the senators that the DESOTO patrols, as well as the 34A operations, would continue, and in fact another 34A raid occurred about this time against the coast of North Vietnam (it was then early morning August 4 Saigon time).

Second Strike?

At 7:40 A.M. Washington time (7:40 P.M. Saigon time) on August 4 [1964], the *Maddox* radioed that an attack from unidentified vessels appeared imminent. *Maddox's* information came from highly classified reports from the National Security Agency, which had intercepted North Vietnamese instructions. An hour later the *Maddox* radioed that it had established radar contact with three unidentified vessels. A nearby U.S. aircraft carrier, the *Ticonderoga,* launched fighter aircraft to the *Maddox's* and the *Turner Joy's* assistance.

Low clouds and thunderstorms on this moonless night made visibility extremely difficult. During the next several hours, confusion reigned in the gulf. The *Maddox* and the *Turner Joy* reported more than twenty torpedo attacks, sighting of torpedo wakes, enemy cockpit lights, searchlight illumination, automatic weapons fire, and radar and sonar contacts.

As the situation intensified, Cy and I met with members of the Joint Staff to consider how to react. We agreed that, assuming the reports were correct, a response to this second unprovoked attack was absolutely necessary. While we had not accepted [former chair of the Joint Chiefs of Staff, ambassador to South Vietnam in 1964] Max Taylor's view that the August 2 attack required retaliation, a second, and in our minds, unprovoked attack against U.S. vessels operating in international waters surely did. Therefore, we quickly developed a plan for carrier aircraft to strike four North Vietnamese patrol boat bases and two oil depots that supplied them. . . .

North Vietnamese attacks on U.S. destroyers on the high seas appeared to be so irrational (in that they were bound to escalate the conflict) that we speculated about Hanoi's motives. Some believed the 34A operations had played a role in triggering North Vietnam's actions against the DESOTO patrols, but others, pointing at 34A's ineffectiveness, found that explanation hard to accept. In any event, the president agreed that a second attack, if confirmed, required a swift and firm retaliatory strike.

The question then became: Did a second attack actually occur?

As I have said, visibility in the area at the time of the alleged attack was very limited. Because of that and because sonar soundings—which are often unreliable—accounted for most reports of the second attack, uncertainty remained about whether it had occurred. I therefore made strenuous efforts to determine what, indeed, had happened. At my request, Air Force Lt. Gen. David A. Burchinal, director of the

Joint Staff, called Admiral Sharp in Honolulu several times to obtain details of the incident.

At 1:27 P.M. Washington time, Capt. John J. Herrick, DESOTO patrol commander aboard the *Maddox*, sent this "flash" message to Honolulu and Washington:

> Review of action makes many reported contacts and torpedoes fired appear doubtful. Freak weather effects on radar and overeager sonar men may have accounted for many reports. No actual visual sightings by *Maddox*. Suggest complete evaluation before any further action taken.

Forty-one minutes later, Sharp telephoned Burchinal and told him that, despite Herrick's message, there was "no doubt" in his mind a second attack had occurred. Captain Herrick sent another message at 2:48 P.M. Washington time, which read: "Certain that original ambush was bona-fide."

I placed several calls myself to obtain as much information as possible. Because the facts remain in dispute even now, thirty years later, I wish to relate some of my conversation (recorded at the time) in detail. At 4:08 P.M., I called Admiral Sharp by secure phone and said, "What's the latest information on the action?"

"The latest dope we have, sir," replied Sharp, "indicates a little doubt on just exactly what went on. . . . Apparently the thing started by a sort of ambush attempt by the PTs." He added, "The initial ambush attempt was definite." However, he mentioned "freak radar echoes" and "young fellows" manning the sonars, who "are apt to say any noise is a torpedo, so that, undoubtedly, there were not as many torpedoes" as earlier reported. Sharp, said the *Turner Joy* claimed three PT boats hit and one sunk, while the *Maddox* claimed one or two sunk.

"There isn't any possibility there was no attack, is there?" I asked Sharp. He replied, "Yes, I would say that there is a slight possibility."

I said, "We obviously don't want to do it [launch the retaliatory strike] until we are damn sure what happened."

Sharp agreed and said he thought he could have more information in a couple of hours.

America Responds

At 4:47 P.M., Cy and I met with the chiefs to review the evidence relating to the alleged second attack. Five factors in particular persuaded us it had occurred: the *Turner Joy* had been illuminated when fired on by automatic weapons; one of the destroyers had observed PT boat cockpit lights; anti-aircraft batteries had fired on two U.S. aircraft overflying the area; we had intercepted and decoded a North Vietnamese message apparently indicating two of its boats had been sunk; and Admiral Sharp had determined there had probably been an attack. At 5:23 P.M., Sharp called Burchinal and said no doubt now existed that an attack on the destroyers had been carried out.

At 6:15 P.M., the National Security Council met at the White House. I outlined the evidence supporting our conclusion and presented our proposed response. All NSC members concurred in the action, and the president authorized the launch of our naval aircraft.

At 6:45 P.M., the president, Dean Rusk, the new Joint Chiefs chairman, Gen. Earle G. "Bus" Wheeler, and I met with congressional leaders to brief them on the day's events and our planned response. Explaining the basis for our retaliation, Dean told the leaders that North Vietnam had made a serious decision to attack our vessels on the high seas, that we should not interpret their action as accidental, that we must demonstrate U.S. resolve in Southeast Asia, and that our limited response would show we did not want a war with the North. The president informed the group that he planned to submit a resolution requesting Congress's support for U.S. combat operations in Southeast Asia should they prove necessary. Several of the senators and representatives said they would support this request.

At 7:22 P.M., the *Ticonderoga* received the president's strike authorization message, as did a second carrier, the *Constellation*, a few minutes later. The first planes took off from the carriers at 10:43 P.M. Washington time. In all, U.S. naval aircraft flew sixty-four sorties against the patrol boat bases and a supporting oil complex. It was considered a successful mission—a limited, but we thought appropriate, reply to at least one and very probably two attacks on U.S. vessels.

It did not take long for controversy to attach itself to the incident. On August 6, several senators disputed our report of what had occurred. The dispute was not resolved, and several years later (in February 1968), a Senate hearing was convened to reexamine the evidence. It also challenged the administration's reporting. In 1972, Louis Tordella, then deputy director of the National Security Agency, concluded that the intercepted North Vietnamese message, which had been interpreted as ordering the August 4 attack, had in fact referred to the August 2 action. Ray S. Cline, the CIA's deputy director for intelligence in 1964, echoed this judgment in a 1984 interview. And James B. Stockdale—a *Ticonderoga* pilot in 1964, who later spent eight years in a Hanoi prison and subsequently received the Congressional Medal of Honor—stated in his memoirs that he had seen no North Vietnamese boats while flying over the two destroyers on August 4, and he believed no attack had occurred. The controversy has persisted until this day.

The Tonkin Gulf Resolution

At 9:00 A.M. on August 6, 1964, Dean, Bus and I entered the Senate Caucus Room and took our seats before a joint executive session of the Senate Foreign Relations and Armed Services committees to testify on the August 2 and 4 events in the Tonkin Gulf and in support of the joint congressional resolution then before both houses.

Dean began his prepared statement by stressing that "the immediate occasion for this resolution is of course the North Vietnamese attacks on our naval vessels, operating in international waters in the Gulf of Tonkin, on August 2nd and August 4th." He continued: "The present attacks . . . are no isolated event. They are part and parcel of a continuing Communist drive to conquer South Vietnam . . . and eventually dominate and conquer other free nations of Southeast Asia." I then described the two attacks in detail, and Bus stated the Joint Chiefs' unanimous endorsement of the U.S.

retaliatory action, which they considered appropriate under the circumstances.

The committees' questioning centered on two separate issues: What had happened in the gulf? And was the resolution a proper delegation of power to the president to apply military force in the area?

Senator Wayne Morse [D-Oregon] vehemently challenged our description of events in the gulf, our military response, and the resolution itself:

> I am unalterably opposed to this course of action which, in my judgment, is an aggressive course of action on the part of the United States. I think we are kidding the world if you try to give the impression that when the South Vietnamese naval boats bombarded two islands a short distance off the coast of North Vietnam we were not implicated.
>
> I think our whole course of action of aid to South Vietnam satisfies the world that those boats didn't act in a vacuum as far as the United States was concerned. We knew those boats were going up there, and that naval action was a clear act of aggression against the territory of North Vietnam, and our ships were in Tonkin Bay, in international waters, but nevertheless they were in Tonkin Bay to be interpreted as standing as a cover for naval operations of South Vietnam.

. . . In reply I said, "Our Navy played absolutely no part in, was not associated with, [and] was not aware of any South Vietnamese actions." As I have explained, the U.S. Navy did not administer 34A operations, and the DESOTO patrols had neither been a "cover" for nor stood by as a "backstop" for 34A vessels. Senator Morse knew these facts, for he had been present on August 3 when Dean, Bus, and I briefed senators on 34A and the DESOTO patrols. That portion of my reply was correct. However, I went on to say the Maddox "was not informed of, was not aware [of], had no evidence of, and so far as I know today had no knowledge of any possible South Vietnamese actions in connection with the two islands that Senator Morse referred to." That portion of my reply, I later learned, was totally incorrect; DESOTO patrol commander Captain Herrick had indeed known of 34A. My statement was honest but wrong.

The hearing then turned to a discussion of the resolution. Its key passages stated:

> Whereas naval units of [North Vietnam] . . . in violation of . . . international law, have deliberately and repeatedly attacked United States naval vessels lawfully present in international waters . . . and Whereas these attacks are part of a deliberate and systematic campaign of aggression . . . against its neighbors, . . . the United States is, therefore, prepared, as the President determines, to take all necessary steps, including the use of armed force, to assist any member or protocol state of the Southeast Asia Collective Defense Treaty requesting assistance in defense of its freedom.

Discussing the proposed language, Dean stressed it granted authority similar to that approved by Congress in the 1955 Formosa Resolution, the 1957 Middle East Resolution, and the 1962 Cuba Resolution. His prepared statement noted that "we cannot tell what steps may in the future be required," and he added: "As the Southeast Asia situation develops, and *if it develops in ways we cannot now anticipate, of course there will be close and continuous consultation between the President and the Congress* [emphasis added]." . . .

During floor debate that afternoon, Sen. John Sherman Cooper (R-Kentucky) had the following exchange with Senator [J. William] Fulbright [D-Arkansas]:

> COOPER: Are we now giving the President advance authority to take whatever action he may deem necessary respecting South Vietnam and its defense, or with respect to the defense of any other country included in the [SEATO] [Southeast Asia Treaty Organization, an anti-communist alliance] treaty?
>
> FULBRIGHT: I think that is correct.
>
> COOPER: Then, looking ahead, if the President decided that it was necessary to use such force as could lead into war, we will give that authority by this resolution?
>
> FULBRIGHT: That is the way I would interpret it.

There is no doubt in my mind that Congress understood the resolution's vast grant of power to the president. But there is also no doubt in my mind that Congress understood the president would not use that vast grant without consulting it carefully and completely.

The Senate and House voted on the resolution the next day, August 7. The Senate passed it by a vote of 88–2, Morse and Ernest W. Gruening (D-Alaska) voting nay; the House approved it unanimously, 416–0.

Authorization for War

Critics have long asserted that a cloak of deception surrounded the entire Tonkin Gulf affair. They charge that the administration coveted congressional support for war in Indochina [Vietnam, Laos, and Cambodia], drafted a resolution authorizing it, . . . and presented false statements to enlist such support. The charges are unfounded.

The resolution grew out of the president's belief that should circumstances ever necessitate the introduction of U.S. combat forces into Indochina—as some of the Joint Chiefs had been suggesting since January 1964—such deployments should be preceded by congressional endorsement. For that purpose, the State Department had drafted a resolution in late May. However, because Max Taylor, as chairman of the Joint Chiefs, had recommended against initiating U.S. military operations at least until the fall—a recommendation that the president, Dean, Mac [national security adviser McGeorge Bundy], and I concurred in—it had been decided to defer presenting the resolution to Congress until after the Civil Rights Bill cleared the Senate in September.

We had this schedule in mind until the North Vietnamese attacks on U.S. vessels led us to believe the war was heating up and to wonder what might happen next. This, in turn, led to our belief that a resolution might well be needed earlier than we had previously anticipated. The president may also have been influenced by what he saw as an opportunity to tie the resolution to a hostile action by Hanoi, and to do so in a way that made him appear firm but moderate, in contrast to

Republican presidential candidate Barry Goldwater's hawkish rhetoric. . . .

Of course, if the Tonkin Gulf Resolution had not led to much more serious military involvement in Vietnam, it likely would not remain so controversial. But it did serve to open the floodgates. Nevertheless, the idea that the Johnson administration deliberately deceived Congress is false. The problem was not that Congress did not grasp the resolution's potential but that it did not grasp the war's potential and how the administration would respond in the face of it. As a 1967 Senate Foreign Relations Committee report concluded, in adopting a resolution with such sweeping language, "Congress committed the error of making a *personal* judgment as to how President Johnson would implement the resolution when it had a responsibility to make an *institutional* judgment, first, as to what *any* President would do with so great an acknowledgement of power, and, second, as to whether, under the Constitution, Congress had the right to grant or concede the authority in question [emphases in original]." I agree with both points. . . .

A Misuse of Power

The fundamental issue of Tonkin Gulf involved not deception but, rather, misuse of power bestowed by the resolution. The language of the resolution plainly granted the powers the president subsequently used, and Congress understood the breadth of those powers when it overwhelmingly approved the resolution on August 7, 1964. But no doubt exists that Congress did *not* intend to authorize without further, full consultation the expansion of U.S. forces in Vietnam from 16,000 to 550,000 men, initiating large-scale combat operations with the risk of an expanded war with China and the Soviet Union, and extending U.S. involvement in Vietnam for many years to come.

The question of congressional versus presidential authority over the conduct of U.S. military operations remains hotly contested to this day. The root of this struggle lies in the ambiguous language of the Constitution, which established the president as commander in chief but gave Congress the power to declare war.

In December 1990, just before the Persian Gulf War, I testified before the Senate Foreign Relations Committee on the possible use of U.S. forces there. A few days earlier, Secretary of Defense Richard B. Cheney had asserted that President Bush possessed the power to commit large-scale U.S. forces to combat in the gulf (ultimately we had 500,000 men and women there) under his authority as commander in chief. Senator Paul S. Sarbanes (D-Maryland) asked my opinion of Cheney's assertion. I replied that I was not a constitutional lawyer and therefore declined to answer. Certain that I would repudiate Cheney's statement, Senator Sarbanes pressed me very hard for a reply.

Finally, I told the senator that he had asked the wrong question. The issue did not come down to legalities. It involved at its most basic level a question of politics: should a president take our nation to war (other than immediately to repel an attack on our shores) without popular consent as voiced by Congress? I said no president should, and I believed President Bush would not. He did not. Before President Bush began combat operations against Iraq, he sought—and obtained—Congress's support (as well as that of the U.N. Security Council).

President Bush was right. President Johnson, and those of us who served with him, were wrong.

Johnson Americanizes the War

Michael H. Hunt

President Lyndon Johnson, convinced that communism had to be contained, began escalating American involvement in the Vietnam War in 1965, using the Tonkin Gulf Resolution passed by Congress in August of that year as the go-ahead for his decision to bomb North Vietnam. Johnson sent ground forces into the war in March 1965. Afraid that his efforts would be misunderstood and criticized by the American people, he downplayed the buildup, a move that inevitably added to his unpopularity.

In the following excerpt from *Lyndon Johnson's War,* author Michael H. Hunt describes the steps Johnson took to Americanize the war in Vietnam in the mid-1960s. Hunt maintains that Johnson battled two opposing inner forces—a desire to serve and improve America, and a willingness to fight and destroy in the name of freedom and humanity.

Michael H. Hunt is a professor of history at the University of North Carolina, Chapel Hill, and is a leading scholar of U.S.–East Asian relations. Some of his works include *Ideology and the U.S. Foreign Policy* and *The Making of a Special Relationship: The United States and China.*

By late 1964 Johnson was in a position to make good on his threats to bomb the DRV and thus in effect to finalize his second major Vietnam decision. The successful air attacks in early August had set a precedent, preparing the U.S. public and calming doubters within the administration. In addition, Congress had not only gone along with the air strikes but also given the executive open-ended permission to do more;

Hanoi had seemingly accepted its punishment and not struck back (as feared) at the vulnerable South Vietnamese regime; and Moscow and Beijing did not react rashly. Johnson's strong but measured response to the Tonkin Gulf attacks proved enormously popular and contributed to his landslide November victory over Barry Goldwater, a conservative Republican who had attacked popular government programs and taken a fervent anticommunist stand. Johnson could assume the powers of the presidency in his own right, with greater authority to push his domestic agenda but also to defend South Vietnam as he saw fit. In early December, having allowed a short interval after his election as the peace candidate, he moved to apply more pressure on Hanoi by bombing supply routes running through Laos. After a pause, he took advantage of a 6 February attack on the barracks of American advisers in Pleiku resulting in the death of eight men. The very day of the enemy attack, Johnson ordered 132 U.S. planes to strike three North Vietnamese barracks.

McGeorge Bundy played the starring role early in 1965 as Johnson moved toward a sustained bombing campaign. On 27 January he had joined McNamara in warning Johnson of a "disastrous defeat" if the United States did not use its power. Later on, the Pleiku attack had caught Bundy in the midst of his first visit to Vietnam. He reacted at once, calling for sustained reprisals aimed at undercutting the morale of both Hanoi and the NLF and correspondingly boosting that of Saigon. For Bundy, bombing thus figured not so much as a decisive step to quickly win the war but rather as a desperate measure to turn the tide of battle running so unfavorable against the Saigon government. He had found that government depressingly paralyzed by internal plotting, seemingly content to let the self-confident Americans handle the fighting, and operating under a cloud of "latent anti-American feeling." By contrast, the enemy showed an "energy and persistence" that puzzled and astonished him as it had Taylor: "They can appear anywhere—and at almost any time. They have accepted extraordinary losses and they come back for more. They show skill in the sneak attacks and ferocity when cornered." But rather than explore the implication of these insights, Bundy resorted to a non sequitur: "[T]he weary country does not want them to win."[1]

Bundy's bombing proposal found quick and general agreement among the president's leading advisers. Johnson now moved quickly to launch the long-contemplated campaign of sustained bombing against North Vietnam (known by its code name Rolling Thunder). By the gradual, controlled application of pressure, he intended to give Hanoi a chance to reflect and retreat before losing all its industrial assets, and at the same time he wanted to reassure the Soviets and Chinese of his restraint. Johnson would monitor the campaign every step of the way from a special White House war room. Each day he would himself carefully pick the next set of targets and then anxiously await the reports on "his boys'" safe return and on the precision and impact of their bombing.

Johnson thought of the escalating air offensive in predictable terms. It was not a brutal "rape" but rather a "seduction" of Hanoi into compliance with U.S. demands to end its "aggression." It was, alternatively, like a Senate filibuster that would encounter "enormous resistance at first, then a steady whittling away, then Ho hurrying to get it over with." What gender and politics didn't explain, frontier imagery might. "We have kept our gun over the mantel and our shells in the cupboard for a long time now," the president observed. "And what was the result? They are killing our men while they sleep in the night. I can't ask our American soldiers out there to continue to fight with one hand tied behind their backs."[2]

Even before beginning the sustained bombing campaign against the North, Johnson had already set the stage for yet deeper American involvement. The decisions to send U.S. ground forces to South Vietnam and to authorize them to play a combat role—the third of Johnson's major steps toward war—had begun to take clear form in late December 1964, when the president had virtually invited his team in Saigon to make the case for a significant U.S. combat presence. Doubtful that air power would prove decisive, he explained that he was prepared to make the difficult decision to have Americans fighting on the ground: "We have been building our strength to fight this kind of war ever since 1961, and I myself am ready to substantially increase the number of Americans in Vietnam if it is necessary to provide this kind of fighting force against the Viet Cong." Leaving no doubt about his position, Johnson cabled his Saigon representatives a month later: "I am determined to make it clear to all the world that the U.S. will spare no effort and no sacrifice in doing its full part to turn back the Communists in Vietnam."[3]

By the end of February 1965, with bombing of the North well under way. Johnson was ready to act. General William C. Westmoreland, since mid-1964 the commander of U.S. ground forces in Vietnam, was reporting a deteriorating military situation. The president responded by ordering 3,500 marines to protect the U.S. airbase at Da Nang. In early April Johnson sent more marines (this time to the area around Hue) and authorized offensive operations. The U.S. ground war had, at least on a small scale, begun.

Lyndon Johnson's speech at Johns Hopkins University the next day, 7 April, capped this pair of decisions on the use of air power and the deployment of ground forces. On the eve of the speech, the administration was already halfway committed to a full-fledged war, but not yet formally, publicly, definitively resolved. The speech made it clear that Johnson was moving rapidly in that latter direction. It came as close as he would get to the war message to Congress required by the Constitution. It warned of what was to come and why. Indeed, the White House staff put as much effort into the address as they would have for a formal request for a declaration of war. The product of a two-week effort, the speech had begun with drafts prepared by Bundy and two other White House staffers, Richard Goodwin and Jack Valenti. As the speech took form, Johnson himself got involved, rewriting the text, trying out portions of the draft on Walter Lippmann, congressional critics, and the press, and weighing the inclusion of a proposal for a billion-dollar development initiative that was to provide a TVA-like program for the Mekong delta as well as schools, health care, and food.

Johnson picked his time and place with a care that reflected his sense of the speech's importance. He had decided the Baltimore university was the right place, and so claimed as his own an invitation already issued to Bundy. But when the Canadian prime minister on a visit to the United States publicly offered advice on how to bring peace to Vietnam, an upstaged Johnson angrily delayed his appearance. After cooling off, he rescheduled the event for the seventh. Throughout that day Valenti continued to refine the prose and pare the length of the speech, while he and Bundy prepared the press. In the evening a serious, subdued Johnson entered the campus auditorium and spoke for thirty minutes into television cameras broadcasting nationwide and to an attentive audience, mostly students, every bit as solemn. He spoke with an intensity reserved for a major state address. There was no humor; only late in the speech did a hint of a smile break on Johnson's face, as he turned from the hard contest unfolding in Vietnam to his dream of peace and plenty.

The speech was vintage Johnson. It put the question clearly: "Why must this nation hazard its ease, its interest, and its power for the sake of a people so far away?" His answers amounted to Cold War clichés. The United States had to stop a brutal war of aggression stage-managed by Beijing against an independent country. Cold War commitments, the pledged word of American presidents, the fear of appeasement, and the hopes for a just world required action. He assured his audience that the use of American air power did not constitute "a change of purpose. It is a change in what we believe that purpose requires." But his disavowal of any "desire to see thousands die in battle—Asians or Americans"—could not obscure his determination to do whatever was necessary to save South Vietnam.

Mixed into the speech, as in Johnson's personality, was a progressive vision that made war a kind of madness, an affront to people around the globe who longed for peace and prosperity. If the speech has a claim to lasting importance, it is because of the way that it brought together and into the open the two irreconcilable impulses battling within Johnson

Confident of Success

From Lyndon Johnson to the combat soldier in the field, America entered the Vietnam War optimistic that winning was just a matter of time, a matter of impressing the enemy with superior military might. Johnson staked everything on that assumption in 1965, and, as historian George C. Herring points out in America's Longest War, *the truth was both depressing and frustrating.*
While visiting the aircraft carrier *Ranger* off the coast of Vietnam in 1965, Robert Shaplen overheard a fellow journalist remark: "They just ought to show this ship to the Vietcong—that would make them give up." . . . The first combat troops to enter Vietnam shared similar views. When "we marched into the rice paddies on that damp March afternoon," Marine Lieutenant Philip Caputo later wrote, "we carried, along with our packs and rifles, the implicit conviction that the Viet Cong would be quickly beaten."
Although by no means unique to the Vietnam War, this optimism does much to explain the form taken by American participation in that struggle. The United States never developed a strategy appropriate for the war it was fighting, in part because it assumed that the mere application of its vast military power would be sufficient. The failure of one level of force led quickly to the next and then the next, until the war attained a degree of destructiveness no one would have thought possible in 1965. Most important, the optimism with which the nation went to war more than anything else accounts for the great frustration that subsequently developed in and out of government. Failure never comes easily, but it comes especially hard when success is anticipated at little cost.

George C. Herring, *America's Longest War: The United States and Vietnam, 1950–1975.* New York: McGraw-Hill, 1979, p. 159.

himself—to serve and construct but also, if necessary, to fight and destroy in the name of what was right.

> For centuries nations have struggled among each other. But we dream of a world where disputes are settled by law and reason. And we will try to make it so.

> For all existence most men have lived in poverty, threatened by hunger. But we dream of a world where all are fed and charged with hope. And we will help to make it so.

> This generation of the world must choose: destroy or build, kill or aid, hate or understand. We can do all these things on a scale that has never been dreamed of before.

> *Well, we will choose life.* And in so doing, we will prevail over the enemies within man, and over the natural enemies of all mankind.[4]

Johnson's concluding remarks were both deeply moving and disturbingly naive. He would bring a better life to the people of Vietnam—on American terms. It would not be the first time blood would flow and bodies crumple in the name of high and humane ideals.

The last of Johnson's critical decisions—the definitive, large-scale commitment of U.S. forces—came in a rush after the Johns Hopkins speech, unfolding with something like inevitability. Johnson remained determined in his defense of a Saigon government whose low morale was further shaken by the appearance of North Vietnamese units, while Ho would not abandon his lifelong commitment to national independence and unification. This profound difference did not "put events in the saddle."[5] The phrase, one George Ball had used in October 1964 when seeking to hold the president back from military action, was tailor-made for the situation in which Johnson now found himself. The Texan was ready to mount up and ride off to rescue a Saigon on the brink of collapse.

The Johns Hopkins speech was followed by a flurry of White House initiatives. The day after, 8 April, a press release went out, revealing the earlier decision to place marine units in the Hue area. Over the next weeks, the president began approving the dispatch of additional units. By mid-May the total number of American troops in Vietnam had climbed to 47,000 and were still rising toward the new ceiling of 82,000.

The tempo of the decision-making slowed briefly in May (in the aftermath of Johnson's decision to send troops into the Dominican Republic to stop a "communist" takeover there). He tried a secret one-week bombing halt to give Hanoi a chance to come to terms. The halt seemed to bring no response (even though Hanoi may have actually signaled a softening of its terms that CIA analysts overlooked). "Hanoi spit in our face," McNamara told LBJ on 16 May.[6] Two days later, bombing resumed, now more intensively than before.

The tempo picked up again in June. Encouraged by a new, permissive attitude in Washington and worried by enemy battlefield gains, Westmoreland asked on the seventh for still more troops. Johnson's response was to authorize both planning for the deployment of an air-mobile division and the beginning of B-52 bombing in NLF areas of South Vietnam (a decision made public on the seventeenth). Johnson explained to a visiting historian that he was not going to have U.S. forces "tucking tail and coming home." He would put pressure on Ho "till he sobers up and unloads his pistol."[7]

McNamara assumed his tried-and-true role of supplying the recommendation on which the president could act. The scenario was a familiar one: a hurried flight to Saigon (in mid-July) and upon McNamara's return a week later the appearance of a set of carefully framed proposals. In these proposals, dated 20 July, McNamara called formally for another, even larger round of troop increases—to raise the American presence from 75,000 as of that date to 175,000, with another 100,000 possibly to follow. While the president had already indicated his general sympathy for sending more troops, McNamara wanted him to go further—to intensify bombing, call up the reserves and national guard, raise conscription, and expand the defense budget. McNamara made plain that all these measures meant that LBJ would in turn have some explaining to do to the U.S. public.

Johnson was now ready to carry his string of Vietnam decisions to their logical conclusion. He immediately embarked on a round of discussions with his senior advisers, nominally to consider McNamara's proposals but in reality to give a last, extended examination to war aims and prospects for success. On 21 July Johnson met for three and a half hours with McNamara, Rusk, Bundy, Ball, William F. Raborn (the new CIA head), Earl G. Wheeler (chair of the Joint Chiefs of Staff), and Henry Cabot Lodge, Jr. (about to take up the post of ambassador to South Vietnam for the second time). The next day the president continued his formal canvassing of Vietnam policy, this time in a two-hour session with the Joint Chiefs, McNamara, and the other civilian leaders in the Pentagon. Finally, on the twenty-seventh, Johnson met with congressional leaders to bring to a close this extraconstitutional process of ratifying the decision for war.

As Johnson took his final steps toward war through the first half of 1965—from bombing to combat operations to a formal military commitment—the best and the brightest marched closely by his side. Walt Rostow, still on the sidelines in the State Department, continued to urge a strategy of victory over this communist insurgency directed against a free South Vietnam. He remained confident the United States could succeed in Vietnam as it had earlier succeeded in putting down insurgencies in Greece, Malaya, and the Philippines. The president, he advised, had only to bomb the North and stymie the insurgents in the South, and eventually Hanoi would have to realize that "its bargaining position is being reduced with the passage of time," and it would thus be compelled to accept defeat, an outcome the United States could encourage by offering "some minimum face-saving formula."[8]

Bundy, who had been shaken by Pleiku and sensed his boss had set a clear course, had become nearly as militant as Rostow. He praised the president for his willingness to escalate, urged him not to be deterred by the risk of a ground war with China, and pushed for intensifying discussions among his advisers on further steps. As Johnson approached his final decision on a major U.S. combat role, Bundy told him not to listen to the critics who saw the United States following French footsteps into a colonial war. U.S. policy was, in Bundy's view, far from colonial; it was, rather, supportive of noncommunist nationalists and intent on stimulating "a non-Communist social and political revolution." And while a tired and divided France had lost the will to fight on, Americans were, in his view, strong, united, and fresh. Finally, the United States fought not for self-interest but to save a country that would otherwise "quickly succumb to Communist domination."[9]

Dean Rusk, emotionally steady and uncompromisingly anti-communist, was serene in the justness of the U.S. cause. He had doubted the wisdom of bombing the North and continued to see the South as the critical battleground. But he finally embraced bombing and the dispatch of troops as desperation measures in late February, stressing to the president the importance of doing whatever was needed "to throw back Hanoi–Viet Cong aggression without a major war if possible." Faced with American bombers and troops, Hanoi and Beijing had sooner or later to recognize that the United States was resolute and hence to abandon an expansionist course doomed to failure. Publicly Rusk lashed out at "the gullibility" and "the stubborn disregard of plain facts" shown by professors critical of Vietnam policy. Could they not see that Hanoi was committing aggression plain and simple and that the failure now to meet the challenge of aggressors with their "appetite which grows upon feeding" would mean paying the same "terrible price" levied on those who failed to stand up to Hitler? To both Johnson and the American public Rusk insisted that appeasement now was sure to result in catastrophe later.[10]

McNamara, to whom fell the responsibility for overseeing this new American conflict, seemed oddly of two minds. He somewhat belatedly bemoaned the heavy military emphasis of operations in the countryside, and even expressed a casual interest in putting the Vietnam issue before some international forum for discussion. But he also showed an impatience for getting down to the details of winning. Hanoi had had its chance to respond, he told Johnson in late April. It was now time to act. The secretary of defense spoke privately with a resolution to match Rusk's. Abandoning Vietnam would produce "a complete shift in the world balance of power" and would have bad domestic repercussions, including "a disastrous political fight" and even erosion of "political freedom." On the other hand, saving Vietnam would (he argued) have a range of benefits, including setting the stage for efforts at economic development and population control in a "gigantic arc from SVN [South Vietnam] to Iran and the Middle East, . . . proving [the] worth of [a] moderate, democratic way of growth for societies."[11]

Maxwell Taylor, the ambassador in Saigon and the only senior adviser with military-command experience, proved the most reluctant. A longtime opponent of Americans fighting conventional wars in Asia, he at first stood against the growing pressure to have American forces assume a combat role, even though he acknowledged that the contest in the South was going badly. The French had failed against guerrillas operating in difficult terrain, and he saw no reason to think Americans would fare better. But as LBJ went ahead with the deployment of U.S. troops—first to protect U.S. bases and then to operate offensively beyond those bases—Taylor, the team player, reluctantly went along. Better to fight than to admit defeat. He would not, however, have to stay in Saigon to help manage the Americanized war. He had agreed to serve in Saigon for only a year, and in early July Johnson announced Lodge's return as ambassador.

In late July Johnson had only to make a public announcement—a final ritual act—to bring the drama of going to war to a close. Johnson wanted to muffle the impact of what he had to say, so he decided to make the announcement not before Congress or in a dramatic special evening address to the nation but rather, without fanfare, at the start of a midday press conference on the twenty-seventh. The American commitment to Vietnam, he declared, had forced on him an "agonizing" and "painful" decision "to send the flower of our youth, our finest young men, into battle." He had resolved to dispatch 50,000 men immediately, raising the total U.S. force to 125,000, with more to go later (an oblique reference to the 175,000-man force he had secretly just authorized for the end of 1965). He was also increasing the draft quota from 17,000 a month to 35,000, while ruling out a call-out of the reserves.[12]

But otherwise a mournful and resigned president side-stepped the hard issues—even tried to obscure them with the simultaneous announcement of a Supreme Court nomination and the appointment of a new head of the Voice of America. Though pressed by reporters, he offered no prediction of how long the war would last and how many men it might take. Nor did he offer estimates of the cost—only a promise to consult with Congress as the bills came due. There would be no state of emergency, no economic controls, no new taxes to cover mounting costs, and certainly no stirring call to rally round the flag. What Johnson's formal announcement began, his responses to reporters completed—the clouding of the significance of the moment. U.S. forces would not seriously fall in harm's way, he promised. Their job would be to guard American facilities and provide emergency backup for Saigon's army, which would still handle offensive operations. He could see no reason why the continuing effort to protect South Vietnam should disrupt domestic prosperity. There was no hint of the long and costly struggle to come.

Notes

1. Bundy to Johnson, 27 January and 7 February 1965, in tabs 10 and 22, National Security Council History, Deployment of Major U.S. Forces to Vietnam, July 1965, National Security File, Lyndon Baines Johnson Library, Austin, Texas [hereafter Vietnam Deployment].

2. Quotes from *Pentagon Papers*, 3: 354; Eric F. Goldman, *The Tragedy of Lyndon Johnson* (New York: Knopf, 1969), 404; and Lyndon Baines Johnson, *The Vantage Point: Perspectives of the Presidency, 1963–1969* (New York: Holt, Rinehart and Winston, 1971), 125.

3. LBJ to Ambassador Taylor, 30 December 1964 and 27 January 1965, in *FRUS, 1964–1968*, 1: 1059, and in tab 13, Vietnam Deployment.

4. *Public Papers of the Presidents: Lyndon B. Johnson* [hereafter *PPP: LBJ*], 1965 (2 vols.; Washington: Government Printing Office, 1966), 1: 394–99 (italics in the original).

5. Ball's memo, reproduced in *Atlantic Monthly* 230 (July 1972): 49.

6. VanDeMark, *Into the Quagmire*, 140.

7. Henry F. Graff, *The Tuesday Cabinet: Deliberation and Decision on Peace and War under Lyndon B. Johnson* (Englewood Cliffs, NJ: Prentice-Hall, 1970), 54.

8. Rostow memo of 20 May 1965, in *Pentagon Papers*, 3: 382.

9. Quote from Bundy memo of 30 June 1965, in tab 354, Vietnam Deployment.

10. Quote from Rusk memo, 23 February 1965, used in talk with LBJ, in tab 82, Vietnam Deployment; Rusk address before the American Society of International Law, 23 April 1965, in *Pentagon Papers*, 3: 733–36.

11. McNamara off-the-record remarks to Arthur Krock, 22 April 1965, in *America in Vietnam: a Documentary History*, ed. William Appleman Williams et al. (Garden City, NY: Doubleday, 1985), 247–48.

12. *PPP: LBJ*, 1965, 2: 794–803.

Chapter 3

America Fights a Losing War

Turning|Points
IN WORLD HISTORY

U.S. Ground Forces Enter Vietnam

Christian G. Appy

The buildup of American combat troops in Vietnam began in March 1965 with the arrival of a battalion of Marines at Da Nang. Hundreds of thousands of soldiers followed in the coming years. At the peak of the war in the late 1960s, approximately 1 million young men were entering or leaving Vietnam each year, and more than half a million troops were fighting in the war.

As author Christian G. Appy points out in the following selection, most U.S. soldiers found their arrival to be a disconcerting, unreal experience. Men who arrived in comfortable commercial jets were shot at as their planes descended. Although they were prepared to meet hostility from the enemy, they were also harassed by war-hardened GIs who scorned their inexperience and naiveté. Appy points out that such bizarre beginnings, coupled with painful feelings of vulnerability, isolation, and confusion, gave new arrivals the first hints of what they would be subjected to during their yearlong term in Vietnam.

Appy is an assistant professor of history at the Massachusetts Institute of Technology.

No one knew what to expect, but what they found was more bizarre and unnerving than anything they had ever imagined. From their first moments incountry, American soldiers were confronted with the war's most troubling questions: Where are we? What are we doing here? Where is the enemy? Whom can we trust? Where is it safe? What is our mission? The answers received provided little comfort or clarity. Instead, the green troops faced a series of confusing and incongruous experiences—ominous portents of a year-long tour of duty against enemies they could not identify, among allies who did not welcome their presence, and on behalf of a policy that was neither meaningful nor realizable.

In the Beginning

In the beginning they arrived by ship. The First and Third Marine divisions, the 173d Airborne Brigade, the First Cavalry Division, the First Infantry Division, the 101st Airborne Division, the Twenty-fifth, Fourth, and Ninth Infantry divisions: most of the major American combat units made their initial arrival in Vietnam by sea, thousands of men carried on large troop transports. In August 1965, for example, 13,500 men of the First Cavalry Division left on seventeen ships from Charleston, Savannah, Jacksonville, and Mobile. These ocean crossings had a familiar look, like something out of World War II newsreels. It was a very black-and-white image—creaky old ships packed to the gills with smelly soldiers suffering from seasickness, frayed nerves, bad food, and petty shipboard duties. The crossing took several weeks and produced nothing more exciting than endless card games.

Though some ships pulled up at dockside in Danang or Cam Ranh Bay and unloaded like ordinary passenger ships, many men (especially those in infantry units) were transferred to landing craft to be unloaded on beaches. This, too, evoked images from World War II—American marines and soldiers, in full combat gear, charging into the surf from their open-mouthed landing craft. They stormed the beaches, expecting the worst. As it turned out, however, the similarity to World War II newsreels soon evaporated. The beaches were almost always quiet. There was no enemy fire, and the enemy himself was nowhere to be seen. Most Americans were undoubtedly relieved. However, for those whose heads were full of romantic visions of the D-day landing at Normandy, the absence of resistance was a bit disappointing. After all, the combat units that made the beach landings in 1965 and 1966 contained the largest portion of enthusiastic volunteers of any time in the war. Eager for battle or not, most found it a strangely surreal beginning, like falling asleep during an old war movie, only to wake up and find oneself flailing in the sand of a tropical beach resort.

The sense of incongruity was perhaps most acute in the arrival of the first major American combat unit on 8 March 1965. The marines waded ashore on Red Beach, ready for bloody combat, and found, instead, a well-orchestrated welcoming committee set up by American and Vietnamese officials. As [author] Philip Caputo describes the moment in *A Rumor of War*, the marines "charged up the beach and were met, not by machine guns and shells, but by the mayor of Danang and a crowd of schoolgirls. The mayor made a brief welcoming speech and the girls placed flowered wreaths around the marines' necks." One month later, the Second Battalion, Third Marines, made a similar landing. In his memoir *Green Knight, Red Mourning*, Richard Ogden recalled that his unit had been told to expect a "hot beach." When no one fired on them, he felt like "the victim of an unfunny hoax." But suddenly a platoon-size group appeared on the horizon. "It must be a Bonsai attack!" Though the American troops were shaking with tension, they were ordered to hold fire. A few seconds later someone yelled, "It's the press corps!" A reporter and cameraman walked right up to Ogden and put a microphone to his mouth: "How do you like the Vietnam war so far, son?"

Too Naive to Be Afraid

During the early stages of the big American buildup of 1965 few of the arriving soldiers anticipated that the war would drag on for years. In fact the most eager men worried that they might get to Vietnam too late and that the war would be over before they had a chance to fight. Matthew Brennan went to Vietnam in December 1965, among a gung-ho group of paratroopers, to join the First Cavalry Division. "Most of us didn't understand what was really happening in Vietnam. We believed that the war had reached its final stages and that we might arrive after the last big battles were won. . . . We were too naive to be afraid."

Landing in Vietnam

Robert Flaherty landed in Vietnam with the Third Battalion, Ninth Marines, in the summer of 1965. After boot camp in the fall of 1964 he was scheduled to receive advanced training as a helicopter mechanic. In early 1965, however, "they started changing a lot of people's orders. All of a sudden they made me a machine gunner. We knew something was wrong when they started changing the MOS's [Military Occupational Specialities]."

When Flaherty boarded a ship for Vietnam, he found the mood a peculiar mixture of intense anxiety and lighthearted bravado. "We were afraid and we weren't afraid. It was bullshit and it wasn't. We didn't know what to expect." One inclination was to dismiss the danger awaiting them in Vietnam. "We had heard about Vietnam in boot camp, but we thought it was just some little rinky-dink thing—a skirmish." Aboard ship, however, stories and rumors began to circulate. There was talk of massive enemy wave attacks, invisible booby traps, and Viet Cong sneaking up in the middle of the night and slitting throats. "By the time these stories got around it was Tarawa all over again." (In World War II more than 1,000 U.S. Marines were killed during the three days it took to defeat the Japanese who occupied Tarawa, a tiny but heavily fortified Pacific island.) "Everybody was getting really jittery, but part of the time we thought the stories were exaggerated, that it couldn't be that bad. We wanted to make-believe that this war was just going to be some month-long gig, some two-month thing that was going to be like Santo Domingo—a few shots fired and everybody goes home."

Flaherty's landing was uncontested. Yet the anxiety and uncertainty of the landing held an important clue about the war: "You never knew when they were going to hit. We'd be expecting a huge firefight and end up picking our nose. And then one day we'd be walking along day-dreaming and— BOOM—they'd spring an ambush. We almost never caught *them* by surprise." It only took a few weeks for Flaherty's unit to realize that Vietnam would hardly be a one-month gig. . . .

Going to War in Comfort

By the end of 1966 most of the major American units had arrived in Vietnam. Once established in-country, brigades and divisions typically brought in additional troops and replacements not by ship or military cargo planes but by commercial jetliner. In 1966, arrival by commercial jet was commonplace. By 1967 it was routine. Throughout the war, most men returned from their tours on commercial planes. The military command called for these "government contract" flights as the only way of handling the rapid movement of troops to and from the war; at the peak of the U.S. ground war, about 1 million Americans were either entering or leaving Vietnam each year. Indeed, in the late 1960s, Tan Son Nhut was the second-busiest airport in the world (after Chicago's O'Hare). The military had neither the ships nor the planes to accommodate such a large and rapid transportation of men while still maintaining their other global movements. The use of commercial flights may have helped to disguise the scale of the U.S. buildup by dispersing and sanitizing it. An enormous fleet of troop-carrying transports continually crossing the Pacific would surely have given a more striking visual representation of the size of American involvement. Chartering commercial jets may not have been calculated by policymakers to conceal the escalation, but it was certainly consistent with Johnson's other efforts to soften the domestic impact of the war.

Soldiers flying to Vietnam on civilian jets had to keep looking at their uniforms to remind themselves they were on their way to a war. Braniff Airlines ran a line from Okinawa to Vietnam for the marines. The planes were "all painted in their designer colors, puce and canary yellow," one veteran recalled. "You would think we were going to Phoenix or something.". . .

After stops in Atsugi, Japan, and in Okinawa, the plane approached Vietnam. The captain offered this farewell message: "Gentlemen, we'll be touching down in Da Nang,

Vietnam in about ten minutes. The local time is now two in the afternoon on the twelfth, and the ground temperature is ninety-six degrees with a clear sky. Please extinguish all cigarettes and fasten your seat belts, please. On behalf of the entire crew and staff, I'd like to say we've enjoyed having you with us on World Airways government contract flight Hotel Twenty-Nine, and we hope to see all of you again next year on your way home. Good-bye and good luck."

Imagine flying to war on an air-conditioned jet, listening to the casual banter of the airline crew, and being reminded to buckle your seat belt. If some men were able to pretend they were aboard an ordinary civilian flight, the fantasy quickly ended upon approach to Vietnam. No planeload of new soldiers was ever shot down, but they sometimes received ground fire. To reduce this risk, pilots made fast, steep, stomach-churning descents. The surreal juxtaposition of the jet's commercial comfort alongside the real and imagined dangers of the landing brought anxiety to a peak. The soldiers were flooded with troubling questions: If we are landing in a dangerous place, why haven't they issued weapons? Will we have to fight our way off? Who's in charge—the civilian jet captain? . . .

Hostile Receptions

Debarking from their planes, new troops often crossed paths with other American soldiers, men who were going in the opposite direction: home to the United States. The same planes that brought new troops to the war served as "Freedom Birds" for the departing soldiers. Crossing paths was a significant and upsetting moment for both groups. It gave the new men a vision of what they might become; to the veterans it presented a vision of what they had been. The contrast was startling. To the new men, the returning veterans looked old, dirty, dull-eyed, jaded, cynical, and smug. To the seasoned veterans, new men seemed ridiculously clean, innocent, awkward, and doomed. There was a strong measure of envy-fed resentment between the two groups. Many new men wished it was their turn to go home on the Freedom Bird. Others envied the veterans' war-tested looks, the disdainful air which seemed to say, "I've seen more [s——] than you can even imagine." For their part, the veterans envied what they perceived as the newcomers' fresh, open naivete and their youthful, bright eyes. The new men were too scared and nervous to approach the nasty-looking veterans, and the latter were too preoccupied with getting out of Vietnam to waste time with the newcomers. . . .

Popular Hollywood movies about World War II were crucial in shaping the images of war held by many young men prior to military service. Soldiers in Vietnam found from the outset a reality radically different from that portrayed on the screen. World War II movies ordinarily depicted whole units of fresh troops moving into war together, sometimes trained and led by battle-tested veterans (like Sergeant Stryker—John Wayne—in *The Sands of Iwo Jima*). As the unit entered combat, men from the rear might be brought in to replace the dead and wounded, and battle-weary units were sometimes relieved. But the movies underscored the fact that American forces were committed "for the duration."

In Vietnam, however, individual tours lasted for one year. Some of the first ship-transported units had trained together and would fight together in Vietnam. Most men arrived in Vietnam as individual replacements, however, and often the other men on the plane were complete strangers. Even when coherent training units flew over together, they were typically divided up and sent as individuals to separate units throughout Vietnam.

In World War II movies, experienced soldiers greeted replacements with attitudes ranging from comradely gratefulness to sardonic bemusement, but they were rarely hostile or insulting to the new men; there was nothing like the hazing reported by Vietnam veterans in which the departing soldiers stood at the gates of war like birds of ill omen. At the end of *Darby's Rangers* (1958), for example, Darby (James Garner) returns to a beachhead after heavy fighting inland. New troops are wading ashore from landing craft. A few of them point to the Ranger insignia on Darby's uniform and stare at him in awe. He snaps them a jaunty salute and strides off into the surf to board the landing craft that will take him back to the rear. . . .

[In a] contrasting example, the opening scene in Oliver Stone's *Platoon*, features a planeload of American troops arriving in Vietnam, eyeing a heap of body bags, and passing a group of homebound grunts [combat soldiers]. "New meat!" one of the veterans calls out. "You gonna love the Nam, man, for-[f——]-ever."

Feeling Abandoned and Vulnerable

Upon first landing in Vietnam, many soldiers were struck by the extraordinary size and impact of the American presence: the rows of military aircraft, the constant buzz of helicopters overhead, the roar of powerful jet bombers landing and taking off, and the military buildings everywhere in sight. Some men drew a measure of comfort from the display of American power and hoped they might spend their entire tours inside one of these enormous American bases; certainly, they assured themselves, no Viet Cong would pose a serious threat to such a place. Other newcomers were unnerved. Amid the hundreds of men and machines moving here and there, they had a piercing sensation of their own insignificance, of how small a part of the whole war they really were, and how little anyone cared about their own well-being. This new world had a life of its own—strange, complicated, and forbidding. Eric Stevens, from Texas, arrived in Vietnam in March 1969:

> We landed in Danang and it's hard to explain the impact: There's Phantoms landing and taking off: SSSHHHUUUGGG, SSSHHHUUUGGG, SSSHHHUUUGGG!!! And there were some people walking around with beards, looking as grungy as can be, and other people walking around looking just as sharp as any military person you ever saw—I mean *slick*. There was a real contrast there: some guys all spit-shined and polished and other guys just back from the field looking rugged and hard-eyed. And you had guys walking around with pump shot-guns they were using to guard the supplies: mostly guarding them from other Americans who stole stuff to sell on the black market. But I couldn't figure any of that out at the time. It was just

a very weird scene. I was safe, but I had no idea how safe. I had no idea what was going on or how I would fit in.

Stevens's first order was to escort some supplies from Danang to Phu Bai. Assuming someone in Phu Bai was expecting his arrival and would be there to meet him, Stevens got on a cargo plane with the two large pallets of equipment he was supposed to deliver. It was nighttime. The plane aborted its first landing attempt.

> "[The crew chief explained] they took a few mortar rounds down there so we're gonna circle around for awhile." I'm really getting nervous because I don't know what's down there. Phu Bai doesn't mean nothing to me. I never heard of it in my whole life. So we landed in pitch dark, only a few lights at the end of the runway. Out of nowhere comes a humungus forklift. It unloads the two pallets I'm with and sets them down right next to the runway and then disappears. Then the crew chief said, "See you later," and then the plane's gone. I'm standing there by myself. There ain't nobody to check in with. Where am I? I see the outline of a building and I get over there and it's the old [abandoned] terminal building that's got holes all shot in it and concertina wire everywhere. I stayed up all night, of course. I laid up on top of the pallets, and I listened to all the night sounds. When the sun come up in the morning, I'm on an airport in Phu Bai and I'm safe as a baby. There wasn't nobody safer than I was that night. But I learned a lot that night. Everything hit home. Dealing with the apprehension of the unknown.

There is more to this statement than the predictable fear we might associate with entering a war zone. There is also a profound feeling of abandonment and isolated vulnerability. The apprehension of the unknown is so terrible because it is so complete and because it is suffered alone. Underlying all of these emotions is the jarring, disorienting recognition that one cannot even trust one's emotions; the war poses such surreal and unpredictable environments and experiences that one might feel most threatened precisely when one is "safe as a baby" and (as soldiers would soon learn) most secure at times of greatest danger.

America Fights a Limited War

Phillip B. Davidson

Influenced by ideological civilian advisers, President Lyndon Johnson waged a limited war in Vietnam. His administration never aimed to overthrow the Communist government in North Vietnam, and never seriously considered using nuclear weapons to achieve its aims. Even conventional bombing raids were restricted, with many strategic targets strictly off limits. Author Phillip B. Davidson claims that Johnson's restraint, clearly exhibited in the Rolling Thunder bombing campaign of 1965–68, was due to a fear of provoking China to enter the war and a belief in the efficacy of a gradual approach to bring the enemy to the bargaining table.

In the following viewpoint, Davidson gives background on the entry of civilians into the field of military strategy and explains the concept of limited warfare. He also details the ideological gap that existed between civilian theorists who counseled Johnson to gradually escalate the fighting and U.S. military leaders who believed in a bolder course of action. Davidson contends that Johnson later regretted his decision to adopt the moderate approach.

Davidson, now retired, was an associate professor of military history at West Point. He served two years in Vietnam as chief intelligence officer under Generals William Westmoreland and Creighton W. Abrams.

From the start, a good deal of the "thunder" of the Rolling Thunder program [the U.S. bombing of targets in Vietnam] came from the United States civilian officials and their military counterparts, who differed widely and vociferously about the aims and the conduct of the campaign. The dispute had deep roots. One was doctrinal and philosophical, another generational, a third ideological. Underneath it all there simmered a novel confrontation in American history—a military-civilian contest for the power to formulate not only military strategy, but military tactics as well. The concept and execution of Rolling Thunder furnished the battleground, but the real battle revolved around the civilian-produced doctrine of "limited war."

Civilian Theorists and Military Strategy

The intrusion of civilians into the field of military strategy dates from the end of World War II. The leaders of the American armed forces came back from their victories in Europe and the Far East proud, idolized—and complacent. In the late forties and fifties, the United States military leaders were not interested in grand strategy or strategic theory, and in this neglect they followed a long American military tradition. Although America had produced first-rate strategists—men like [General Robert E.] Lee, [Admiral Alfred Thayer] Mahan, and [General Douglas] MacArthur—they were the exceptions. The Americans had won every war since (and including) their own Civil War by an overwhelming combination of superior manpower and weight of materiel, a superiority which minimized the importance of strategy. After World War II, a few officers picked at the subject, but the post-war services produced no strategic thinkers worthy of that title. The advent of the atomic bomb encouraged this delinquency. Here was a weapon so powerful, so new, that it seemed to nullify all of the old laws of strategy (the value of mass, surprise, and the initiative, for example), and while some bold officers wrestled with this new monster, most looked on in confusion and apathy. In the late forties and fifties, the military in effect abdicated its traditional role as the formulators of the country's military strategy.

Into this gap infiltrated the civilian theorists, with backgrounds in one of the physical sciences or in economics. Herman Kahn, of the Hudson Institute, was perhaps preeminent. Other prominent thinkers and writers of the fifties include Bernard Brodie, Robert E. Osgood, Thomas C. Snelling, and Samuel P. Huntington. Among these men, military experience was minimal or totally lacking. However, they viewed this lack as no disadvantage. They believed that the atomic bomb had changed everything about warfare, and therefore, past military experience counted for little. Using the techniques of operations analysis and systems analysis, of statistics, of the theory of games and economic-type modeling, these civilian theorists developed their own strategic concepts. Some had validity; some were bizarre. These theories went largely unchallenged by the military, who considered them to be academic and useless exercises played by a bunch of eggheads. Later, the admirals and generals would rue this casual disregard.

The Theory of Limited War

One of the theories developed by the civilians was that of "limited war." They based this concept on two assumptions: first, the United States had to contain communism, which was expanding by means of local or indigenous wars; second, a nuclear war with China or the Soviet Union must be avoided. In the broadest application of the theory, the academic analysts proposed a strategy of *gradualism*, . . . "*not* to apply maximum force toward the military defeat of the adversary; rather it must be to employ force skillfully along a continuous spectrum—from diplomacy, to crises short of war, to an overt clash of arms—in order to exert the desired effect upon the adversary's will." Osgood, in his book *Limited War Revisited*, states, "This principle held an appealing logic for the new breed of United States liberal realists who had discovered the duty of managing power shrewdly in behalf of world order." Inherent in this doctrine was a distrust of the military. The liberal academicians believed that, given an opportunity, the military would dangerously escalate any war in their desire to "win" it. To negate this impulse, the doctrine of limited war stressed that the president must have the means of command and communications to enable him to tailor force to a specific political purpose anywhere in the world.

Until the Korean War, the strategy of limited war languished as nothing more than an interesting theory in the classrooms of academia, in the pages of esoteric magazines, and in the "think tanks" of consultants. The Korean War brought the doctrine into prominence. The Korean War *was* a limited war, and to some, it succeeded in accomplishing its primary purpose of containing Communist aggression. This war highlighted also the basic dispute between military strategists (MacArthur) and the proponents of limited war ([Harry] Truman, et al). This brought the doctrine into the open, but domestic politics and emotion prevented any rational and studied debate of its merits and faults. In 1961, the Kennedys—liberal, young, trendy, contemptuous of all past theories—ardently embraced the limited war concept. Once in office, President Kennedy set about improving the limited warfare capabilities which [President Dwight] Eisenhower had allowed to decay. Kennedy brought into the Departments of State and Defense a number of young "whiz kids," all adherents to the theory of limited war and world order.

Shortcomings of Gradualism

Thus, the fundamental dispute about Rolling Thunder between the civilians and the military turned around the aims and philosophy of that program. The civilians, led intellectually by Assistant Secretary of Defense for International Security Affairs (ISA) John T. McNaughton, espoused a program of *gradually* applied pressure through air power on North Vietnam, beginning with carefully selected and generally unremunerative [unprofitable] targets. In essence, this philosophy maintained that Hanoi [capital of North Vietnam] would "get the signal" that the United States was serious about the war in Vietnam, and they would cease supporting the Viet Cong [Communist guerillas in South Vietnam]. Its restrained inauguration and philosophy offered President Johnson maximum flexibility, in that the pressure could be increased. Its initial restraint would probably not panic the Soviets or the Chinese into entering the war. Unfortunately, from this policy of gradualism Hanoi received almost precisely the opposite signal from the one the United States wanted to transmit. The signal Hanoi got was that the United States was *not* serious about fighting or ending the war in Vietnam.

The strategy of gradualism suffered from other serious shortcomings. United States air power was committed piecemeal and on limited targets (many unimportant), and some air targets were restricted. Gradualism allowed the North Vietnamese time to build up their air defenses and to build alternate installations. In the final analysis, gradualism forced the United States into a lengthy, indecisive air war of attrition [wearing down the enemy]—the very kind which best suited [North Vietnamese leaders] Ho [Chi Minh] and [Vo Nguyen] Giap. A war of attrition takes time—a commodity of which the Vietnamese Communists had plenty, and one of which the United States (although its leaders did not grasp this in 1965) had very little.

Led by General [John] McConnell, the air force chief of staff, and Admiral [Ulysses S. Grant] Sharp, CINCPAC [Commander in Chief, Pacific], the military urged the president from the beginning to launch an air campaign which would take advantage of mass and surprise. The attacks would strike at airfields, petroleum storage areas, and industrial facilities throughout North Vietnam. They wanted to hit the North hard and keep on hitting it hard. They argued that this was the way to use air power, and that Hanoi would best get the "message" regarding the seriousness of United States intentions from its own destruction. This bolder, more violent course had hazards, too. There could be some effect on world opinion and on the support for the war in the United States to see the Americans play the "bully boy" and beat up a small opponent, and a devastating air campaign against North Vietnam might force Russia and China to take an active hand in the war.

"Old Fogies" Versus "Whiz Kids"

The gulf between the president's military and civilian advisers went far beyond a difference of doctrinal opinion as to the employment of United States air power against North Vietnam. Between the two groups existed a generational gap. The military men were of the Depression generation. By heritage, training, and experience, they were hardbitten and tough. The civilians were of the post–World War II generation, by birth used to affluence and by education attracted to innovative ideas. The uniform services had been taught from their plebe years in the service academies that war is violent, and that the best way to employ violence is in an all-out assault against the enemy. Violence is violence, their creed taught, and when you try to ameliorate it, you invariably get into trouble. To the civilians, this kind of theory

---

A Frustrating Experience

As commander of U.S. forces in Vietnam from 1964 to 1968, General William Westmoreland was one of the key architects of U.S. military strategy. He consistently pushed for greater commitment to the conflict, however, and expresses the frustration of fighting a limited war in the CNN special "The Cold War," a portion of which can be found on the Internet at CNN Cold War— Interviews: William Westmoreland.

At the outset, the president made the statement that he would not geographically broaden the war, and that meant that military actions were confined to the territory of South Vietnam. The enemy was not operating under such restraints, and therefore over the years the border area of Cambodia and Laos were used freely by the enemy. But by virtue of the policy of my government, we could not fight the overt war or deploy military troops overtly into those countries. And that was a major problem. A major problem. That gave the enemy a sanctuary that was of benefit to him. I mean, when he moved into the South Vietnamese soil, he was defeated, he took great casualties; but then he moved across into Cambodia or to Laos, licked his wounds, and restored his military capability. And that is why the war lasted so long. It was a frustrating experience for us. . . .

William Westmoreland, "On Fighting a Limited War," *The Cold War*, Cable News Network, 1998. http://cnn.com/SPECIALS/cold.war/episodes/11/interviews/westmoreland.

was overly simplistic and outdated. To them, the Vietnamese War was a limited war, for a limited objective, to be fought with limited means. They believed that the violence of war could be and should be tailored to the objective of the war.

Finally, the gap was ideological, the most unbridgeable of all chasms, except perhaps the gulf of disparate religion. The military were social conservatives, middle-class products of West Point and Annapolis, with the Spartan outlook and ideals of those institutions. They were staunchly anti-Communist, intensely patriotic men, believers in the traditional values of the American system, and in "my country right or wrong." The civilians ranged in ideology from liberals to leftists. They were largely the products of the "enlightened" schooling of the Ivy League universities. In outlook, they were more flexible, less doctrinaire than the military. They, too, were patriots, but not in the same way the generals and admirals were. The civilians could perceive faults in the American system, and they wanted to cure them. They believed not in the realities of a great power conflict, but in an "interdependent world order" in which the use of military force had become outdated.

The gulf was widened by mutual mistrust and contempt. The civilians feared that the military, if not restrained, would lead the country into World War III. The military were afraid that the civilians with their fancy theories would piddle around and lose the Vietnam War. To the civilians, the generals and admirals were "old fogies" and warmongers. To the military, the civilians were "whiz kids," military neophytes who had "never heard a shot fired in anger." [General William] Westmoreland, typical of the military group, disparages them on at least two occasions as "field marshals." Of course, the above characterizations are too hard and fast to include all of the civilians and all of the military. [Secretary of State] Dean Rusk and [State Department policymaker] Walt Rostow were hawkish [pro-war] to the end, and John McCone, then director of the CIA, supported the military position. Maxwell Taylor, then ambassador in Saigon, came out originally for the graduated response, although he later changed his view.

Johnson Sides with the Civilians

All of this bitter dispute left one man in the middle—President Lyndon Baines Johnson. Having gotten into the war (no doubt reluctantly), he now sought to hedge his action by siding with the civilians and choosing the weakest options of air attack against North Vietnam. Johnson, unfamiliar with war, saw the bombing in terms of domestic American politics, in which he was an expert. The aircraft, the bombs, the destruction itself were only bargaining tools, and he believed in his politician's heart that Ho Chi Minh would bargain. After all, Johnson had risen to the presidency by exploiting the old maxim that every man has his price, and to Johnson, Ho had his—if he (Johnson) could only find it. Thus, the weak start of Rolling Thunder would allow Johnson the maximum flexibility in sounding Ho out.

The dispute over the basic aims and broad philosophy of Rolling Thunder had a raucous twin in the day-to-day conduct of the program. The airmen could bomb only relatively minor targets, none north of the 19th Parallel. Attack sorties were stringently limited, and the military were galled not only by the ineffectiveness of the program, but even more so by the target selection system. Johnson, [Secretary of Defense Robert] McNamara, and their civilian underlings not only established the philosophy of the program, they decided what targets should be hit, the number of planes to be used, and on occasion, even the type and weight of bombs to be employed. To see Johnson and McNamara huddled over maps and aerial photographs planning air strikes would have been ludicrous, had the consequences not been so serious. As a result of the restrictions and the interference of the "self-appointed air marshals" (Westmoreland's words), Rolling Thunder's initial efforts were futile. In a political sense, they were also ineffective. Ho Chi Minh ignored all of the "signals" Johnson was trying to send him.

Nobody knows if the more aggressive program advocated by the military would have brought Ho Chi Minh to the negotiating table in 1965. In 1972, a program of heavy air attacks plus the mining of the port of Haiphong drove the North Vietnamese to negotiations. But the situation in 1972 was different than that of 1965, and so no valid conclusions may be drawn. Lyndon Johnson did draw some conclusions, however. Several years later, he told General Westmoreland that his (Johnson's) "greatest mistake was not to have fired, with the exception of Dean Rusk, the holdovers from the Kennedy administration." The army historian S.L.A. Marshal reports, "In the last month of his life, it is said, LBJ told a confidant: 'I am aware of my main mistake in the war: I would not put enough trust in my military advisers.'" But by 1973 it was too late, and the bad advice of his civilian staff in 1965 exacted a severe price.

The Tet Offensive Shakes America's Confidence

Phillip B. Davidson

The Tet Offensive, a turning point in the war, was a series of simultaneous attacks on major cities of South Vietnam carried out in early 1968 by Vietnamese Communist forces. The attacks began during the cease-fire to observe Tet, the Vietnamese New Year. Taken by surprise, U.S. and South Vietnamese forces rallied and beat back the enemy, who suffered heavy casualties.

In the following selection, author Phillip B. Davidson describes the offensive and discusses the effect it had on the American people, who had been led to believe by the Johnson administration that North Vietnamese forces were too weak to carry out such an assault. Davidson contends that both media misrepresentation of the attacks and President Johnson's weak leadership led to a feeling of national demoralization. That feeling effectively turned the offensive into a psychological loss for America, and motivated Johnson to scale back U.S. involvement in the war.

Davidson served two years in Vietnam as chief intelligence officer under Generals William Westmoreland and Creighton W. Abrams. He was an associate professor of military history at West Point and is now retired.

If 1967 was the Year of Decision in Vietnam, 1968 was the Year of Culmination. The year 1968 saw:

a. one of the most decisive battles in American history;

b. an American military triumph transformed into a political and psychological defeat for the United States;

c. an American president announce that he would make no effort to continue in office;

d. the manifest bankruptcy of the ground strategies which both adversaries in Vietnam had been pursuing, and the subsequent adoption of new strategies by both sides; . . .

e. the beginning of serious negotiations to end the war.

The trigger for these historical events was [North Vietnamese General Vo Nguyen] Giap's Tet offensive of late January 1968, an event long planned by the Politburo [Communist Party leadership] and for a short period expected by the Americans. By the beginning of 1968, both sides had completed their preparations for what each knew would be a large, and probably decisive, battle. The North Vietnamese and the Viet Cong [Communist irregulars] were positioning men and supplies to launch their Great Offensive. In mid-January, specially trained commando units called sappers began to infiltrate into the cities and towns with their weapons concealed under loads of farm products. At the same time, Main and Local Force units began to move toward their objectives, the towns and cities of South Vietnam. On the American side, [commander of U.S. ground forces in Vietnam] General [William C.]Westmoreland, his staff, and his subordinate commanders took up a stance of watchful anticipation. As January drew to an end, Westmoreland curtailed operations by United States troops and repositioned them to counter whatever Giap might try.

Attack!

Between midnight and [3 A.M.], 30 January [1968], Viet Cong forces attacked six cities or towns in the middle section of South Vietnam. The initial success of the attacks varied, but by daylight all Communist forces had been driven from their objectives. No other towns or cities in South Vietnam were attacked on that night as the six attacks were premature. According to prisoners of war, the nationwide attacks had originally been set for the night of 29–30 January, but just before D-day, Giap ordered a twenty-four-hour delay until the night of 30–31 January. Some of the VC [Viet Cong] attacking units apparently did not receive the change of date, or if they did, could not notify their assault units, already moving into their attack positions. The premature attacks of 29–30 January cost Giap dearly, for he lost much of the key element on which the success of his Great Offensive depended—surprise.

January 30 was a hectic day for the Americans and their Allies. . . . Westmoreland called his senior commanders, warning them to expect heavy enemy attacks on the cities and headquarters in their areas that night, and placed his entire command (including the air force and navy) under a maximum alert. He went to see [South Vietnam's] President [Nguyen Van] Thieu and persuaded him to order all South Vietnamese military personnel on Tet leave to return at once to their units. Some made it; most, however, did not.

The evening presented an incongruous spectacle in South Vietnam. On one hand the South Vietnamese people, refusing to believe that even the Communists would violate the sanctity of Tet, celebrated with parties and fireworks. The Americans and the RVNAF [Republic of Vietnam's Air Force] on the other hand, furiously prepared for the onslaught which they knew was sure to come that night. . . .

During the night (30–31 January), Giap launched his countrywide offensive against the cities and towns of South Vietnam. The assaults on most of the cities were soon beaten off, although heavy fighting continued in Saigon for about two weeks and in Hue for almost a month. For Giap and the Communists, the Great Offensive failed with enormous casualties. The Communists lost around 45,000 men of the 84,000 with which they initiated the attacks. While this loss figure must be viewed with the skepticism always reserved for enemy strength and casualty figures, there is no doubt that Communist losses (almost entirely Viet Cong) were disastrous. Not only were Viet Cong losses heavy, but they were concentrated in their political leadership cadres who had surfaced during the attacks. In truth, the Tet offensive for all practical purposes destroyed the Viet Cong.

Not only did Giap's Great Offensive come to grief, but the Great Uprising never "arose." The ARVN [Army of the Republic of Vietnam—South Vietnam] troops did not surrender or defect, and the South Vietnamese people refused to join the Viet Cong even in those towns where the VC held temporary sway. On the contrary, the Southerners rallied to the support of the South Vietnamese government. . . .

Reaction in the United States

Within the United States, the Tet offensive produced a flash flood of confusion and dismay, overwhelming all who would attempt to guide or stem it. The reasons for this depression varied. Some were easily discernible on the surface of the American scene, some buried deep in the national psyche. One reason for this sudden national lurch towards defeatism was the surprise of the Tet offensive. The American people had for some months been assured by no less authoritative figures than President Johnson, Ambassador [Ellsworth] Bunker, and General Westmoreland that we were winning the war in Vietnam, and that there really was a "light at the end of the tunnel." (Incidentally, General Westmoreland has declared on several occasions that he only used the phrase "light at the end of the tunnel" once, and that in a backchannel [private message] from himself to General [Creighton] Abrams. Even then, he put the phrase in quotation marks, indicating that it was not his wording. Westmoreland states that Ambassador Henry Cabot Lodge originated and used the term.) And these judgments that we were winning the war were correct. In late 1967, the Allies *were* winning the war, and the Communists *were* losing it.

The press and television contributed also to this aura of American triumph. [Investigative reporter and author] Edward J. Epstein reported in 1973 that ". . . in reexamining the nightly newscasts of this period (1967) the dominant impression is of continuous American successes and enemy losses." [Newsman] Walter Cronkite reflected the national mood after the Tet attacks when he exclaimed, "What the hell is going on. I thought we were winning the war."

This optimistic outlook prevailed despite the fact that in December 1967, key American officials were sounding the alarm that a major enemy offensive in South Vietnam was coming. On 18 December 1967, General [Earle] Wheeler, the chairman, JCS [Joint Chiefs of Staff], in a speech before the Detroit Economic Club warned, ". . . there is still some heavy fighting ahead—it is entirely possible that there may be a Communist thrust similar to the desperate effort of the Germans in the Battle of the Bulge in World War II." This warning was ignored by the news media, and thus the American people. On 20 December General Westmoreland in Saigon fired off a message to Washington, forecasting ". . . an intensified countrywide effort, perhaps a maximum effort, over a relatively short period." This warning was held closely within the Pentagon and the White House and not disseminated further.

Finally, on 23 December 1967, President Johnson, in Australia to attend memorial services for Prime Minister Holt, who had accidentally drowned, told the Australian Cabinet in a closed meeting that "We face dark days ahead" and that he ". . . foresaw the North Vietnamese using 'kamikaze' tactics in the weeks ahead." This forewarning never got out of Australia. Thus, while the president knew and accepted Westmoreland's forecast of an imminent major enemy offensive, Johnson made no effort to warn the American people. On the contrary, in his State of the Union message delivered on 17 January 1968, he sidestepped Vietnam with a series of platitudes dealing with the possibility of negotiations. The president later admitted that his failure to tell the people in his State of the Union message that a major enemy offensive was coming in Vietnam was a serious mistake.

So, the American public, blissfully unaware of the approaching Communist attacks, was struck a paralyzing blow by the surprise and intensity of the Tet offensive. Military philosophers have known for centuries that a sudden surprise blow against an enemy flank or rear brings paralysis and panic. Such attacks not only upset an enemy's plans, they cause *psychological dislocation*. It was this same psychological dislocation which struck the American public, its news media, and finally its governing elite. This psychological trauma of the American public was exacerbated by two separate, but connected, failings—the United States news media misreported the Communist offensive as an American defeat, and Lyndon Johnson failed to exercise presidential leadership in the crisis.

Misrepresentation by the Media

First, the failure of the news media. From the start of the Tet offensive, both the press and the television networks hammered on the theme that Tet was an American (and South Vietnamese) disaster. History offers no better example of the truth of the old adage, "the pen is mightier than the sword"—a maxim, of course, now requiring modernization to add the words, "and the TV screen." Only recently has the media's misreporting of the Tet offensive been spotlighted. [Media critic and author] Peter Braestrup wrote: "Rarely had contemporary crisis-journalism turned out, in retrospect, to have veered so widely from reality. Essentially, the dominant themes of the words and film from Vietnam (rebroadcast in commentary, editorials, and much political rhetoric at home) added up to a portrait of defeat for the Allies. Historians, on the contrary, have concluded that the Tet offensive resulted in a severe military-political setback for Hanoi in the South. To have portrayed such a setback for one side as a defeat for the other—in a major crisis abroad—cannot be counted as a triumph for American journalism." In 1978, on the TV program "Firing Line," chaired by [political commentator] William Buckley, Braestrup said bluntly, ". . . the Tet offensive in particular, in contrast to other times in the war, was badly covered by the media." Dr. David Culbert, a history professor at Louisiana State University, who spent three years studying the media's reporting of the Tet offensive, censured the news managers for portraying a "North Vietnamese military and political disaster as a stunning victory. . . ."

Braestrup argues that a factor which contributed to the spurious reporting of the offensive was the media's penchant for substituting "analysis" for facts. These "analyses" he characterized as "the hasty reactions of the half-informed" and as a "serious lapse of journalistic self-discipline." In effect, what Braestrup says is that the reporters simply filled in their own "facts" when they did not have the true ones.

Finally, Braestrup points out that a mind-set quickly developed among reporters and editors that "Tet was a disaster, not only for the highly-visible 10 percent of the South Vietnamese population caught up in the urban fighting, but actually or imminently, for the allied armies, the pacification effort, the Thieu government."

While the misrepresentation of the Tet offensive by the print media as an Allied defeat shook the American people, it was the television coverage which shattered public morale and destroyed the support for the war in the United States. [Ambassador] Gen. Maxwell Taylor wrote: "In forming the popular concept of what had happened during the Tet offensive, TV was the dominant factor. The picture of a few flaming Saigon houses, presented by a gloomy-voiced telecaster as an instance of the destruction caused in the capital, created the inevitable impression that this was the way it was in all or most of Saigon. This human tendency to generalize from a single fact to a universal conclusion has always been a prime cause for the distorted views regarding Vietnam and certainly contributed to the pessimism in the United States after the Tet offensive in 1968."

President [Richard M.] Nixon backed up General Taylor's view, stating categorically that television's reporting of the Tet offensive demoralized the home front. Howard K. Smith of the American Broadcasting Company said of the television network's coverage during this period, "Viet Cong casualties were one hundred times ours. But we never told the public that. We just showed pictures day after day of Americans getting hell kicked out of them. That was enough to break America apart."

Braestrup points out in his book that even after the uncertainties surrounding the original attacks had lifted and Giap's defeat was readily ascertainable, the "major media were producing a kind of continuous black fog of their own, a vague conventional 'disaster' image . . . in the case of *Newsweek*, NBC, and CBS . . . the disaster theme seemed to be exploited for its own sake." Walter Cronkite made a hurried tour of Vietnam in late February 1968 and shortly thereafter on national television dolorously called Tet an

American defeat, saying on 27 February that "the only rational way out will be to negotiate, not as victors but as an honorable people." President Johnson watching this program lamented to his press secretary, George Christian, "If I've lost Cronkite, I've lost middle America." . . .

Weak Leadership

The news media's distortion of the Tet offensive as an American defeat and the carping of the war's critics about the immorality of the struggle still might have been overcome in February and early March 1968 had President Johnson exercised forceful leadership. He did *not* go on television a day or two after the offensive started and tell the American people that their forces had suffered some tactical surprises, but that the United States and its South Vietnamese Allies were winning. He did *not* say emphatically that the news media was wrong in reporting Tet as an American defeat and that it was in reality a victory. Johnson made no Rooseveltian "Day of Infamy" speech and made no effort to rally a disoriented, divided, and demoralized nation. Instead, he ordered Westmoreland to go on television in Saigon and tell the people that Giap's offensive was failing. When that proved ineffectual, he ordered Westmoreland's key staff officers . . . to explain the war on national television. That effort turned out even worse. At the president's behest, Secretary of State [Dean] Rusk followed by Secretary [of Defense Robert] McNamara appeared on domestic TV to tell the American people the real story. All to no avail. In a crisis, Americans want to hear from their president, and they want to hear straight talk, positive plans, and some sign of courageous leadership. From Johnson, the people got none of these.

Johnson's lack of leadership at this critical time remains a mystery. Johnson's memoirs ignore the failure. Walt Rostow, Johnson's national security adviser, in his excellent book *The Diffusion of Power*, avoids the matter. Of course, there is always the old shopworn explanation that Johnson did not want to arouse the beast of vengeance in the American people who then would demand that he take some intemperate action which could widen the war. There is, no doubt, some truth in this explanation, but it will not totally suffice. A presidential speech on national television could have informed the country of the true situation of Tet without leading to an escalation of the conflict. There must, therefore, have been other reasons.

Braestrup and others furnish them. It is Braestrup's thesis that Johnson himself was unnerved by the press and television coverage of the war. The president knew from his official sources what was actually going on in Vietnam, but from the newspapers and the TV screen (to which by all reports he was unusually sensitive) he was getting a different and demoralizing story. At best the president was confused, at worst, intimidated.

That this phenomenon (confusion and disorientation resulting from conflicting information from two variant sources) upset and unsettled the president is credible. One has only to listen to the reaction of Harry McPherson, President Johnson's counsel and one of his speechwriters: "I felt that we were being put to it as hard as we ever had. I would talk to Walt Rostow and ask him what had happened. Well, I must say I mistrusted what he said because like millions of other people who had been looking at television, I had the feeling that the country had just about had it. I suppose that from a social-scientist point of view it is particularly interesting that people like me—people who had some responsibility for expressing the presidential point of view—could be so affected by the media, as everyone else was, while downstairs was that enormous panoply of intelligence-gathering devices."

Thus, the greatest casualty of the media's misreporting of Tet was the president himself. Confused, apprehensive, aware that events were fast spinning out of control, Johnson froze. The fleeting moments passed when he might have informed, inspired, and led the country. The president had lost the first two battles of the campaign being waged for the mind and soul of America following the Tet offensive. He had lost the battle of the mind to the news media, and he had forfeited the battle of the soul to his antiwar critics.

President Johnson
Changes Direction

Larry Berman

By early 1968, antiwar feelings were running high in the United States, and polls reflected the unpopularity of President Lyndon Johnson and his policies. The Communist Tet Offensive in January shocked Americans, who had believed the enemy was too weak to mount such an attack.

Dissension reached as high as Johnson's cabinet and advisers. Secretary of Defense Robert McNamara's resignation in late 1967 was the most conspicuous sign of trouble. A request from General William Westmoreland for additional troops shortly after Tet increased the tension in the White House. Johnson, who supported Westmoreland but feared a public outcry, asked incoming Secretary of Defense Clark Clifford to head a task force to consider Westmoreland's request. As author Larry Berman describes in the following viewpoint, Clifford's efforts produced unexpected results and sparked a significant change of course in the war.

Berman is a professor of political science at the University of California, Davis. In addition to *Lyndon Johnson's War*, his works include *The Americanization of the War in Vietnam* and *Approaching Democracy*.

President [Lyndon] Johnson had given [Secretary of Defense Clark] Clifford only until March 4 [1968] to arrive at an acceptable recommendation for meeting [Gen. William C.] Westmoreland's request for troops. "I was directed," Clifford later wrote in his memoirs, "as my first assignment, to chair a task force named by the President to determine

Excerpted from Larry Berman, *Lyndon Johnson's War*. Copyright © 1989 Larry Berman. Reprinted with permission from W.W. Norton & Company, Inc.

how this new requirement could be met. We were not instructed to assess the need for substantial increases in men and matériel; we were to devise the means by which they could be provided."

Clifford was not only new at the helm of defense but he found that those like himself on the periphery of intelligence data and information were at a distinct disadvantage vis-à-vis those individuals with extensive experience on Vietnam's problems. "Thrust into a vigorous, ruthlessly frank assessment of our situation by the men who knew the most about it," Clifford wrote, he proceeded somewhat cautiously.

A Vietnam Reappraisal

Among the documents Clifford researched was the study known as *The Pentagon Papers*, which detailed how the civilian officials in the Defense Department sought to discredit the JCS [Joint Chiefs of Staff] and MACV [Military Assistance Command Vietnam] military analysis. The study had been commissioned by [former Secretary of Defense] Robert McNamara on June 17, 1967, in an attempt to assess where the U.S. military policymaking process on Vietnam had failed. The task force of 36 civilian and military analysts had had access to virtually all classified material from the Office of the Secretary of Defense, the CIA, and the State Department. The result was a history of over twenty years of deception by the Defense Department to perpetuate U.S. military power in Southeast Asia with total disregard for the effects of that policy on American and Vietnamese citizens. [*The Pentagon Papers* was published by the *New York Times* in June 1971 after Daniel Ellsberg, a former defense department official and critic of the war, leaked the top-secret study.]

One background paper in particular, "Alternative Strategies," authored by the assistant secretary of defense for systems analysis, Alain Enthoven, was a blistering McNamara-like attack from a "whiz kid" turned whistle-blower:

> Our strategy of attrition has not worked. . . . We became
> mesmerized by statistics of known doubtful validity, choos-

ing to place our faith only in the ones that showed progress. We judged the enemy's intentions rather than his capabilities because we trusted captured documents too much. . . . In short, our setbacks were due to wishful thinking compounded by a massive intelligence collection and/or intelligence failure. . . . We have achieved stalemate at a high commitment.

Enthoven's paper was supported by the analyses of Deputy Secretary of Defense Paul Nitze and Assistant Secretary of Defense for International Security Affairs (the Pentagon's "Little State" Department) Paul Warnke.

Clifford also questioned the Joint Chiefs and those advisors who knew the most about Vietnam. He recalled his attempts at fact finding in "A Viet Nam Reappraisal":

"Will 200,000 more men do the job?" I found no assurance that they would. "If no, how many more might be needed—and when?" There was no way of knowing. "What would be involved in committing 200,000 more men to Viet Nam?" A reserve call-up of approximately 280,000, an increased draft call and an extension of tours of duty of most men then in service. "Can the enemy respond with a build-up of his own?" He could and he probably would. "What are the estimated costs of the latest requests?" First calculations were on the order of $2 billion for the remaining four months of that fiscal year, and an increase of $10 to $12 billion for the year beginning July 1, 1968. "What will be the impact on the economy?" So great that we would face the possibility of credit restrictions, a tax increase and even wage and price controls. The balance of payments would be worsened by at least half a billion dollars a year. "Can bombing stop the war?" Never by itself. It was inflicting heavy personnel and materiel losses, but bombing by itself would not stop the war. "Will stepping up the bombing decrease American casualties?" Very little, if at all."

The Joint Chiefs had expected the new secretary of defense to be more supportive of the bombing program than his predecessor because of his past hawkish views, but

Clifford now requested to see the military plan for attaining victory in Vietnam:

> I was told that there was no plan for victory in the historic American sense. Why not? Because our forces were operating under three major political restrictions: The President had forbidden the invasion of North Viet Nam because this could trigger the mutual assistance pact between North Viet Nam and China; the President had forbidden the mining of the harbor at Haiphong, the principal port through which the North received military supplies, because a Soviet vessel might be sunk; the President had forbidden our forces to pursue the enemy into Laos and Cambodia, for to do so would spread the war, politically and geographically, with no discernible advantage. These and other restrictions which precluded an all-out, no-holds-barred military effort were wisely designed to prevent our being drawn into a larger war.

Clifford also asked the Joint Chiefs,

> What is the best estimate as to how long this course of action will take? Six months? One year? Two years? Not only was there no agreement, I could find no one willing to express any confidence in his guesses. Certainly, none of us was willing to assert that he could see "light at the end of the tunnel" or that American troops would be coming home by the end of the year. After days of this type of analysis, my concern had greatly deepened. I could not find out when the war was going to end; I could not find out the manner in which it was going to end; I could not find out whether the new requests for men and equipment were going to be enough, or whether it would take more and, if more, when and how much; I could not find out how soon the South Vietnamese forces would be ready to take over. All I had was the statement, given with too little self-assurance to be comforting, that if we persisted for an indeterminate length of time, the enemy would choose not to go on.

Clifford finally asked, "Does anyone see any diminution in the will of the enemy after four years of our having been there, after enormous casualties and after massive destruction from our bombing?" The answer was that there appeared to be no diminution in the will of the enemy.

Clifford Reports

Johnson received the Clifford task-force report on March 4 [1968]. The report recommended meeting Westmoreland's immediate military situation by deploying 22,000 additional personnel (approximately 60 percent of which would be combat and three tactical fighter squadrons). The task force also recommended approval of a 262,000 Reserve call-up in order to help restore the strategic Reserve. But the report contained none of Clifford's private doubts or questions. Instead, it called for a major new study designed to give Westmoreland "strategic guidance" for the future. It was quite possible that an additional 200,000 American troops or double or triple that quantity, would not be enough to accomplish U.S. objectives.

Upon receiving the task-force report, Johnson convened a meeting of the principals. Now, for the first time, the president heard Clifford outline the problems facing the president.

> Your senior advisers have conferred on this matter at very great length. There is a deep-seated concern by your advisers. There is a concern that if we say yes, and step up with the addition of 206,000 more men that we might continue down the road as we have been without accomplishing our purpose—which is for a viable South Vietnam which can live in peace. We are not convinced that our present policy will bring us to that objective.

Clifford then turned to the tragic irony of the previous autumn's progress report.

> For a while, we thought and had the feeling that we understood the strength of the Viet Cong and the North Vietnamese. You will remember the rather optimistic reports of General Westmoreland and Ambassador Bunker last year. Frankly, it came as a shock that the Vietcong–North Vietnamese had the strength of force and skill to mount the Tet

offensive—as they did. They struck 34 cities, made strong inroads in Saigon and in Hué. There have been very definite effects felt in the countryside.

Clifford emphasized that the 206,000 request was not just another call for more troops. The new request brought the president to the clearly defined watershed of going down the same road of "more troops, more guns, more planes, more ships?" And, "do you go on killing more Viet Cong and more North Vietnamese and killing more Vietcong and more North Vietnamese?" Clifford now shattered any illusions the president may have held with respect to military progress.

There are grave doubts that we have made the type of progress we had hoped to have made by this time. As we build up our forces, they build up theirs. We continue to fight at a higher level of intensity. Even were we to meet this full request of 206,000 men, and the pattern continues as it has, it is likely that by March he [General Westmoreland] may want another 200,000 to 300,000 men with no end in sight. The reserve forces in North Vietnam are a cause for concern as well. They have a very substantial population from which to draw. They have no trouble whatever organizing, equipping, and training their forces. We seem to have a sinkhole. We put in more—they match it. We put in more—they match it. I see more and more fighting with more and more casualties on the US side and no end in sight to the action.

The Sinkhole

President Johnson now found himself in a difficult situation. The American people had been told that General Westmoreland would get all he required. Failure to meet the request of his field commander would leave Johnson vulnerable to the charge that he was not supporting soldiers in the field. . . .

In virtually every respect, [however,] General Westmoreland's 205,000 request represented the failure of U.S. strategy. The reinforcements would bring the total American military commitment in ground forces to three-quarters of a million—yet the United States would be no closer to victory than in 1965 at the outset of the Americanization of the war. Progress had been made but the objective of an honorable peace in Vietnam was nowhere in sight. It was becoming increasingly evident that no amount of military power would bring North Vietnam to the conference table—at least not in an American presidential election year. Why should anyone believe that 750,000 would break the enemy's will?

Tet had been, in the words of General Bruce Palmer, who was deputy to General Westmoreland and later served as Vice-Chief of Staff, "an allied intelligence failure ranking with Pearl Harbor in 1941 or the Ardennes Offensive in 1944." George Kennan, former diplomat, presidential advisor, and author of the containment doctrine, now bitterly denounced administration policy as a "massive miscalculation and error of policy, an error for which it is hard to find any parallels in our history." At a campaign dinner for Senator Eugene McCarthy, Kennan charged that the military effort was "grievously unsound, devoid throughout of a plausible, coherent and realistic object."

American public opinion would not tolerate a long drawn-out military campaign with high casualties. Westmoreland's strategy of search and destroy was based on the faulty premise that a military victory was conceivable if U.S. forces just destroyed enough Viet Cong. This was a sound doctrine in World War II, but was not realistic in the Vietnam war. Vietnam could not be won by attriting the enemy alone. . . .

Changing Course

The war had become a sinkhole. The notion of American omnipotence and inevitable victory was shattered during Tet. The Tet offensive had contradicted the president's public pronouncements. "I am convinced I made a mistake," Johnson later wrote, "by not saying more about Vietnam in my State of the Union report on January 17, 1968." Cable traffic and intelligence reports all confirmed a buildup of enemy forces, but after presenting optimistic scenarios in

November, President Johnson could hardly have done otherwise. "In retrospect, I think I was too cautious. If I had forecast the possibilities, the American people would have been better prepared for what was soon to come." Tet had revealed that despite over 525,000 men, billions of dollars, and extensive bombing, the United States had not stopped the enemy from replacing his forces. The rate of the war and the capacity to sustain it were controlled not by America's superior technology, but by the enemy.

President Johnson had tried to control public perceptions of the war's progress. He appears to have believed he could utilize the prestige of the presidency to legitimize statistics— as though they could stand alone as proof that there was no policy stalemate. Faith in numbers replaced a visible demonstration of presidential leadership.

Between the final meeting of the "wise men" [White House foreign policy and senior advisors] and President Johnson's March 31 speech [a major address to the nation focusing on Gen. Westmoreland's troop request], Clifford took control of the speech-drafting process. He informed [Secretary of State Dean] Rusk and [National Security Advisor Walt] Rostow that the country could not accept a war speech; the president as candidate and as Commander in Chief needed a peace speech. Democracy could not survive without majority support for a nation's war policy. LBJ had lost that link. Clifford assigned responsibility for drafting the speech to [presidential aide] Harry McPherson, whose views were well known amongst the principals. Clifford and McPherson have provided lengthy oral-history interviews which describe how they literally set out to save their president from the hawks. "Together we'll get our country and President out of this mess," Clifford decided. "Is he with us," a phrase from the French Revolution, became the secret code for those working for disengagement. The speech became the format for a bombing halt at the twentieth parallel of North Vietnam which would be tied conditionally to Hanoi's favorable response for negotiations.

The president was scheduled to deliver his speech at 9:00 P.M. EST [on March 31, 1968]; McPherson was still working on the draft in his White House office when LBJ telephoned:

> "Do you think it is a good speech?" the president asked his aide. McPherson thought it was. "Do you think it will help?" McPherson thought it would, particularly at home. "Do you think Hanoi will talk?" The aide was much less certain—the chances seemed to him to be less than 50–50. "I'm going to have a little ending of my own to add to yours," the president told his aide and friend. McPherson had heard that it was in the works, and he caught a hint the day before of what Johnson might do. "Do you know what I'm going to say?" Johnson asked. There was a pause. Yes, he thought so. "What do you think?" "I'm very sorry," said McPherson softly. "Okay," responded the President with a Texas lilt in his voice—"so long, pardner."

Johnson's Surprise

In his speech . . . , Lyndon Johnson announced a partial suspension of the bombing against North Vietnam. "There is no need to delay talks that could bring an end to this long and this bloody war. Tonight, I renew the offer I made last August—to stop the bombardment of North Vietnam. We ask that talks begin promptly, that they be serious talks on the substance of peace. We assume that during those talks Hanoi will not take advantage of our restraint. We are prepared to move immediately toward peace through negotiations. So tonight, in the hope that this action will lead to early talks, I am taking the first step to de-escalate the conflict. We are reducing—substantially reducing—the present level of hostilities. And we are doing so unilaterally, and at once." The president then stunned the nation by announcing, "believing this as I do, I have concluded that I should not permit the Presidency to become involved in the partisan divisions that are developing in this political year. With America's sons in the fields far away, with America's future under challenge right here at home, with our hopes and the world's hopes for peace in the balance every day, I do not believe that I should devote an hour or a day of my time to any personal partisan causes or to any duties other than the awesome duties of this office—the Presidency of your country. Accordingly, I shall not seek, and I will not accept, the nomination of my party for another term as your President." . . .

When the president uttered his March 31 words, "I will not accept . . ." Johnson's colleagues, friends, and political observers unanimously viewed his decision as a positive, forward, and constructive step for national unity and peace in Vietnam. A Harris survey immediately following Johnson's announcement revealed a complete reversal in the president's job approval rating at the start of March. Approval in April stood at 57 percent, in March it had been 43 percent; disapproval had dropped in one month from 57 percent to 43 percent. Stepping aside brought Johnson more praise than any of his actions in the past year. . . .

In Retrospect

Lyndon Johnson chose to Americanize the war in July 1965; he chose to accept General Westmoreland's attrition strategy; he chose not to mobilize his country for war; he chose and encouraged others to paint optimistic scenarios for the American public; he chose to hide the anticipated enemy buildup prior to Tet because, in an election year, he had hoped for a military miracle—perhaps Westmoreland would turn the tide when the enemy began its final desperate assault.

It was left to Clark Clifford as secretary of defense to convince Johnson that Vietnam had become a sinkhole. The irony was that Secretary McNamara had been banished from the administration for the same advocacy. [Undersecretary of State] George Ball had been listened to but not heard. Johnson's decision to remove himself from the renomination race represented the ultimate recognition that the Vietnam war had become interwoven with his personality and his presidency. "I shall not accept" was the president's admission that Vietnam had become, against his every desire, Lyndon Johnson's war.

Chapter 4

America's Disillusionment

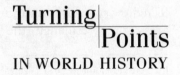

Turning|Points
IN WORLD HISTORY

Antiwar Protests Rock America

Robert D. Schulzinger

American involvement in Vietnam initially enjoyed strong support in the United States, but as the conflict continued without signs of an eminent conclusion, public opinion changed. Disapproval of President Lyndon B. Johnson's limited approach to fighting increased. Some individuals, labeled "doves," thought America should negotiate a quick settlement with the Communists in order to get out of Vietnam. Others, nicknamed "hawks," believed the war should be waged more vigorously to bring the Communists to their knees.

In the following viewpoint, author Robert D. Schulzinger traces the growth of the antiwar movement, emphasizing that it was composed of a variety of groups—some radical, some moderate—with a variety of conflicting demands and objectives. Dissension and violence within the movement repulsed many sympathizers, but, despite these shortcomings, growing numbers of ordinary Americans participated in protests as the years passed. Schulzinger points out that there is conflicting evidence that the antiwar movement helped hurry the end of the war. It did, however, change perceptions Americans held regarding their country and their government.

Robert D. Schulzinger is a professor of history and director of the International Affairs Program at the University of Colorado at Boulder.

Controversy over the war in Vietnam brought vast changes to the United States in the 1960s. The war profoundly affected every institution in American life: universities, Congress, the presidency, the Democratic Party, the armed forces, labor unions, religious organizations, and the mass media. At the beginning of U.S. involvement in the war most Americans trusted their leaders to make appropriate choices, and the public held most large organizations in high regard. . . .

By 1968 this landscape had changed beyond recognition. A sizeable portion of the public no longer believed that government officials waged the Cold War properly. Many thought that the war in Vietnam had become a burden which the country no longer could afford. Quickly labeled "doves" by the mass media, these people wanted the United States to reduce its role in Vietnam and reach a negotiated settlement with the North Vietnamese and the NLF [National Liberation Front; Communist-dominated political organization in South Vietnam]. Many others, often a larger proportion of the public, believed that the U.S. involvement in the war had initially been a proper course of action, but they now thought that leaders had badly mismanaged the conduct of a war which seemed to drag on endlessly without the traditional indicators of success. These so-called hawks wanted the United States to fight the war more vigorously and end it soon.

The desire for a speedy end to the fighting crossed all lines as the public grew disgusted with the war. The largest political demonstrations since the 1930s took place as opponents of the war demanded the end of U.S. participation. Some of the most dramatic demonstrations against the war took place on college and university campuses. Many protesters challenged the basic assumptions of U.S. foreign policy in the Cold War. By 1968 opposition to the war forced Lyndon Johnson to withdraw from the presidential race, while the Democratic Party nearly tore itself apart over the Johnson administration's policy in Vietnam. For a generation most Democratic members of Congress had advocated the containment of communism as the proper foreign policy for the United States, but a group of Democratic senators and representatives opposed the Johnson administration's policy in Vietnam. As this group grew from about eleven in 1965 to more than thirty in 1968, many of the members also questioned the basic assumptions of American foreign policy. They concluded that Vietnam represented an overextension of U.S. resources. The majority of Democratic office-holders continued to support Johnson and his Vietnam policy, but many did so out of a sense of duty rather than conviction. . . .

Early Expressions of Protest

From the early days of anti-war protest in 1965, opponents of the war in Vietnam confronted the dilemma faced by anyone who considers a public issue one of right or wrong. Political activists wanted to convince a majority of the public or elected representatives to adopt their course of action. That required patience, subtlety, and the willingness to allow people with different points of view a graceful way to change their minds. But if the issue truly involved morality it was hard for the activists to accept that more Americans supported the war than opposed it. In the fall of 1965 a Gallup Poll revealed a huge majority of 70 percent supported the war and that people between the ages of twenty-one and thirty backed the war more strongly than did any other group. That fall, college students expressed pro-war feelings at least as strongly as they did anti-war sentiments. Sixteen thousand students at Michigan State University signed a petition backing Johnson, 2,000 at the University of Michigan and 175 at the Harvard Law School sent telegrams to the White House supporting Johnson's position.

Being outnumbered only frustrated anti-war activists. The bitterness led to dramatic acts, most of which hardened public attitudes against the anti-war movement. The violence and self-defeating activities of a few anti-war activists also deepened the divisions among opponents of the war. As time went on the differences over tactics—non-violence versus direct action, political involvement designed to change the minds of politicians versus demonstrations designed to raise the costs of continuing the war for both the public and government officials—tended to overshadow the agreement among opponents of the war that the fighting should end.

Two political suicides in late 1965 raised the stakes. On November 2, 1965 Norman Morrison, a Quaker active in the peace and civil rights movements, held his eighteen-month-old daughter in his arms near the entrance to the Pentagon, poured kerosene over himself and the child, and set themselves afire. Bystanders rescued the child, but Morrison died. He had previously expressed despair at the "terrible predicament" of speaking out against the killing without reversing government policy. The day he killed himself he read the anguished cry of a French priest in Vietnam who had "seen my faithful burned up in napalm." Morrison thought his previous efforts to organize letter writing campaigns to members of Congress futile. . . . A week later Roger LaPorte, a twenty-two-year-old participant in the Catholic Worker Movement's opposition to the war in Vietnam, also took his life in a gasoline immolation in front of the United Nations headquarters in New York. Before he died LaPorte said, "I'm a Catholic Worker. I'm against all wars. I did this as a religious action." . . .

The two suicides did not inspire others to follow. Religious pacifists encouraged people to live their lives for peace. Practically, that meant continuing the sorts of political organizing, rallies, and opposition to the draft that had so frustrated Morrison and LaPorte. In 1966 liberals and moderate pacifists overshadowed radicals in their opposition to the war. . . .

The Movement Grows

Anti-war protest activities exploded during 1967 with the largest demonstrations yet demanding a negotiated settlement, reduction of the U.S. role, and even withdrawal. White House aides who spoke with students in early 1967 noted that they had "deeply troubled attitudes about Vietnam." In 1967 more ordinary citizens without ties to traditional peace groups, religious pacifist organizations, or the New Left [radical liberals] attended marches and vigils, wrote members of Congress, and told friends, neighbors, co-workers, or fellow students that in one way or another they wanted the war to end. A myriad of organizations opposed to the war either sprang up or were rejuvenated: Another Mother for Peace, Clergy and Laity Concerned about Vietnam, the Student Mobilization Committee to end the War, Women Strike for Peace. More popular support for opposition to the war, however, did not translate into tangible measures to end it. Antiwar activity produced more demonstrations of support for the President. The Johnson administration, always suspicious of its critics, increased its program of infiltrating and provoking the anti-war movement. . . .

In February 1967, [civil rights leader] Martin Luther King Jr. spoke out forcefully against the war. For the previous year he had privately voiced misgivings about the course of U.S. policy in Vietnam, but said that his civil rights work took up all of his time. He changed as the war seemed to absorb more energies of the administration and the momentum for civil rights drained after the elections of 1966. In February King called for an alliance of the civil rights and peace movements "until the very foundations of our country are shaken." Later he became the co-chairman of the Clergy and Laity Concerned About Vietnam, a prominent liberal religious coalition opposed to the war. He called the government "the greatest purveyor of violence in the world today." He characterized American involvement in Vietnam as a "symptom of a far deeper malady," the reflexive fear of revolution that had led the United States to oppose people throughout the underdeveloped world who wanted to assert their rights. "Somehow this madness must cease," he said. "The great initiative in this war is ours. The initiative to stop it must be ours." As he anticipated earlier, King's outspoken opposition to the war caused a breach with other civil rights leaders, the national media, and the Johnson administration. Roy Wilkins, Executive Director of the NAACP [National Association for the Advancement of Colored People], denied that Vietnam had hindered the advancement of African Americans. The national board of the NAACP rejected King's call to merge the civil rights and anti-war movements. Vice President Hubert Humphrey criticized King publicly. Behind the scenes John Roche, Johnson's aide in charge of liaison with intellectuals, told the President that King had

Feeling that U.S. involvement in Vietnam was hindering the progress of civil rights legislation, Martin Luther King Jr. began to speak out against the war.

"thrown in with the commies." Roche recommended that "the Communist origins of the operations must be exposed, the leaders discredited."

Most of the various anti-war organizations had no ties to the Communist Party, Hanoi, or Moscow. Many groups worked uneasily together to sponsor a variety of protests against administration policy in the spring, summer, and fall of 1967. The Spring Mobilization to End the War in Vietnam began as an effort to unite liberals, pacifists, and radicals. Organizers hoped to undermine the Johnson administration's "claim to legitimacy through the electoral process." Eventually some liberal groups such as Women Strike for Peace, SANE [Committee for a Sane Nuclear Policy], and the Fellowship of Reconciliation, uneasy with the radicalism they anticipated at some rallies, declined to be official sponsors. They wanted the massive protests to be "anti-administration, but not anti-American." But the refusal of national liberal organizations officially to endorse the protests did not dampen attendance at huge rallies in San Francisco and New York on April 15 [1967]. The rally in San Francisco drew fifty thousand people; the one in New York two hundred thousand. . . . Some young demonstrators shouted "Hey, hey, LBJ, how many kids did you kill today?" and "Hell no, we won't go." In New York Martin Luther King Jr. called on the United States to "honor its word" and "stop the bombing of North Vietnam." His wife, Coretta Scott King, addressed the rally in San Francisco, also urging an end to the bombing of the North. . . .

The massive rallies were important for showing how many people opposed the war and giving many people a sense that they had done something to try and end it. . . . People went to these rallies for a variety of reasons: to hear speakers, to show support for the few hundred young men who burned their draft cards, to join a festival of music and art, or just to show that they did not like what the war did to the United States. For the most part, people who attended anti-war protests were middle class and better educated than the public at large. College students and other young people made up a substantial portion of the audience. Crowds were mostly white, although there was substantial representation among African Americans who drew the same connection between the push for civil rights and the war in Vietnam that had encouraged Martin Luther King Jr. to speak out against the war.

Organizers of the protests considered the demonstrations huge successes because they showed that a significant number of people did not like the war, and believed that the demonstrations gave "visibility to the ever-widening base of the antiwar movement" and produced cover for "many new groups and persons to enter the political struggle against this war." Protest rallies alone, however, did not seem to brake the momentum of the war. The public remained in flux, confused and disheartened by the war but unwilling to advocate withdrawal. Polls taken in the summer of 1967 revealed that a majority could not specify the war aims, but a plurality did not believe it had been a mistake to enter the war. Majorities opposed increasing troop levels and withdrawal. Approval of Johnson's handling of the presidency dropped to 38 percent in October 1967. While most leaders of the anti-war movement understood that their views did not represent the thinking of a majority of the public, they gradually came to believe it did not take a majority to change policy. If somehow the Johnson administration could appreciate that the cost of the war at home had risen too high, the government might change course. . . .

Violence Escalates

Widespread demonstrations occurred from California to Washington in October [1967], culminating in a giant march on Washington on October 20–21. The activities ranged from hundreds of vigils, to picketing outside the White House, to acts of civil disobedience. A group called Resistance organized turn-ins of draft cards. Over 1,100 young men across the country turned in their draft cards on October 16 as thousands more female supporters and adults of both genders applauded and endorsed their actions. In the days before the march on the Pentagon 3,500 radical demonstrators tried to shut down the army induction center in Oakland, California. Police officers waded into the crowd waving clubs, sending twenty people to the hospital. Three days later ten thousand angry people showed up in front of the induction center to fight with two thousand police officers. In Madison, Wisconsin, sixty people were injured when police attacked students demonstrating to stop representatives of the Dow Chemical Company, the maker of napalm, from recruiting on campus. . . .

About one hundred thousand people began gathering in Washington on Friday, October 20. That afternoon a group organized by the Resistance went to the Justice Department to deliver a collection of draft cards turned in by protesters. . . . The next morning over one hundred thousand people gathered at the Lincoln Memorial to begin the largest antiwar demonstration held up to that point at the capital. After a few hours of denunciations of Johnson and speeches demanding immediate negotiations, a bombing halt, and withdrawal of troops, about fifty thousand of the demonstrators slowly walked across the Arlington Memorial Bridge to a

Pentagon parking lot. Nearly all of the marchers milled around, gave flowers to the soldiers, sat down in the parking lot, and sang protest songs. . . . A group called the SDS [Students for a Democratic Society] Revolutionary Contingent rushed the entrance to the Pentagon and were thrown back by military police. Police then sprayed tear gas on other demonstrators. Some ran in panic or went limp for arrest; a few threw bottles or taunted the police. About six hundred people entered an area declared off-limits before the march and were arrested. Forty-seven demonstrators and police officers went to the hospital.

Press accounts of the rally at the Lincoln Memorial and the Pentagon pointed out the diversity of the crowd and how the vast majority had been non-violent. Commentary focused, however, on the behavior of a few. David Brinkley of NBC News characterized the march as "a coarse, vulgar episode by people who seemed more interested in exhibitionistic displays than any redress of grievances." Barry Goldwater called it a "hate-filled, anti-American, pro-communist violent mob uprising." Opinion polls revealed that the public believed by a 3 to 1 margin that people thought anti-war demonstrators endangered the safety of Americans fighting in Vietnam. Seventy percent agreed that the anti-war demonstrations encouraged the NLF and North Vietnamese to fight harder. Johnson took comfort in these numbers, and demanded heightened government efforts to link the anti-war movement to Moscow or Hanoi. . . .

Impact of Opposition

By the end of 1967 the war in Vietnam had come home in ways that neither supporters nor opponents of it expected or fully comprehended. The growth of opposition to the war had wrecked the consensus constructed by Johnson in [the election of] 1964. Distrust of the government was at its highest point since the Second World War. But the anti-war movement had not convinced most people to support its views either.

At the time and for a generation after the events of the middle 1960s, participants in the movement and outside analysts argued over its tactics. Sometimes the discussions became so intense and the points at issue so arcane [obscure] that observers concluded that the existence of the arguments themselves detracted from the success of the anti-war movement. Certainly it was diverse, noisy, divided, and angry. . . . The fringe of the anti-war movement engaging in violence attracted more attention than the hundreds of thousands of ordinary people who occasionally marched, went to vigils, or wrote members of Congress. The tumult within the anti-war movement turned away as many people as it recruited. At its most basic level the discussion of the tactics of anti-war protesters addressed the question of whether the movement shortened or prolonged the war. Sympathizers with liberal protesters, such as Charles De Benedetti in his massive study, *An American Ordeal: The Antiwar Movement of the Vietnam Era*, argue that the responsible form of protest favored by the traditional peace groups stood a good chance of shortening the war. Unfortunately, De Benedetti and other liberals claim, radical elements in the anti-war movement adopted such extreme positions and engaged in such foolish acts of romantic revolutionary violence that more people came to revile anti-war activities than supported them. Tom Wells, another veteran of the anti-war movement, argues exactly the opposite position in *The War Within: America's Battle over Vietnam*, claiming that the very disruptions of the anti-war movement eventually made it impossible for the United States to continue the fight.

The anti-war movement did not end the war in Vietnam, but it did alter, almost irrevocably, the perceptions of ordinary citizens of their society and their government; it also altered the perceptions of leaders toward the public. Secretary of State Dean Rusk claimed that he overestimated the patience of the public to fight a long war. By the end of 1967 that patience had worn out.

Tragedy at My Lai

David L. Anderson

In November 1969, America learned that U.S. Army lieutenant William L. Calley had been charged with multiple murders of Vietnamese civilians in a village called My Lai. Disillusioned with a struggle that had been going on for five years and had taken more than forty thousand American lives, the public saw the incident as one more sign of the immorality of the war and the need to get out of Vietnam.

In the following selection from his book *Facing My Lai: Moving Beyond the Massacre*, author David L. Anderson describes the incident, then discusses how psychological pressure, poor leadership, and America's approach to waging war in Vietnam combined to produce the atrocity. Anderson also examines the military's slow response to investigate the incident, as well as the difficulty of convicting those who participated.

Anderson served in the U.S. Army Signal Corps in Vietnam and is now a professor of history and chair of the Department of History and Political Science at the University of Indianapolis. He also wrote *Trapped by Success: The Eisenhower Administration and Vietnam, 1953–1961*.

Although the words *My Lai* and *massacre* will forever be linked in the historical record, the enormity of the evil of that day is scarcely remembered. For many Americans, it is one of a host of unpleasant and uncomfortable images and associations from the Vietnam War that they seek to forget. As the divided public reaction to the Calley verdict also revealed, the explanation of what happened was elusive and has continued to confound those who seek to understand and to ease the psy-

Excerpted from David L. Anderson, *Facing My Lai: Moving Beyond the Massacre*. Copyright © 1998 University Press of Kansas. Reprinted with permission from the University Press of Kansas.

chic pain of the evil and horror of Vietnam. Who was responsible and who was to blame? Time has a way of healing, according to the old adage. Time also erases or blurs memories. Forgetting and healing are not necessarily synonymous.

What Really Happened

Some facts about My Lai are generally accepted. On March 16, 1968, troops of Charlie Company, First Battalion, Twentieth Infantry Brigade, American Division combat air assaulted a village in South Vietnam's Quang Ngai Province. Known to Americans as My Lai 4, Vietnamese called it Thuan Yen. It was part of a hamlet called Tu Cung, which was part of a larger village called Son My. In GI slang it was "Pinkville," a name derived from shading on military maps that indicated a densely populated area.

Charlie Company was part of Task Force (TF) Barker, a temporarily assembled strike unit of three infantry companies and an artillery battery commanded by Lieutenant Colonel Frank Barker. TF Barker's mission was to locate and destroy Vietcong [communist] main-force combat units in an area that had long been a political and military stronghold for the enemy. Captain Ernest L. Medina commanded Charlie Company and Second Lieutenant William L. "Rusty" Calley commanded the company's First Platoon.

Shortly before 8:00 A.M., helicopters landed the company outside My Lai. Expecting Vietcong resistance, the first and second platoons entered the village with weapons firing. By noon every living thing in My Lai that the troops could find—men, women, children, and livestock—was dead. The total of Vietnamese civilians killed numbered 504, according to North and South Vietnamese sources. The casualties of Charlie Company were one self-inflicted gunshot wound in the foot. The company's report to the division commander, Major General Samuel W. Koster, listed 128 enemy killed in action (KIA) and three weapons captured. Two days later, the division's newsletter proclaimed: "TF Barker Crushes Enemy Stronghold."

What really happened at My Lai? . . . Why did many, but not all, of the men of Charlie Company persist for over three hours in brutalizing and executing all the unarmed, unresisting villagers? . . . Why did not someone in command stop the slaughter? . . . Why did it take a year and a half before the horrible facts of the events at My Lai became public, and then only through the prodding of a conscience-stricken GI, Ron Ridenhour, who was not even present at My Lai? Why was Lieutenant Calley the only person there that day ever to receive any judicial punishment?

There has been no general agreement on the answers to these questions. The U.S. Army eventually investigated the massacre and gathered volumes of testimony and other evidence that detailed the gruesome facts of that March 16. Several criminal prosecutions ensued, but in the courts of law guilty verdicts proved difficult to obtain. Similarly, in the judgment of history, much of the truth about My Lai remains ambiguous. One of the most contentious questions has been whether My Lai was an aberration or an operation. Was the cold-blooded brutality unique or at least an extreme deviation from the admittedly harsh tactics of a counterinsurgency war? Or was it routine or at least close to normal for a war that was conducted with lethal modern weapons among an inscrutable and racially distinct population? Was the atrocity produced by a breakdown of leadership and discipline in one unit, or was it an inevitable and all-too-familiar product of a war that was a bureaucratic abstraction of body counts, attrition strategy, and global deterrence? . . . How one answers these questions about the past determines how one lives with the traumatic memories in the present and guards against such disasters in the future.

Three Explanations

In examining the My Lai massacre, three explanations emerge. Although they tend to point the finger of blame in three directions, they are complementary and, in combination, help reveal who or what was responsible. One explanation is that a mental breakdown by some individual members of Charlie Company produced this atrocity. The culprit is emotion, ranging from fear, rage, and vengeance on one extreme to no human feeling at all on the other. This interpretation cites mounting psychological pressures on the men. On February 12 [1968], a bullet from an unseen sniper had killed Specialist Four Bill Weber. His death was the company's first in Vietnam. Over the next month there were more deaths and terrible wounds from land mines and booby traps, but no face-to-face encounters with enemy troops. The men became increasingly brutal in their treatment of Vietnamese civilians they encountered on their patrols, and the officers tolerated this behavior. On March 15 the company held an emotional memorial service for Sergeant George Cox, a popular squad leader who had been blown apart by a booby trap the previous day. Immediately after the service, Medina briefed the men on the next morning's operation at My Lai. The service and briefing merged into a kind of ritualistic preparation for bloody vengeance. Regardless of what were Medina's specific orders before going into My Lai, the troops were primed to kill, and kill they did. For some the villagers were the unseen enemy that had been killing and maiming their friends for weeks, and for others the victims were scarcely human at all. The soldiers' behavior was so shocking that attention can be misdirected toward them and shifted away from what others were doing.

Poor leadership is a second explanation for the atrocity, and it puts the burden primarily on the company, battalion, and division officers. Medina, Barker, Colonel Oran K. Henderson (the new brigade commander supervising his first combat operation), and Koster are the chief culprits here. Calley himself fits both the first and second explanation, because his rank gave him command responsibility while his inexperience made him susceptible to breakdown. Either from actual orders or from the informal climate in the division, many of the men believed they had license to kill. Ridenhour suspects that the higher officers may purposefully have planned an operation to brutalize the village and others. A similar, somewhat smaller, and never fully prosecuted incident occurred with Bravo Company of TF Barker at the nearby village of My Khe. In this counterterrorism scenario, a brutal attack on a village in a Vietcong-controlled area would be a demonstration to the local people, something like a criminal gang burning out a small business to convince others in the neighborhood to pay protection money. It is likely that Henderson and Koster were in "Charlie-Charlie" (command and control) helicopters over My Lai, and it is certain that Medina and Barker were close by. Did these officers make no move to stop the ground action because it was going according to plan? Even if not planned, Colonel William Eckhardt, who supervised the My Lai prosecutions, notes that Medina quickly knew the men were on a rampage and did nothing to stop it. Medina and those above him may have kept a discreet distance to create plausible deniability later.

A third explanation is that the massacre flowed from what could be called the American way of war in Vietnam. The United States used high technology and vast material resources to inflict maximum suffering and damage on the enemy while minimizing pain and loss to U.S. forces. Military historian Russell Weigley has noted that "war creates a momentum of its own; the use of violence cannot be so nicely controlled and restrained as strategist . . . would have it." The culprit is body count or kill ratio—that is, counting the number of enemy KIA or comparing enemy KIA to American KIA. In a war where the enemy often wore civilian clothes, the bodies were often counted using the "mere gook rule" that "if it's dead and it's Vietnamese, it's VC [Viet Cong]." Secretary of Defense Robert McNamara's Pentagon devised this war by the numbers, and General William C. Westmoreland, the commander of all forces in Vietnam, tried to implement it through an attrition strategy sometimes labeled "search and destroy." The destruction was accomplished not just by soldiers' firing into villages with M-16s and rocket-propelled grenades (RPGs), but also by artillery, napalm bombs, and B-52 carpet bombing in so-called "free-fire zones." All of this violence was the product of a global strategy to deter the ambitions of America's powerful enemies. How many Vietnamese civilians had to die to prove a point to Moscow and Beijing? What point was being proved? There was no relationship between means and ends. . . .

Slow to Act

These considerations are important in trying to obtain some closure as to how this atrocity could have happened, but of equal or even greater long-term significance is the aftermath, including the cover-up, uncovering, trials, and finally the response of the military and the public. The dark secret of March 16 was held within the American Division for a year. A complaint by Warrant Officer Hugh C. Thompson, Jr., had been forwarded up the brigade chain of command almost immediately. A helicopter pilot, Thompson was not part of Charlie Company but was in the aviation unit assigned to cover the ground assault on My Lai. Realizing what the ground forces were doing, he landed and rescued the few civilians he could. The actions of Thompson and his crew were a singular and powerful expression of compassion and moral courage amid a scene of human depravity. His formal report of brutal and unprovoked murder of civilians was not investigated or acted upon by brigade or division headquarters. Did the senior officers in charge simply not believe the brash young pilot? Had they become insensitive to violence against civilians? Were they knowingly hiding their own culpability and failure of leadership?

The uncovering began more than a year after the event, when Ron Ridenhour, a recently discharged GI, wrote a letter. He sent copies to the army and to several members of Congress. It asked for a public investigation of "something very black indeed," namely, the possible killing of every man, woman, and child in the village of My Lai. Without this letter, the crimes at My Lai might never have been investigated. Ridenhour had not been in Charlie Company or at My Lai, but he knew several men who were. He had heard them describe that day in chilling detail. His sense of justice and patriotism compelled him to track down other witnesses, to search for more grim facts, and ultimately to speak out. In his letter he quoted Winston Churchill: "A country without a conscience is a country without a soul, and a country without a soul is a country that cannot survive."

Numerous investigations ensued. The Department of the Army Inspector General and the Criminal Investigation Division of the Army determined, largely through interviews with members of Charlie Company and other witnesses such as Thompson and his crew, that the laws of land warfare had been violated. General [William C.] Westmoreland, who was then Army Chief of Staff, created a special investigation panel headed by Lieutenant General William R. Peers. With the army's image already damaged by the long and increasingly controversial war in Vietnam, Westmoreland was as concerned about the apparent cover-up by senior officers as he was about the brutality in the village. Peers returned a stunning report that graphically described the carnage and called for the indictment of twenty-eight officers. At the top of Peers's hit list was General Koster, who had moved on to become commandant of West Point, one of the army's most honored assignments.

Naming suspects and getting convictions proved to be very different propositions. Because many months had passed since the crimes, many of those involved were out of the service, and the Nixon administration's Justice Department resisted bringing civilians before military courts-martial. Evidence had been destroyed, and key witnesses either could not or would not remember important details. In addition, military law allowed commanders to review the merits of charges brought against members of their command. As a result of these factors, Koster and several other senior officers escaped the court-martial process entirely. Lieutenant General Jonathan Seaman harshly censured Koster for failing to investigate Thompson's complaint and for ignoring other evidence of wrongdoing. In a nonjudicial action, the former American commander was demoted to brigadier general and stripped of his Distinguished Service Medal; he soon retired, his once promising career finished. Although Seaman may have been correct that there was not enough evidence to proceed to open trial, the public-relations impact of his decision was enormous. Since Koster's censure was administered privately, the dropping of the formal charges made it appear that one general was simply protecting another and letting others take the blame and punishment for My Lai.

Unwilling to Believe

From the time that Ridenhour wrote his letter, he had feared the military would not pursue the cases. He began trying to get his story to the press but could find no real interest. After the arrest of Calley in September 1969, an investigative reporter in Washington, Seymour Hersh, began to look into the Calley case, not knowing about Ridenhour or the broader investigation. Slowly the story began to come out. Hersh began publishing a series of reports, and he found Ridenhour, who was a fountain of information. On November 20 the *Cleveland Plain Dealer* published photographs of the massacre taken by Ron Haeberle, a combat photographer who had been present. Shortly afterward, Paul Meadlo appeared on the *CBS Evening News*. The press and public had to acknowledge that something horrible had happened at My Lai.

The story became front-page news, but the initial reaction was disquieting. Many Americans simply refused to believe that the allegations could be true, and others accused the accusers of trying to tear down the armed forces. Thirteen members of Charlie Company, including Captain Medina, were eventually charged with murder. All were acquitted or had their charges dropped except for Calley. Colonel Barker had died in Vietnam in a June 1968 helicopter crash. Twelve officers were accused in the cover-up, but only Colonel Henderson stood trial. He was acquitted after several witnesses declared under oath that they could not recall the events about which they were being questioned.

Calley, then, was the only person convicted of My Lai related crimes. A military court of six officers found him guilty of premeditated murder and sentenced him to life imprisonment at hard labor. Responding to public criticism of the verdict and especially the complaint that this one junior officer was being singled out, [President Richard] Nixon as commander-in-chief moved Calley from the stockade at Fort Benning [Georgia] to house arrest and said he would review the case. Privately, Secretary of the Army Stanley Resor and, publicly, Captain Aubrey Daniel, who had prosecuted Calley, took strong issue with the president's action. They argued that the president's interference denigrated the military justice system and that it placed the U.S. government in the position of condoning a crime that, in Resor's words, stood "alone in infamy." After various appeals and reviews, Calley served only four and a half months in the military prison at Fort Leavenworth [Kansas].

Facing the Darkness

Like Resor and Daniel, many military professionals underst[and] that there [is] no defense or excuse for the cold-blooded mass murder at My Lai. The U.S. military role in Vietnam ended in 1973, and career officers throughout the Army began to take a hard look at the institution to which they remained loyal. Many of them saw a host of mistakes made in management and organization of the military, and they set out to reform the system and restore its fallen honor. In military staff and command schools and colleges, My Lai and the law of war became important subjects of study.

Answers to disturbing questions about My Lai remained difficult to fashion because the event itself was so painful to recall. For many years Americans sought to repress the entire Vietnam War experience in both their own minds and the nation's collective memory. Vietnam, after all, represented defeat and failure. . . .

[But] if American political and military leaders and U.S. citizens are going to face the darkness and heal the wounds of Vietnam—both collectively and individually—they are going to have to confront the war in all of its reality. The massacre at My Lai is part of that reality, indeed, one of the most daunting parts of that reality.

Crisis in the Military

Gabriel Kolko

By 1970, demoralization of troops in Vietnam was a serious problem that threatened the war effort as well as America's standing as a military superpower. A significant breach in relations existed between officers who were often concerned only with career advancement and combat troops who risked their lives daily in ugly and meaningless skirmishes with the enemy.

In the following viewpoint, author Gabriel Kolko describes resistance practiced by rebellious American troops in the 1970s. He maintains that the crisis in morale was serious enough to warrant the withdrawal of combat troops in order to save the United States from monumental failure in Vietnam. Kolko wrote for the *New York Times*, *Le Monde Diplomatique*, the *Nation*, the *New Republic*, and other publications during the Vietnam War. He has also written several highly influential books on U.S. history and foreign policy.

The Vietnam War tested every dimension of America's limited-war capacity: its weapons, strategy, and, ultimately, its armed forces. But while earlier experience had shown how finite firepower was in coping with local wars against highly motivated enemies, the United States was completely unprepared for human failures in its own armed forces. By the time [President Richard] Nixon came to office, this was a growing, serious problem; by 1970 it was a major crisis, with obvious implications for America's freedom to protract the war in Vietnam and for its ability to intervene elsewhere in the future. . . .

Excerpted from Gabriel Kolko, *Anatomy of a War: Vietnam, the United States, and the Modern Historical Experience*. Copyright © 1985 Gabriel Kolko. Reprinted with permission from the author.

Inexperience and Careerism

About one-tenth of the Army was composed of officers during the 1960s, and for those who were professionals, particularly those from West Point, a tour in South Vietnam was essential to career advancement. . . . Mainly confined to safe and often extremely comfortable rear bases, careerism became the leitmotif [dominant and recurring theme] of all of their actions during a glorious half year. Lower-level officers, generally ROTC graduates who were not making the Army a career, were most likely to be sent into the field and exposed to the same risks as common soldiers. From a military viewpoint, they lacked both the experience and the motivation to make good leaders. For the professionals, producing impressive numbers often meant goading men to action, falsifying data on enemies killed or targets destroyed, or both. Once they left, the war was someone else's problem. Deception, cynicism, and brutality were built into such a system. Bombs and shells were dropped to produce results which could be translated into medals, complimentary reports—and promotions. Nearly nine out of ten generals who served in Vietnam thought careerism was a problem, 37 percent considering it a serious one. One of its effects was a huge breach in relations between officers and men. Well before the war ended, critics outside the military and a few disgruntled former officers were airing such problems. . . .

Top Priority: Survival

Brutality throughout the war was almost wholly the result of superior orders, and the GI was the instrument of his officers. The average platoon and company operation suffered from serious constraints, making them inefficient instruments of warfare. Even junior officers usually spent six months in combat situations, their subordinates one year, and the constant rotation of forces led to minimal group cohesion, with the soldier's primary loyalty, if any, being to his buddies and their mutual passion to survive twelve months and get shipped out. If an officer pressed his men, he was not likely to succeed in motivating them without taking their instinct of self-preservation into account. The most popular officer was the unambitious lieutenant who took no unnecessary risks and was responsible to his men and not his superiors. Such units had high morale and solidarity and minimum losses; . . . Senior officers complained that the troops in such units were likely to bunch together and avoid engagements. They could not always do so, but after 1968 it was commonly conceded that whenever possible platoons "[d]on't fight a fire-fight or a contact; they wait it out." " ' Search and evade' (meaning tacit avoidance of combat by units in the field) is now virtually a principle of war," Colonel Robert D. Heinl wrote in a much noticed account in June 1971, "vividly expressed by the GI phrase, 'CYA (cover your ass) and get home!' "

The GI's lack of political commitment was one of the Army's fatal weaknesses. The grunt regarded Vietnam as someone else's country, and he became increasingly sensitive to the immaculate officers back at comfortable bases who were urging him on to greater risks. The soldier soon learned to distrust everyone but those comrades who had shown solidarity with him in battle. Paradoxically, many, perhaps most, grew increasingly to resent the ARVN [Army of the Republic of Vietnam] and the Vietnamese people, and while such blanket hostility is one reason for the countless crimes against civilians that were committed, it also had military implications when cooperation with the ARVN was necessary. . . .

All of these forces and relationships operating in America's military created a grave liability for its entire war effort. However efficient its parts technically, as a human organization the American military was so weak that with time it became more of a factor in the overall military balance. The personal responses of the foot soldier to his predicament and dangers . . . the soul- and mind-deadening techniques of warfare, the stress on numbers killed, the tension, heat, and degradation—this surreal mélange was destined to create major human problems, which in turn had far-reaching military implications. . . .

We Can Never Win

Marine lieutenant Philip Caputo landed in Vietnam in 1965 with the first ground combat units, served a sixteen-month tour of duty, then later returned to Vietnam as a correspondent for the Chicago Tribune *during the war. Some of his observations on morale among those men with whom he served are documented in the CNN special "The Cold War," a portion of which can be found on the Internet at CNN Cold War—Interviews: Philip Caputo.*

I remember sitting at this wretched little outpost one day with a couple of my sergeants. We'd been manning this thing for three weeks and running patrols off of it. We were grungy and sore with jungle rot and everything else like that, and (we had) taken about nine, 10 casualties on a recent patrol. This one sergeant of mine, Prior was his name, said, "Lieutenant," he says, "I don't see how we're ever going to win this." And I said, "Well, Sarge," I says, "I'm not supposed to say this to you as your officer—but I don't either!" So there was a sense, at least in my platoon and maybe in the whole company in general, that we just couldn't see what could be done to defeat these people.

Philip Caputo, "On Morale," *The Cold War,* Cable News Network, 1998.
http://cnn.com/SPECIALS/cold.war/episodes/11/interviews/caputo.

Whatever the personal responses of the GI to his frustration before 1968, morale failed to impress senior officers as a real problem. During 1968–69 troop morale began visibly to break down, and from 1970 onward the human collapse of the Americans in Vietnam ceased to be simply an individual or psychological issue and became a highly publicized major organizational question involving discipline and, ultimately, the very capacity of the U.S. armed forces to function.

The difficulties began with drugs, the GI's anodyne [source of comfort] for the minutes and days of terror and boredom. . . . Heroin and marijuana were cheap and readily obtainable by 1968, when their use began to rise sharply. The drug epidemic that followed was to some extent related to the sheer boredom among enlisted men, as long days on bases replaced search-and-destroy missions. Some generals in Saigon regarded drug use among soldiers as the single most serious personnel problem, even though the Pentagon maintained an embarrassed silence as long as possible, until the press and Congress forced the issue in mid-1971. The Pentagon then attempted to argue that only 5 percent of the GIs were hard-drug users. In 1973 it conceded that 35 percent of all Army enlisted men who had been in South Vietnam had tried heroin and that 20 percent had been addicted at some time during their tour of duty there. Some estimates of its regular use are much higher. The use of marijuana, of course, was much more common. Since the MACV [Military Assistance Command, Vietnam] had neither the will nor the capacity to stop the drug traffic, early in 1972 some key U.S. bases began allowing prostitutes into the barracks in the hope of reducing drug usage.

Racial conflict among troops grew out of inherited legacies compounded by the distinctive experiences of blacks in Vietnam. Overrepresented in combat or in menial tasks, and led by very few black officers, blacks in Vietnam were much more under the influence of radical and militant currents than their white counterparts were. Black pride was the rule; Eldridge Cleaver, Malcolm X, and Cassius Clay were their most admired heroes. One-fifth of all black troops in South Vietnam in 1970 declared they hated whites, and over one-third disliked them but tried to get along with them. Blacks were the most politically conscious group among the GIs, and also the most frequent drug users. By 1968, senior officers were reporting to the Pentagon, "Racial incidents and disturbances have become a serious and explosive problem." The Army did not deny that it had a race problem, but defended itself by arguing irrelevantly that it was one endemic in American society and not of its own making. Still, since armed men were supposed to be fighting a common enemy rather than each other, racism became another factor weakening discipline and morale among already dissatisfied soldiers. Significant riots began as early as 1968, reaching the Navy in 1972. Part of the Army's response was to attempt to restrict symbols of black nationalism.

Breakdown of Authority

This combination of the enlisted man's contempt for his officers, the officers' desire to squeeze more combat out of their subordinates, drugs, and racism produced a profound breakdown and the emergence of "fragging," the attempted murder of officers by soldiers, usually with grenades.

Troop attacks on officers occurred during both world wars when troops refused to face the dangers of battles. During the Vietnam War fraggings were expanded to include attacks by black soldiers against white officers for racial reasons as well as the efforts of drug peddlers and users in the military to prevent discipline. The number of actual fraggings, especially in the first category, is difficult to document, but minimum figures for 1969–72 are 788 confirmed cases, resulting in 86 deaths. Other official data raise the number to 1,016, and some estimates are twice that. These levels were far higher than those of earlier wars, which involved many more men. . . . Acts of mutiny, insubordination, and disobedience to orders rose from 252 in 1968 to about twice that in 1971, yet it was fragging and the threat of it which most profoundly affected officers. . . .

Equally disturbing was the spread of disobedience to the Navy and Air Force. In the Navy resistance took the form of sabotage during 1972, particularly on war-related ships. A major fire aboard the aircraft carrier *Forrestal* in July, antiwar petitions with one thousand signatures on another, and myriad incidents produced a House inquiry which reported, "The subcommittee has received a list of literally hundreds of instances of damage to naval property wherein sabotage is suspected. . . . The magnitude of the problem . . . is alarming."

Even more disturbing was the demoralization of the Air Force during the closing months of 1972. "It is an impersonal thing," the commander of the B-52 base on Guam said; the airman doing his job "without too much question about whether he is killing anybody on the ground. I don't think it enters his mind." Still, tactical aviation pilots were concerned that they would be the last to die against the DRV's [Democratic Republic of Vietnam—North Vietnam] superb air defenses. In November some began diverting their missions. When the B-52s were sent to bomb Hanoi during Christmas 1972, in the final act of the war, tactical aircraft failed to show up to attack antiaircraft defenses, and fifteen B-52s were shot down. At least one B-52 commander was tried for refusing to fly, but others threatened to follow him. According to one official study, there was a "near mutiny" among some B-52 crews, a crisis only the signing of the Paris accords averted. . . .

Weakened Military Capacity

The importance of the erosion of the various military services, particularly of the Army, to the military and political evolution of the war should not be underestimated. While political leaders in Washington largely ignored these developments, the generals and admirals fully appreciated them. "Somehow, the Vietnamese communist soldier has absorbed enormous motivation," retired General Hamilton H. Howze, one of the Army's most senior personalities, wrote in 1971. "A force that lacks good discipline will take a terrible shellacking from one that has it." Could the Army be employed again in South Vietnam if necessary? In public the Pentagon avoided the issue, but Peter R. Kann, the *Wall Street Journal*'s authoritative Saigon correspondent, in November 1971 voiced a common feeling that "sapped by problems of drugs, race, discipline and morale, the U.S. military's very ability to fight if called upon to do so is increasingly in question." By that time, moreover, the Pentagon was publicly confessing that the war had weakened the physical and moral capacity of the Army throughout the world, in part because GIs who had been in South Vietnam had transferred their habits and attitudes elsewhere. It was essential, in the view of more and more civilians and military in the Pentagon, to get the vast bulk of its forces out of South Vietnam and to reform the entire personnel structure as quickly as possible. By late 1972, after the intense stress of Navy and Air Force operations off Vietnam seriously cracked the morale and discipline of those two services, there was a virtual unanimity among admirals and generals that solving these problems was a prerequisite to once again making American military power in the world credible.

The withdrawal of troops was therefore essential not only in order to gain political time at home but also to save the military from even graver problems. Had Nixon tried to reverse the process—and [Secretary of Defense Melvin R.] Laird was not about to let him, partly for these reasons—he very likely would have produced a far more serious defeat of American power. Such perceptions of the state of the military wove in and about diplomatic and political affairs for the remainder of the Vietnam War. The United States' technology had been its most precious illusion and threat, but that was now disintegrating as the human organization around the machines ceased either to believe or to obey.

Whatever the crisis in American strategy, doctrine, and weaponry before Vietnam, . . . it paled by comparison with that which existed after a decade of effort. For the concept of America's might was based exclusively on the existence and capabilities of tactics and weapons, not on the skills and attitudes of those who operated them; without highly committed personnel the United States, with all its arms, might prove impotent. The steps by which this monumental failure occurred had not been remotely imagined in the strategy seminars of the military, the elite universities, and the think tanks or in the analyses of the entire foreign policy establishment. Now that the inconceivable was a reality, the constraints on those in power were all the greater. . . . The collapse of conventional wisdom had proved total, as strategy, sophisticated weapons, and well-groomed politicians and generals seemed irrelevant and pathetic before their resourceful, dogged Vietnamese foe.

America Negotiates
a Meaningless Peace

Joseph A. Amter

Peace negotiations between the United States and North and South Vietnam had reached an impasse when President Richard Nixon took office in 1969. South Vietnam's President Nguyen Van Thieu refused to negotiate with the Communists in Hanoi; they in turn insisted on the withdrawal of all U.S. forces and the removal of the existing South Vietnamese regime, to be replaced by a coalition government. U.S. demands included that all North Vietnamese troops be withdrawn from the South.

To move forward, National Security Adviser Henry Kissinger began secret negotiations with the North Vietnamese in Paris in 1971. Seeking to end the war before presidential elections in November 1972, Kissinger eventually made extraordinary concessions. The United States agreed to withdraw completely from Vietnam, accept the presence of several North Vietnamese divisions in South Vietnam, and recognize the political legitimacy of the Provisional Revolutionary Government (PRG), created in June 1969 to serve as a Communist counterpart to the Saigon government. In return, Hanoi agreed to drop its insistence on Thieu's resignation. Kissinger triumphantly announced that "peace was at hand." Thieu, however, accused the United States of betrayal, and Nixon refused to sign the agreement.

In the following excerpt, Joseph A. Amter details subsequent developments in the peace process. He points out that several more months of brutal fighting initiated by the United States made no difference in the final terms of the treaty, which was finally signed by the United States, South

Excerpted from Joseph A. Amter, *Vietnam Verdict: A Citizen's History*. Copyright © 1982 Mrs. Joseph A. Amter. Reprinted with permission from The Continuum International Publishing Group, Inc.

Vietnam, the PRG, and North Vietnam in early 1973. The agreement allowed the United States to withdraw from the war, but in fact, none of the participants intended to honor its terms, and fighting continued until 1975.

Amter founded the Peace Research Organization Fund in 1962 and served in 1965 as co-chair of the White House Conference on International Cooperation.

[After National Security Advisor Henry Kissinger] announced that "peace is at hand," [on October 26, 1972] [President Richard] Nixon pursued his plan to achieve total victory by the most savage aerial attack on North Vietnam of the entire war, in an effort to force Hanoi to surrender. Kissinger agreed to meet with [North Vietnamese negotiator] Le Duc Tho again on November 20, after the election was over. In the meantime, the United States concentrated on supplying Saigon with every available weapon. The United States sent [South Vietnamese] General [Nguyen Van] Thieu a huge supply of tanks, helicopters, bombers, and fighter aircraft. The delivery of weapons, all soon to be lost to the North Vietnamese, cost this country several billion dollars and weakened our other bases around the world. South Vietnam, meanwhile, emerged "with the fourth largest air force in the world—more than 2,000 aircraft— even though its pilots had not yet been checked out to fly some of the more sophisticated planes."

North Vietnam watched in amazement as U.S. cargo planes and ships unloaded equipment that General Thieu could use to continue the war. Operation Enhance Plus was open-ended. The Nixon administration was trying to squeeze its entire military aid program for South Vietnam for the coming year into a matter of weeks, before any peace agreement was reached.

Power Play

Enhance Plus was crucial to the Nixon-Kissinger strategy for ending the war on America's terms. They felt confident that such pressure would strengthen their negotiating position and force Hanoi to yield to their terms. From Nixon's point of view, Enhance Plus served two purposes. The program bolstered the Saigon regime and made Thieu more amenable to an eventual peace treaty. The President sent General [Alexander] Haig to Saigon to supervise the delivery. Haig warned Thieu that the time would come when the United States would be forced to leave Vietnam and that he should cooperate with the White House. He made it plain that the South Vietnamese leader should concentrate on how to survive after the United States left Vietnam.

Project Enhance Plus had the additional objective of showing Thieu that the United States meant to stand behind him. To emphasize this point, President Nixon ordered new air strikes against North Vietnam just as Enhance Plus began. North Vietnam accused Nixon of "strengthening the Nguyen Van Thieu clique to prepare for new aggressions," but Le Duc Tho did return to Paris for another meeting with Kissinger. At that meeting, Le Duc Tho issued the following statement:

> If the U.S. protracts the negotiations, delays the conclusion
> of the agreement, and continues the war, the Vietnamese will
> have no other way than to resolutely carry on their fight until
> genuine independence, freedom and peace are achieved.

The United States responded by introducing new demands that reopened issues already agreed upon in October 1972. Kissinger now asked that the DMZ [Demilitarized Zone] be recognized as a provisional boundary, that North Vietnam withdraw some troops from the South, and that Hanoi give further recognition of the sovereignty of South Vietnam. Kissinger also outlined some of Thieu's objections. Le Duc Tho conceded some minor points but refused to discuss fundamental changes in the agreement. When Washington introduced further new demands on November 25, the North Vietnamese asked for a recess. The two sides appeared deadlocked once again.

As Kissinger left Paris, he threatened that the war would be intensified unless Hanoi yielded. In one cable to Kissinger, Nixon said:

If they were surprised that the President would take the strong action he did prior to the Moscow summit and prior to the election they will find now, with the election behind us, he will take whatever actions he considers necessary to protect the U.S. interest.

Nixon then made a secret commitment to Thieu that if the North Vietnamese in any way breached the projected agreement, the United States would come to Saigon's rescue. "You have my absolute assurance," Nixon wrote, "that if Hanoi fails to abide by the terms of the agreement it is my intention to take swift and severe retaliatory action." The President assured his inner circle that he intended to keep this secret commitment. He also directed the Pentagon to finish work on a special plan to carry out the commitment, should it become necessary. . . .

Breakdown in Negotiations

Kissinger and Le Duc Tho resumed their discussions the first week of December 1972 in Paris. The two representatives hashed through all the issues again, but neither side retreated from its respective position. Kissinger held firm on the major changes that both Nixon and Thieu wanted in the October agreement, and threatened North Vietnam with further bombing attacks if Hanoi did not concede. Tho, for his part, hoping to force Kissinger to negotiate more realistically, started drawing back on some of the concessions Hanoi had already made. In particular, the North Vietnamese representative hinted that the release of political prisoners held by Thieu might have to coincide with the release of the American POWs.

Kissinger refused to compromise and the talks broke down again on December 13, 1972. Kissinger returned to Washington and met with Nixon the next day. They decided to issue an ultimatum to Hanoi: Yield to U.S. demands within three days or face a bombing campaign. Moving quickly, Kissinger explained the situation to Admiral [Thomas] Moorer of the Joint Chiefs and asked how many B-52s were available for an attack on North Vietnam. The answer apparently satisfied the White House, for when the arbitrary deadline ran out on December 17, Nixon immediately ordered the greatest air attacks of the war against Hanoi and Haiphong.

To justify the bombing, Kissinger told the American people that North Vietnam was at fault and had sabotaged the talks in Paris. He said that Hanoi had introduced "one frivolous issue after another" as part of a great "charade," and each time "a settlement was . . . within our reach, [it] was always pulled just beyond our reach." . . .

Christmas Bombing

For the next twelve days, from December 18 to December 30, the United States bombed Hanoi and Haiphong with more ferocity than at any time in the history of the Vietnam War, dropping over 35,000 tons of bombs in the middle of North Vietnam's two major urban centers. Nixon and the Pentagon unleashed two hundred B-52s; the giant strato-fortresses flew in groups of three, carrying 500- and 750-pound bombs, which, when dropped, literally engulfed rectangular areas, one mile long and one-half mile wide, of the city. The military expected that population centers as well as military targets would be wiped out, and in most cases the target areas emerged as heaping mounds of rubble. The rubble represented the Pentagon's admitted goal—"crippling the daily life of Hanoi and Haiphong and destroying North Vietnam's ability to support forces in South Vietnam."

The Christmas bombings of 1972 caused massive destruction and suffering. More than 2,000 civilians died in Hanoi alone. Entire neighborhoods were obliterated, transportation facilities completely destroyed, and important hospitals devastated. The Bach Mai hospital, Hanoi's most up-to-date medical facility, with over 900 beds, was left in ruins. Foreign reporters described fifty-foot craters and uprooted trees in the very heart of Hanoi.

President Nixon told one columnist that he ordered the bombings because "the Russians and Chinese might think they were dealing with a madman and so had better force North Vietnam into a settlement before the world was consumed by a larger war." Many people agreed that only a madman could have ordered the kind of destruction carried out by the B-52s on civilian population centers.

In fact, when the Christmas bombings were over, the United States had actually lost ground in the effort to end the war on its terms. Nixon had underestimated the determination of the North Vietnamese people. The attack against Hanoi had been anticipated; many important offices and many of the people had been moved out into the countryside, where the air attacks were less intense. The President also underestimated the skill of the North Vietnamese defense forces. The B-52s came under steady fire from North Vietnam's SAM [surface-to-air] missiles. Between thirty-three and thirty-five of them, carrying almost 100 U.S. airmen, went down in twelve days. The official figure of only fifteen planes lost was almost certainly in error. The new-found accuracy of North Vietnam's gunners shocked the Pentagon, so much so that by the end of December the Joint Chiefs strongly urged an end to the bombings.

Finally, Nixon underestimated his critics at home and around the world, who condemned the Christmas bombings as "war by tantrum" or "Stone Age strategy." From the Pope's outcry against the "harsh . . . war actions" to the British view that here was "a man blinded by fury or incapable of seeing the consequences of what he is doing," outrage was the standard response. The *Washington Post* described Nixon's air blitz under the headline "TERROR BOMBING IN THE NAME OF PEACE," while other sources of world opinion agreed with [Soviet Premier] Leonid Brezhnev's judgment, politically inspired or not, that Nixon's decision to level Hanoi was nothing more than barbaric.

Agreement in Paris

The White House announced on December 30 [1972] that Henry Kissinger and Le Duc Tho would hold their next meeting in Paris on January 8, 1973. In light of the subsequent agreement, many people have assumed that the Christmas air raids were responsible for ending the war. But the truth is that Nixon's last brutal fling achieved little or nothing for the United States. The agreement worked out in January 1973 differed little from the one reached the previous October. . . .

More than once Henry Kissinger had bragged that, if worse came to worse, he could "reduce Le Duc Tho to tears" with America's B-52s. When Kissinger arrived at the January peace talks, Tho greeted him with the icy comment, "I am a personal victim of yours," as if the North Vietnamese representative had heard of Kissinger's boasts. After a stormy first day, the two sides got down to business on January 9 and finally worked out a peace agreement by January 13, 1973. The United States had clearly yielded in its demands. For example, Kissinger agreed to allow migration and movement across the DMZ, thus recognizing the temporary nature of the dividing line. The United States also agreed to upgrade the National Council of Reconciliation and Concord, allowing it to stand alongside Thieu's government; the council would be responsible for future elections. Indirectly, Kissinger even gave in to Hanoi on the issue of recognizing the Vietcong. One of the two peace documents was signed by representatives of the Vietcong. The United States agreed that the National Liberation Front [communist dominated political organization in South Vietnam] would share power with the Thieu government in a divided South Vietnam. According to [authors Bernard and Marvin] Kalb:

> Nixon got the prisoners back, Tho got the Americans out, Thieu got to keep his hold on power, and the PRG [Vietcong government] got a degree of political legitimacy in South Vietnam. Everybody got something, but nobody got everything.

There was no guarantee that the Thieu regime would survive after the United States finally withdrew from South Vietnam. Despite their secret commitment to Thieu, both Nixon and Kissinger must have known that South Vietnam's future was bleak. The United States could bolster Thieu's regime, escalate the war until the very end, and even, if necessary, work to subvert the final agreement, but Kissinger himself admitted, "The most that could be salvaged from the

U.S. involvement in Vietnam was a 'decent interval' between an American pullout and the possibility of a Communist takeover." The United States had become involved in the war to save South Vietnam from Communism; the terms of the peace agreement did not safeguard that goal.

Provisions of the Treaty

The chief provisions of the Paris agreement signed on January 27, 1973, were:

1. A cease-fire in place throughout all of Vietnam, and an end to all ground, air, and naval combat operations. This important provision tacitly recognized the right of North Vietnam to retain the bulk of its military forces in South Vietnam. No withdrawal of North Vietnamese troops from the South was required.

2. A complete withdrawal of U.S. military forces within sixty days (including all advisers and technicians), the removal of U.S. war materiel, and the dismantling of all U.S. bases.

3. A return of all military prisoners of war from both sides within sixty days.

4. A prohibition against sending new military personnel (including advisers, technicians, or police) into South Vietnam, and a prohibition against sending new war materiel into South Vietnam. Both sides were permitted to replace weapons and war materiel that had been destroyed, damaged, worn out, or used up—but only on a one-for-one replacement basis. No new types of weapons could be introduced.

5. A three-party Council of National Reconciliation and Concord would be established. The Council would include representatives from Thieu's government, from the National Liberation Front, and from the neutralist factions. Its job would be to organize and help supervise free, democratic elections in South Vietnam. Thieu's government and the NLF would hold two-party conferences to work out the initial arrangements. Until the elections, all people in South Vietnam would have personal freedom, freedom of speech, freedom of the press, freedom of meetings, organization, and political activity, and freedom of movement and residence.

6. A new International Commission for Control and Supervision (ICCS) would be formed to supervise the cease-fire, the withdrawal of U.S. forces and the dismantling of U.S. bases, and the return of POWs. The ICCS could only investigate and report violations; it would have no authority to punish violations.

7. A Joint Military Commission made up of representatives from the United States, Thieu's government, the NLF, and North Vietnam would be formed in Saigon (with branches throughout the country) to enforce the Paris agreements.

8. All foreign countries would end all military activities in Laos and Cambodia as soon as possible. Then all foreign military forces were to be withdrawn.

9. The United States would discuss reconstruction aid with North Vietnam. The terms of this provision were very vague in the public document, but several sources allege that Kissinger promised huge amounts of U.S. aid to North Vietnam.

The terms of the treaty showed that the last three months of the war, from October 1972 to January 1973, were totally meaningless, a futile propaganda exercise. From a broader perspective, the final four years of the war gained nothing and meant nothing. All those months of fighting caused indescribable suffering in the United States and in Vietnam.

Violating the Peace

A "peace treaty" had been agreed upon, but as time passed it became apparent that neither party signed it in good faith. Enhance Plus . . . evidenced Nixon's determination to bolster the Thieu regime. A U.S. military presence was maintained in South Vietnam by simply replacing military personnel with large numbers of U.S. "military civilians"—soldiers without uniforms. . . .

Nixon's determination to nullify aspects of the peace agreement encouraged General Thieu to do the same. In the closing days of the war, both the ARVN [Army of the Republic of Vietnam] and their North Vietnamese/Vietcong adversaries occupied hundreds of villages in disputed territory.

When the cease-fire went into effect, both sides were to remain in place. But General Thieu did not abide by this provision. For the next several months, in complete violation of the treaty, he unleashed the South Vietnamese armed forces against hundreds of disputed villages, using both aircraft and artillery against his own people. Within the first few months of 1973, the forces of General Thieu had driven the Communists out of hundreds of towns and villages under their control at the time of the cease-fire.

Thieu also conducted a terribly harsh—and illegal—campaign of terror against internal enemies and political opponents in South Vietnam. Although the peace treaty specifically guaranteed the freedoms of speech and assembly, as well as the freedoms of movement and residence, General Thieu undertook severe policies against his enemies. . . .

The North Vietnamese had no greater interest than Thieu in the final implementation of the Paris accords. They had supreme confidence that after a decent interval had elapsed, they would ultimately be victorious. In the meantime, they simply went through the motions of complying with the Paris agreement. The State Department at one time issued a white paper outlining all of the North Vietnamese actions in violation of the treaty. Many of these were true.

The apparent patience and restraint of North Vietnam appeared to be deeply frustrating to President Nixon. He was still totally committed to the concept of winning in Southeast Asia. Under the pressure of Watergate, he attempted to focus the attention of Congress and the American people again on the Vietnam problem and to prepare them for the necessity of resuming the war when the time came that he would need to fulfill his secret promise to Thieu. He thus emphasized North Vietnamese cease-fire violations, allegations, for example, that North Vietnam had not withdrawn completely from Cambodia and Laos. The Paris agreement had not set any specific time limit for their withdrawal, so Nixon was almost certainly correct that there were still some North Vietnamese in those countries after the cease-fire. Without giving the North Vietnamese a reasonable time to withdraw their remaining forces, Nixon ordered U.S. bombers to attack. By the end of the month of February, the Seventh Air Force was flying over sixty B-52 missions per day against Cambodian targets. These aircraft, flying out of Thailand, came under the authority of the new air force headquarters at Nakhom Phanom Air Field on the Thai border.

Nixon also continued to maintain the massive U.S. supply program to Saigon. After January 1973 the White House actually increased the amounts of aid to General Thieu, and allowed South Vietnam to take over all U.S. bases intact, contrary to the peace agreement. Hanoi responded with a modest resupply program of its own. The North Vietnamese built a paved road to the South and sent in food and logistical supplies, but the Pentagon discovered through its reconnaissance that relatively little military equipment came down Hanoi's road into South Vietnam after the cease-fire. Nevertheless, on March 15, Nixon threatened for the first time to take unilateral action if necessary to force North Vietnam to stop their "infiltration" into the South. Nixon then resumed aerial reconnaissance flights over North Vietnam in April 1973. In the past, reconnaissance flights had usually signaled the resumption of full-scale bombing against the North.

End of an Era

About ten days after the Paris agreement was signed, Kissinger flew to North Vietnam for talks on war reconstruction aid as required by the accords. The two sides agreed that, in mid-March [1973], Washington and Hanoi would begin negotiations in Paris. These talks moved along so smoothly that by March 27 most of the problems were solved, but in April 1973 Nixon called a halt to the talks and publicly threatened North Vietnam with renewed bombing.

Before these bombing threats could be put to the test, however, the presidential house of Watergate cards, so carefully built over the past ten months, began to fall down upon Nixon's head. On April 30, 1973, Nixon was forced to announce the resignations of his two top aides, H.R. Haldeman and John Erlichman, his attorney general, Richard

Kleindienst, and his legal counsel, John Dean. From that day onward Nixon was unable to maintain effective control over his foreign policy. . . .

Only four days after Nixon was forced to fire Haldeman, Erlichman, Kleindienst, and Dean on April 30, the House Democrats voted to cut off funds for the bombing of Cambodia. On May 19, 1973, the full House voted likewise. Still Nixon persisted. The cut-off would not become law until the Senate passed the measure. Meanwhile, Nixon continued to pound Cambodia day after day.

Nixon's final attempt to somehow achieve victory in Vietnam came the following month when [Soviet Premier] Brezhnev visited the United States. Nixon entertained Brezhnev at [Nixon's home in] San Clemente [California], where he again tried in vain to enlist Russia's support in forcing North Vietnam to accept U.S. terms. On the last day of Brezhnev's visit, the U.S. House of Representatives agreed to a Senate bill calling for an immediate cutoff of all funds for U.S. bombing in Cambodia. Although Nixon vetoed the bill, he was a beaten man. Reluctantly, he agreed to stop all U.S. bombing in Indochina on August 15, 1973.

An era of direct U.S. military involvement in Indochina ended when the last bomber to strike Cambodia returned to its base in Thailand. For almost thirty years the United States had been involved in Southeast Asia. For four and a half years, Richard Nixon had fought a deadly war in Southeast Asia to achieve total victory. At long last Congress finally put an end to the war, which fact Nixon continue[d] to lament. [He wrote in 1980:]

> The war in Vietnam was not lost on the battlefields of Vietnam. It was lost in the halls of Congress, in the boardrooms of corporations, in the executive suites of foundations, and in the editorial rooms of great newspapers and television networks. It was lost in the salons of Georgetown, the drawing rooms of the "beautiful people" in New York, and the classrooms of great universities. The class that provided the strong leadership that made victory possible in World War I and World War II failed America in one of the crucial battles of World War III—Vietnam.

Chapter 5

Legacy
and Lessons
of the War

Turning | Points
IN WORLD HISTORY

South Vietnam Falls to the Communists

James P. Harrison

The Paris Peace Agreement of January 1973 marked the official end of America's involvement in the Vietnam War, but it did not bring about an end to fighting. Later that year, the South Vietnamese Army went on the offensive against the Communists and, in response, the North staged repeated attacks against the South. President Richard Nixon and his National Security Adviser Henry Kissinger had promised to support South Vietnam's president Nguyen Van Thieu in case of Communist aggression, but both men became involved in the Watergate scandal and proved powerless to provide assistance.

Hostilities came to a head in the spring of 1975 when North Vietnam staged a massive offensive against the South. In the following selection, James P. Harrison details the push that toppled Nguyen Van Thieu's government and marked the end of more than thirty years of war in Vietnam. Harrison emphasizes the weakness of the South Vietnamese Army and the ease of its defeat despite America's previous efforts to strengthen it.

Harrison is a professor of history at Hunter College in New York City and is the author of *The Endless War: Vietnam's Struggle for Independence*, *The Long March to Power: A History of the Chinese Communist Party*, and *Mastering the Sky: A History of Aviation from Ancient Times to the Present*.

The march of Communist armies into Saigon on April 30, 1975, stunned the world. It marked the end of over thirty years of one of history's most brutal wars and the fiftieth anniversary of the founding of the first Vietnamese Marxist group. Coming only two years after the withdrawal of American forces in 1973, it also made glaringly apparent the extent to which the United States, and earlier France, had prolonged a war in which the Communists had already taken predominant power thirty years before.

What happened and why during the final offensive in 1975, as in earlier years and decades, will long be debated. Enemies of the Communists argue, as they did a generation earlier about similar events in China, that if the United States had continued or increased its aid to the existing anti-Communist government, or earlier had placed less restraint on the operations of U.S. forces in South Vietnam, the Communists could not have won.

Such arguments ignore the fact that the Communists had already won power twice in North Vietnam, in 1945 and 1954, and were close to power in South Vietnam also in 1945 and 1954, and again in 1964. Massive United States intervention in 1965, like that of the French in 1945, attempted at terrible cost, to stop the Communists. But the whole concept of considering Communist "aggression" in such a situation as an external threat that could be stopped by military force short of genocide obscures rather than clarifies the significance of the over thirty years of warfare in Vietnam that preceded the final Communist offensive. Throughout both wars Vietnamese fought Vietnamese, and even though the Communists used a "foreign" ideology, it was equally evident that the greater direct foreign presence by far, especially until 1973, was on the side of the anti-Communists. . . .

Spring Offensive, 1975

Following the withdrawal of direct U.S. military intervention as arranged by the January 1973 "peace accords" and following continued intransigence by the Nguyen Van Thieu government, North Vietnamese divisions in conjunction with southern forces struck to achieve what turned out to be their final, and greatest, victory in the spring of 1975. As often before, the Communists were the first to apply major force, but they did so in response to innumerable hostile, if smaller, actions on the part of their adversaries. And they did so as the heirs to over a generation of leadership of the Vietnamese Revolution. What the United States had intervened to prevent a decade earlier—a northern invasion of the south—became a reality in 1975, and a classic case of self-fulfilling prophecy.

As early as July, 1973, . . . the Communist Party's Central Committee called for new initiatives on the part of Communists to counter Saigon's actions in the South; and in March 1974 the Party's Military Committee decided to move toward the final offensive. . . . Communist troops were instructed to move, but with extreme caution, lest the United States reintervene, and only as military progress allowed, with the expectation either of new negotiations, or of a final military victory at best the following year, in 1976. But initial victories precipitated others in a manner that even the most optimistic Communist decision makers could not have foreseen.

The first push was a preliminary test of Saigon's defenses and the U.S. response. It began in December [1974] and on January 6, 1975, Communist forces were able to capture and hold their first provincial capital, that of the province of Phuoc Long, some eighty miles north of Saigon, following three weeks of combat. On the next day they seized the strategic "black virgin" mountain just north of the key western city of Tay Ninh. These victories, together with reports of information on Saigon's expectations obtained from a spy high in Thieu's entourage, moved the Party's Political Bureau, in urgent session from December 18 to January 8, to order an acceleration in the planned offensive.

Then after regrouping and final preparations, Communist armies began the great spring offensive of 1975, almost exactly twenty-one years after the defeat of the French at Dien Bien Phu. . . . On March 10, 1975, following diversions toward the strategic cities of Plei Ku and Kon Tum, the Communists struck a hundred miles farther south at Ban Me Thuot, a town of 70,000 and capital of Dar Lac province. According to one apparently apocryphal story, some sixty-five years before, Ban Me Thuot had been the site of a tiger hunt by American President Teddy Roosevelt.

But now it was the Communists who carried the big stick, and even though the estimated one or more million troops in all regions of the South under Saigon's command considerably exceeded the total number of Communist troops north and south, at Ban Me Thuot the Communists enjoyed a five to one superiority in troops. They also enjoyed almost complete surprise, helped by a Communist agent working at Saigon's Central Intelligence headquarters, where he prepared fake maps to show the greatest concentration of Communist troops around Plei Ku and Kon Tum rather than at Ban Me Thuot. Moreover, thanks to careful preparations and an increased flow of supplies over new roads buttressing the "Ho Chi Minh trail" linking North and South Vietnam, the Communists even enjoyed superior armament in this battle. . . . Because of these detailed preparations, the general handicap of having no air power was minimized; with surprising ease, Liberation Army troops captured Ban Me Thuot after thirty-two hours of fighting. . . .

Widespread Panic

Following the fall of Ban Me Thuot came the blunder that accelerated beyond control the collapse of Thieu's forces. General Nguyen Van Thieu, the leader of South Vietnam for a decade, knew better than to minimize the loss of Ban Me Thuot, the key to the Central Highlands; and on March 14 [1975], after consultation with only two of his field commanders, he decided to withdraw entirely from the Highlands and to concentrate on the defense of coastal areas. This decision led to a devastating panic, first in the Highlands and soon all along the densely populated coastal plains, as hundreds of thousands of refugees joined retreating government troops in scenes of confusion seen on television sets around the world.

It was this panic as much as, or even more than, Communist military victories that sealed the fate of South Vietnam. In scenes of mad futility, soldiers and refugees sought to claw their way onto overloaded ships, aircraft, and helicopters,

Final Days

The Communist offensive of early 1975 met with little resistance in South Vietnam, where the ARVN buckled and panicked without the backing from American troops who once reinforced them. Poised to leave the country in the final days of the war, Chicago Tribune *correspondent Ronald Yates describes the fatalism of the time in one of his final reports.*

It is a time for waiting, a time to wonder where the next rocket will explode, where the next North Vietnamese victory will be, when Saigon will fall.

There is a strange, sad giddiness in Saigon after the short, but effective rocket barrages on the city Sunday—like the feeling one gets when the score is 56 to 0 late in the fourth quarter and your team is the one with zero.

You aren't happy about the thrashing your team got, but at this point the most merciful thing is for the game to end.

Despite the talk of fighting to the death and never surrendering that one hears from politicians around Saigon these days, most Vietnamese have resigned themselves to the fact that the war is finally drawing to a close.

"It is not what we wanted," says a Vietnamese doctor, "but it is what we must accept. The South has lost. It is fini [finished]."

That phrase: "It is fini," is perhaps the most often heard phrase in Saigon these days. Every day journalists are asked by cabdrivers, ARVN soldiers, street hustlers, shop owners: "You stay for end? You wait for Saigon to die?"

Ronald Yates, "A Time to Wait for Next Rocket," *Chicago Tribune,* April 28, 1975, p. 1.

only to be stampeded, even crushed to death in the wheel-wells, or shaken from departing aircraft like so much chaff in the wind. Within weeks, long columns of desperate people, dubbed "convoys of tears," added another million to the previous millions of refugees, one-half million streaming into the single city of Da Nang. . . .

The refugees, of course, were seeking to escape the horrors

of war and their fears of the Communists, but certainly also their fears of retaliatory anti-Communist bombing. In their anguish, hardly obscured by the clouds of dust marking the end of the dry season, they seemed to supply final proof of the changing of the Mandate of Heaven, the ancient Chinese idea that Heaven's favor was a precondition of rule. For no matter the motives of the refugees, the loss of authority of the Saigon government was all too evident.

The panic continued to spread as the entire Central Highlands, long considered absolutely essential to the sovereignty, as well as the military security, of South Vietnam, were abandoned almost overnight. Plei Ku and Kon Tum, 90 and 115 miles to the north of Ban Me Thuot, were abandoned March 16 and An Loc to the south on March 18. Saigon had bitterly defended all three strategic towns against earlier Communist offensives, and the news of their fall shocked the country and the world. Moreover, local Viet Cong rather than North Vietnamese troops were the first to enter Plei Ku.

Communists "Liberate" Southern Towns

There followed one by one the surrender of important coastal towns, proceeding more or less from north to south. Quang Tri, which changed hands in bitter fighting at the time of the spring 1972 Communist offensive, fell on March 19, then farther south, Tam Ky on March 24. On March 25, local sympathizers declared Quang Ngai "liberated" even before the entry of Communist forces.

The most damaging losses yet ensued, those of the nineteenth-century imperial capital of Hue on March 26, and on March 29 that of the country's second city, Da Nang. Hue had long represented the sentimental capital of the entire country as it was from there that the last independent government before the French, the Nguyen dynasty, had ruled. After its capture by the Communists for several weeks during the Tet offensive of 1968, Hue had been virtually "destroyed in order to save it," so important was its value judged by Saigon. Da Nang was, after Saigon, the South's second largest city and a principal American base area.

By the end of March, therefore, the northern half of South Vietnam, including two of its three principal cities, had come under Communist control. The south was much more than cut in half, a great fear of earlier years. Moreover, an estimated one-half of Saigon's troops had been lost. The overwhelming majority of them simply disappeared, . . . with Vietnamese of all ranks, military as well as civilian, deciding the Communists had, indeed, won. The essential calculation immediately became to establish peace and come to terms with the victors, as another Chinese adage, long accepted by Vietnamese, telling applied; "He who wins is king, he who loses is a bandit."

Nonetheless, publicly, Saigon and Washington claimed the collapse could be stopped, and that the Saigon area and agriculturally rich southern delta could be held against the Communists. Still, Washington began the evacuation of nonessential personnel on March 31. On the same day, in Hanoi, the Political Bureau confirmed its March 25 decision to advance target dates and "liberate Saigon before the rainy season," that is, before the end of May.

Total Victory

The relentless advance continued. Qui Nhon and Nha Trang fell on April 1 [1975], and on the fourth, the mountain resort of Da Lat. On the same day occurred the crash of an American airlift plane attempting to carry some 300 orphans out of the country, one of the most traumatic of the final horrors of the war.

Then, amid talk of a coup d'état against Thieu, on April 8, a South Vietnamese pilot, apparently a clandestine Party member, bombarded the Presidential Palace in Saigon. Ironically, this was only the second time during the long years of war that Saigon had witnessed directly a few of the millions of tons of bombs dropped on the country, and on both occasions the bombs came from Saigon's own planes.

After a slight pause, on April 16, Phan Rang, less than 200 miles from Saigon, fell to the Communists, as did Phnom Penh, the next day; then Phan Thiet on the nineteenth, and on the twenty-first, the last strategic post,

40 miles east of Saigon, Xuan Loc. Saigon sought to make an effective stand there, and for almost two weeks seemed to be succeeding. Its troops held out for twelve days, supported by heavy air strikes, including the only use in the war of the dreaded CBU-55 bomb, [Cluster Bomb Unit, which sprayed asphyxiating gases and thousands of small, metal fragments across an area up to a half mile wide] and a three to one superiority in heavy guns. But in the end, not even this most stubborn government stand of the final offensive could endure, as instructed, "to the last man." In early April also, there was heavy fighting to the south of Saigon at Thu Thua, only 12 miles away, and for control of the "rice road," Highway 4.

With the fall of Xuan Loc on April 20 the game was up; the belated resignation of Nguyen Van Thieu followed the next day. For a week, his successor, Tran Van Huong, who had been prime minister twice before, in 1965 and 1968–1969, tried to patch together a government capable of negotiation with the Communists. It was much too little and much too late, as was the still briefer presidency of Duong Van ("Big") Minh, who replaced Huong on April 27. Minh had been one of the principal architects of the ouster and murder of [President Ngo Dinh] Diem on November 1, 1963, and had emerged as one of the leaders of the so-called Third Force following his ouster by another general, Nguyen Khanh, in January 1964.

The Communists would accept nothing short of total victory now, and the advance proceeded with relentless finality. With the fall of the port of Vung Tao on April 28, exit by sea was cut off, and on the next day the United States ordered final evacuation of remaining Americans by helicopter. An accelerated evacuation from Than Son Nhut airport had begun on the twenty-first, but had been slowed and then halted by increased Communist shelling. . . .

On April 30, 1975, jubilant Communist troops entered Saigon. In a final extraordinary irony, the man who transmitted Big Minh's final cease-fire order, a one-star general named Nguyen Huu Hanh, was none other than a longtime Communist agent who fed information to Communist units from Saigon's Joint General Staff. Fittingly, and with feelings one can imagine . . . he embraced the Viet Cong captain who liberated his unit's headquarters. At 11:30 A.M., other Communist troops raised their flag above the Presidential Palace signaling the triumph of the Provisional Revolutionary Government. By May 3, the Mekong Delta to the south and remaining areas were declared "liberated," and Saigon became Ho Chi Minh City, thirty years after revolutionaries first so named it.

Veterans: The Painful Price of Service

Arnold R. Isaacs

Caught in controversy that surrounded the Vietnam War, veterans encountered public hostility rather than welcome-home parades on their return to the United States. Even friends and family who appreciated their loved one's service were too confused or embarrassed to talk about the war. Vets often felt shunned and alone as they attempted to cope with their memories and their reentry to civilian life.

In the following viewpoint, author Arnold R. Isaacs describes the isolation felt by Vietnam veterans and compares their return reception with more positive receptions given to veterans of other wars. Isaacs points out that, because many Vietnam vets felt overlooked and rejected, they rejected the government that had belittled their sacrifice. President Jimmy Carter's offer of amnesty to draft evaders in 1977 added to veterans' anger because it validated the perception that avoidance of the conflict was justifiable and service a misjudgment.

Isaacs spent the last years of the war as a correspondent for the *Baltimore Sun* newspaper. Since 1981 he has taught about Vietnam at Towson University in Towson, Maryland. He is the author of *Without Honor: Defeat in Vietnam and Cambodia* and is coauthor of *Pawns of War*.

"You don't go to war, come home, and not talk about it," Bobby Muller said from his wheelchair. But America's soldiers returning from Vietnam came back to a silence that, for years, silenced them as well.

Excerpted from Arnold R. Isaacs, *Vietnam Shadows: The War, Its Ghosts, and Its Legacy*. Copyright © 1997 Arnold R. Isaacs. Reprinted with permission from Johns Hopkins University Press.

"We lost the war in Vietnam, and that's why we don't talk about it," said a man in the audience the night Bobby Muller spoke. It was early 1979, nearly four years before the Vietnam Veterans Memorial dedication, almost ten years after Muller took a bullet in spine near a place called Con Thien in the Republic of Vietnam [South Vietnam].

He had wept with pride at the Marine Corps hymn after he enlisted, Muller recalled that night in Baltimore; had gone willingly to the war that crippled him, and then discovered that in his own country, nobody seemed to care. "Goddamn it, no one feels responsible," he said. "Everyone thinks, hey, it wasn't my war! I didn't do it. It all got delegated to a couple of schmucks [fools] out there in that country, and when they come back—hey, man, it's your bad luck."

Deep Confusion

In the discussion that evening, people tried, with evident difficulty, to grapple with the troubled silence that seemed to surround Vietnam and its veterans. One man, of an age to have been in World War II or maybe in Korea, put his finger on one cause: No one knew what to say about this more recent war; not the people at home, not the soldiers themselves. The national experience in Vietnam never rested on any foundation of understanding, and so the men who fought there "were not standing on anything," he said. "There was no solid ground under them. Those of us in previous wars had solid ground, we knew where we came from, knew who we were and why we were there."

A woman wanted to know "how does all this relate to the violence that sort of has come out of Vietnam?" She didn't mean the war itself; she meant riots and snipers and shootings and store holdups in Baltimore and elsewhere in America. Others pointed out that American society and moral codes changed for many more reasons than just the Vietnam war, but she shook her head, unconvinced. Somehow she knew the war did it, and nothing anyone said could change her mind.

People spoke of the My Lai massacre [the mass murder of Vietnamese civilians by U.S. soldiers in 1968] and Lt.

William Calley [convicted of playing a significant role in the massacre], of the destruction of Dresden [in World War II], the firebombing of Japan, the Germans. "The horrible thing is that we were the ones," said a young woman, in obvious confusion and with many long pauses. "Maybe we weren't exactly like Hitler, we can't compare ourselves to that—but I don't think we can compare this war to World War II at all. . . ." No one was suggesting—quite—that American soldiers in general were murderers or war criminals. But the words were spoken: "Calley," "Dresden," "Nazis," "body count." And they had an evil sound. It was painful to imagine how they might sound to Bobby Muller in his wheelchair on the stage or to the other veterans sitting with him or in the audience. Yet in its very incoherence and fragmented quality, the discussion that evening in a way explained the moral fog Vietnam had left in American minds: a confusion so deep that for many years, Americans found no way to speak about it to themselves and, consequently, no way to speak to their own returning soldiers, either.

Strangers in Their Own Society

The folklore that grew up around that homecoming, telling of soldiers routinely being cursed or spit on, was almost certainly exaggerated. But the sense of being silenced, which *felt* a good deal like being shunned, was part of almost every soldier's experience. And the hurt was deep. "I want to go back to Vietnam and make it different," wrote a former Army nurse named Kathy Gunson some years after her return. "I want to come home to a marching band and a red carpet. I want to hear a 'thank you.' I want to hear 'I'm sorry.' " Another veteran, Jamie Bryant, remembered:

> It was the spookiest thing. . . . In over ten years, there has really never been anybody who has asked me: "What happened to you over there? What was it like?" It's like having a whole year of your life that didn't exist. When you first get back, you don't think about it much. Then you begin to wonder why no one asks the questions. Then you begin to feel like maybe it really isn't something you should talk about.

Many never did. Not infrequently, veterans reentered civilian life and told nobody, not even wives or girlfriends, that they had served in Vietnam. The absence of words meant more than an absence of gratitude or sympathy or respect. Unable to speak about the war, many veterans also had no way to find a reason or purpose in what they had lived through, no way to complete their experience by telling about it and thus coming to understand it.

The great majority were able to find some pride in their own conduct. If you asked, they would tell you they went, did their job, conquered their fear, didn't let down their friends. Like soldiers in any war, they had learned something about endurance and comradeship and about their own inner resources. But if their discoveries gave some purely personal meaning to their experience, it was not the same as finding an explanation, a worthwhile *reason*. Thus the war remained "like a piece of buried shrapnel," as one of them wrote, in a hidden and tender place within them. And like bearers of some terrible secret that could never be told, the returning soldiers felt themselves strangers in their own society. When he came home, the writer Larry Heinemann recalled years afterward, "I had the distinct feeling (common among returning veterans, I think) that this was not my country, not my time."

Sense of Alienation

It was that sense of alienation that separated the Vietnam veterans from those of earlier conflicts. The difference was not so much in the wars themselves, since the tension and boredom and petty restrictions and stupidities of military life and the terrors and exhaustion of combat don't vary much from one war to another. ("When somebody is shooting at you and you are shooting back," the veteran and novelist Jack Fuller once wrote, "all wars are pretty much the same.") What made Vietnam and America's other wars so different was how they were assimilated afterward into the veterans' and the nation's experience.

Men who fought in World War II or Korea might be just as haunted by what they had personally seen and done in combat. But they did not come home, as the Vietnam vets did, to a country torn and full of doubt about why those wars were fought and whether they had been worthwhile. Nor did they return as symbols of a great national failure. Whatever troubling private memories they brought back with them, those earlier veterans did not have to grope for an explanation of what their experience had meant and what its purpose was. Their country—its political and intellectual leaders, its journalists and educators, its movies and popular novels—gave them the answer. They had been heroes in a necessary cause, they were told, and eventually most of them came to believe it was true. But those who fought in Vietnam were told . . . nothing. Even several decades later, Americans reached no common understanding, no comforting myth that could give sense or logic to that war, or absolve soldiers who had trouble coming to terms with the violence they had participated in.

"In past wars," Jack Smith, a psychologist and Marine Corps veteran, told the author Myra MacPherson, "through cleansing acts, society *shared* the blame and responsibility" with those who had done the fighting. "Victory banners, medals, and parades were ways of recognizing the tasks they did in the country's name," Smith added, but the country refused to give its name to Vietnam. "The responsibility and blame was left on the heads of the guys who fought it. They were left to sort out who was responsible for what." Another psychologist, John Wilson, explained to a *Los Angeles Times* reporter: "All cultures recognize that when we send some one to battle, it's difficult psychologically. . . . After the battle, most cultures also have a ritualized way of welcoming back the warrior and giving him a new identity and a new status in society. But we didn't do it for Vietnam veterans. . . . Many men felt isolated after Vietnam. They had to create meaning and make sense of what they did in Vietnam— and they had to do it alone."

Tarnished Honors

If parades and medals were rituals of reconciliation, perhaps it was inevitable that an unreconciled war like Vietnam sometimes turned those rituals inside out, as on an April afternoon in Washington in 1971 when hundreds of veterans marched past the U.S. Capitol and, instead of receiving medals from a grateful government, threw away their decorations to protest the war. The reverse imagery was complete, down to the eight-foot-high temporary security fence below the Capitol's west front physically keeping apart the veterans and the government whose uniform they had worn.

At the head of the procession were parents of three men who had died. Gail Olson, a high-school band teacher from Russell, Pennsylvania, wore his son's fatigue jacket and carried a bugle. After blowing taps, he stepped to a microphone that had been set up next to the barricade so the demonstrators could stop, if they wanted to, and say something. Olson said into the mike: "My son's name was Sergeant William Olson. We're playing taps for all the dead—Vietnamese, Laotian, Cambodian, all our wonderful sons. Let us pray there will be no more, no more." Next was Evelyn Carrasquillo of Miami, who carried a U.S. flag and her son's medals mounted in a frame. "I will not turn my back on this country . . . but we've done our best for the Vietnamese," she said. "It's time to get out. Let's stop the war now." Unlike the veterans, she kept the medals—"all I have left of Alberto." The third Gold Star parent was Anna Pine, of Trenton, New Jersey, who carried her son's medals up to the microphone and then stepped away, weeping, with the medals still in her hand. Later she returned and threw them over the fence with the others.

Then, for two hours, the veterans filed by and tossed away their medals. Some simply dropped them over the fence. Others hurled them as hard as they could, as if aiming at the Capitol dome far overhead. Some men walked on crutches; a few were pushed in wheelchairs. Some of those who stopped to speak into the microphone sounded angry, some just sounded sad. "I'm turning in all the [s——] that wasn't issued and I had to buy it," one man said. Another said: "This is for all the dudes in Third Battalion, Charlie Company, Ninth Marines, who didn't make it." Another said:

"Here's a Vietnamese Cross of Gallantry, which God knows I didn't earn until just now."

One of the men who marched that day was a tall, lean former Air Cavalry trooper with lank black hair named Ron Ferrizzi, who threw away a Purple Heart and a Silver Star he'd been awarded for pulling another soldier out of a burning helicopter. "My wife wanted me to keep these medals so my son would be proud of me," Ferrizzi told me. "But I'm not proud of them. It's all garbage. It doesn't mean a thing." He turned and walked away into the crowd. I watched him go, thinking with a pang that if Ron Ferrizzi had joined the fire department, say, instead of the Army, and if he'd been decorated for saving someone from a fire in his hometown in Pennsylvania instead of in Vietnam, he'd have kept that decoration, no doubt, and his son would be proud of him when he got old enough to understand, and he would be right to be proud. I thought about going after Ferrizzi to tell him that. But I didn't.

The next time I saw Ron Ferrizzi, twenty-three years later in the framing shop he and his wife Kathy owned in North Philadelphia, I mentioned that long-ago impulse. Ferrizzi shook his head. Nobody could take away what he'd done to earn those medals, he said, and throwing away the actual decorations was a necessary part of rejecting a war he passionately believed was wrong. "I was so relieved. It was like the seas parted for me. It was like physically striking back," he said. And there was another powerful reason: his two sons. "I never wanted my kids to come up to me and say, when am I going to get a chance to get my medals?"

Kathy Ferrizzi didn't disagree. But she still sounded a little sad when she remembered her own feelings at the time: "I was brought up, if you had medals you were proud of them, your children were proud of them, and they were handed down. And here he was throwing them all over the wall. I wasn't that thrilled. I didn't think that was the right thing to do.

"I never thought he was wrong about the war," she added. "I just asked him not to give back his medals."

Dishonored Sacrifice

The veterans' march in 1971 was one of the last major anti-war protests, but it was not the last time Vietnam veterans would discard their medals. Nearly six years later, furious at President Jimmy Carter's amnesty for draft evaders, a former marine sergeant in North Carolina named Dale Wilson called on other outraged veterans to turn in their decorations to protest Carter's action. Wilson, whose grievous wounds in Vietnam had cost him both legs and his right arm, had not been bitter when he returned home, he wrote in a letter to his local newspaper, the *Statesville Record & Landmark*. He had enlisted in the Marine Corps "feeling that it was my patriotic duty to serve my country," he wrote, and even after being wounded, only days before he was due to rotate home, felt lucky that he had survived to see his country again.

But Carter's amnesty, Wilson felt, defiled his sacrifice and the service of every soldier who had fought in the war: "Now I am faced with the fact that those who ran when our country called can come back and take the jobs and positions in the community of those who deserve them: the United States veteran." Like Ron Ferrizzi, Wilson had a young son, and like Ferrizzi he felt his decorations were too tarnished to pass on. He would have kept them for his son, he wrote, "but as the war has been recognized as a mistake, I feel there is no honor in medals obtained through dishonorable conflict." A week after his letter was published, Wilson and other angry veterans, some from as far away as Pennsylvania and Ohio, gathered on a parking lot next to a Statesville grocery store. There, they nailed their decorations, and for good measure, an artificial limb, to the wall of an outhouse they had brought to the site—"a symbol," Wilson declared, "of the universal political platform which promises relief and ends up with——." When all the decorations had been hung on the wall, Doris Millet, whose son had been killed in Vietnam, touched a match to the outhouse, which had been soaked in kerosene, and with Wilson and the others, watched it burn to ashes.

The fact that men with such different opinions on the war as Dale Wilson and Ron Ferrizzi both ended up making the identical gesture of rage spoke volumes about how deeply Vietnam had torn the national spirit. Whether they were flung away by veterans at the Capitol protesting the war or by veterans on a North Carolina parking lot protesting the amnesty program, those discarded medals represented personal courage and sacrifice that deserved to be honored whether the war was justified or not. Tainting that honor for so many veterans might not have been the worst thing Americans did to themselves in Vietnam. But it was no small crime, either.

The Long-Term Effect of the War on U.S. Foreign Policy

George C. Herring

The Vietnam War continued to haunt the United States for decades after the conflict ended. The nation had been torn apart emotionally, the triumph of communism in Vietnam shook its confidence, and Americans were left feeling adverse to all overseas entanglements that might become foreign policy quagmires. These feelings were termed the "Vietnam syndrome," the tendency to see America's involvement in the Vietnam War as wrong, to question government intervention in other countries, and to resist proposals to send American troops abroad.

In the following excerpt from his book *America's Longest War*, historian George C. Herring examines the long-term effects of Vietnam on America's foreign policy. He points out that, although American intervention in theaters such as the Persian Gulf has helped restore national confidence, painful memories of Vietnam still linger. Such memories can be beneficial, Herring concludes, particularly if they motivate the United States to proceed cautiously in future foreign policy commitments.

Herring is a highly respected scholar and the author of numerous essays, articles, and books, including *LBJ and Vietnam: A Different Kind of War*. He is an alumni professor of history at the University of Kentucky and was visiting professor of history at the U.S. Military Academy at West Point in 1993–1994.

Much like the effect of World War I on the Europeans, Vietnam's greatest impact was in the realm of the spirit. As no

Excerpted from George C. Herring, *America's Longest War: The United States and Vietnam, 1950–1975*. Copyright © 1996 McGraw-Hill, Inc. Reprinted with permission from McGraw-Hill.

other event in the nation's history, it challenged Americans' traditional beliefs about themselves, the notion that in their relations with other people they have generally acted with benevolence, the idea that nothing is beyond reach. It was a fundamental part of a much larger crisis of the spirit that began in the 1960s, raising searching questions about America's history and values, marking a sort of end of American innocence.

The fall of Saigon [in 1975] had a profound impact. Some Americans expressed hope that the nation could finally put aside a painful episode from its past and get on with the business of the future. Among a people accustomed to celebrating peace with ticker-tape parades, however, the end of the war left a deep residue of frustration, anger, and disillusionment. Americans generally agreed that the war had been a "dark moment" in their nation's history. Some comforted themselves with the notion that the United States should never have become involved in Vietnam in the first place, but for others, particularly those who had lost loved ones, this was not enough. "Now it's all gone down the drain and it hurts. What did he die for?" asked a Pennsylvanian whose son had been killed in Vietnam. Many Americans expressed anger that the civilians did not permit the military to win the war. Others regarded the failure to win as a betrayal of American ideals and a sign of national weakness that boded poorly for the future. "It was the saddest day of my life when it sank in that we had lost the war," a Virginian lamented. The fall of Vietnam came at the very time the nation was preparing to celebrate the bicentennial of its birth, and the irony was painfully obvious. "The high hopes and wishful idealism with which the American nation had been born had not been destroyed," *Newsweek* observed, "but they had been chastened by the failure of America to work its will in Indochina.". . .

Shattered Consensus and New Nationalism

Nowhere was the impact of Vietnam greater than on the nation's foreign policy. The war shattered the consensus that had existed since the late 1940s, leaving Americans confused and deeply divided on the goals to be pursued and the methods used. Even before the war had ended, the traumatic experience of Vietnam, combined with the apparent improvement of relations with the Soviet Union and China and a growing preoccupation with domestic problems, produced a drastic reordering of national priorities. From the late 1940s to the 1960s, foreign policy had consistently headed the ranking of national concerns, but by the mid-1970s it placed well down on the list. The public was "almost oblivious to foreign problems and foreign issues," opinion analyst Burns Roper remarked in late 1975.

The Vietnam experience also provoked strong opposition to military intervention abroad, even in defense of America's oldest and staunchest allies. Polls taken shortly before the fall of Saigon indicated that only 36 percent of the American people felt the United States should make and keep commitments to other nations, and only 34 percent expressed a willingness to send troops should the Russians attempt to take over West Berlin. A majority of Americans endorsed military intervention only in defense of Canada. "Vietnam has left a rancid aftertaste that clings to almost every mention of direct military intervention," the columnist David Broder observed.

The indifference and tendency toward withdrawal so manifest immediately after the war declined sharply in the next decade. Bitter memories of Vietnam combined with the frustration of the Iranian hostage crisis to produce a growing assertiveness, a highly nationalistic impulse to defend perceived interests, even a yearning to restore the United States to its old position in the world. The breakdown of détente, the steady growth of Soviet military power, and the use of that power in . . . Afghanistan produced a profound nervousness about American security. The defense budget soared to mammoth proportions in the early 1980s, and support for military intervention in defense of traditional allies increased. Under the leadership of President Ronald Reagan, the nation embarked on a new global offensive against the Soviet Union and its clients.

The new nationalism was still tempered by lingering memories of Vietnam. Many Americans remained deeply skeptical of 1960s-style globalism and dubious of such internationalist mechanisms as foreign aid or even the United Nations. Fifteen years after the end of the war, a whopping majority still believed that intervention in Vietnam had been a mistake, producing strong opposition to military intervention abroad. Thus in the aftermath of Vietnam, the public mood consisted of a strange amalgam of nostalgia and realism, assertiveness and caution.

In the very different climate of the 1980s, the debate over Vietnam that had not taken place at the war's end assumed a central place in the larger and at times quite vocal debate over U.S. foreign policy. The basic issue remained the morality and wisdom of intervention in Vietnam. Concerned that in a new and even more dangerous Cold War a resurgent militance might lead to further disastrous embroilment, liberals urgently warned of the perils of another Vietnam. Fearful, on the other hand, that the so-called Vietnam syndrome had sapped America's will to defend legitimate interests and stand firmly against the evil of communism, some conservatives, including most notably President Reagan, spoke out anew on what they had always believed was a fundamental reality: that, as Reagan repeatedly proclaimed, Vietnam was "in truth a noble war," a selfless attempt on the part of the United States to save a free nation from outside aggression. Other conservatives conceded that the United States might have erred in getting involved in Vietnam in the first place, but they went on to insist that an important interest had been established that had to be defended for the sake of U.S. credibility throughout the world.

Lessons Learned

The second great issue on which Americans also sharply disagreed concerned the reasons for U.S. failure in Vietnam. Unwilling to concede that success had been beyond reach, many of the leading participants in the war concluded that America's failure had been essentially instrumental, a result of the improper use of available tools. General [William C.] Westmoreland [former head of military forces in Vietnam], Admiral [U.S. Grant] Sharp [commander of U.S. forces in the Pacific], and others blamed the "ill-considered" policy of "graduated response" imposed on the military by civilian leaders, arguing that had the United States employed its military power quickly, decisively, and without limit, the war could have been won. Some conservatives indeed concluded that timid civilian leaders had prevented the military from winning the war, a view that worked its way into the popular culture. "Sir, do we get to win *this* time?" the movie hero Rambo asked upon accepting the assignment to return to Vietnam and fight the second round single-handedly.

Others viewed the fundamental mistake as the choice of tools rather than the way they were used, and they blamed an unimaginative military as much as civilians. Instead of trying to fight World War II and Korea over in Vietnam, they argued, the military should have adapted to the unconventional war in which it found itself and shaped an appropriate counterinsurgency strategy. Still other commentators, including some military theorists, agreed that military leaders were as responsible for the strategic failure as civilians, arguing that instead of mounting costly and counterproductive search-and-destroy operations against guerrillas in South Vietnam, the United States should have used its own forces against North Vietnamese regulars along the seventeenth parallel to isolate the north from the south.

The lessons drawn were as divergent as the arguments advanced. Those who felt that the United States lost because it did not act decisively concluded that if the nation became involved in war again, it must employ its military power quickly and without limit to win before public support began to erode. Those who felt that the basic problem was the formulation rather than the execution of strategy insisted that military and civilian leaders must examine more carefully the nature of the war they were in and formulate more precisely the ways in which American power could best be used to attain clearly defined objectives.

Such lessons depended on the belief systems of those who pronounced them, of course, and those who had opposed the war reached quite different conclusions. To some former doves, the fundamental lesson was never to get involved in a land war in Asia; to others, it was to avoid intervention in international trouble spots unless the nation's vital interests were clearly at stake. Some commentators warned that policymakers must be wary of the sort of simplistic reasoning that produced the domino theory and the Munich analogy. Others pointed to the weakness of South Vietnam and admonished that even a superpower could not save allies who were unable or unwilling to save themselves. For still others, the key lessons were that American power had distinct limits and that to be effective, American foreign policy had to be true to the nation's historic ideals.

The Vietnam Syndrome

Throughout the 1980s, the ghost of Vietnam hovered over an increasingly divisive debate on the proper U.S. response to revolutions in Central America. Shortly after taking office in 1981, Reagan committed U.S. prestige to defending the government of El Salvador against a leftist-led insurgency, in part in the expectation that success there might exorcise the Vietnam syndrome. When the quick victory did not materialize, the administration expanded U.S. military aid to El Salvador, created a huge military base in Honduras, and launched a not-so-covert war to overthrow the Sandinista government of Nicaragua. The administration insisted that the United States must support non-Communist forces to avert in Central America the bloodshed and misery that followed the end of the war in Vietnam. At the same time, the military and the Defense Department made it clear that they would not go to war under the conditions that had prevailed in Vietnam. On the other side, dovish critics ominously and repeatedly warned that U.S. intervention in Central America would lead straight into a quagmire like Vietnam.

The issues were squarely joined in the Persian Gulf War of 1991, which seemed, at times, to be as much about Vietnam as about Saddam Hussein's conquest of Kuwait. Those who opposed going to war to liberate Kuwait warned that "Iraq was Arabic for Vietnam" and predicted a Vietnam-like quagmire in the desert. President George Bush, however, expressed from the outset his determination that the war in the Persian Gulf "would not be another Vietnam," and he and his military advisers, many of whom had fought in Vietnam, conducted the Gulf War largely on the basis of its perceived lessons. The President made it clear that American troops would not be forced to fight with "one hand tied behind their back," as had allegedly been the case in Vietnam, and the military employed maximum force as rapidly as possible to ensure a speedy victory. Media coverage was rigidly censored to prevent, as many claimed had happened in Vietnam, its stimulating antiwar sentiment. When the United States and its allies swiftly and decisively defeated Iraq, Bush in a euphoric victory statement exulted: "By God, we've kicked the Vietnam syndrome once and for all!"

The President's eulogy turned out to be premature. To be sure, success in the Gulf War helped restore the nation's confidence in its military institutions and weakened inhibitions against military intervention abroad. It did not, however, expunge deeply encrusted and still painful memories of an earlier and very different war. The President's own actions made this quite clear. In refusing to drive on to Baghdad and seek total victory over Iraq, Bush himself heeded fears of the political entanglements and military quagmire that might result from involvement in an alien and hostile area.

In the aftermath of the Gulf War, the ghosts of Vietnam still lingered. Emotional debates in 1993 and 1994 over possible military intervention in the brutal ethnic conflict in the former Yugoslavia called forth old and still bitter memories. A journalist surveying opinion in the American heartland in May 1993 found "an abiding fear that the Balkans are another Vietnam, a deep-seated angst that tends to outweigh concern that another holocaust is in the making." A number of senators, including Vietnam veterans like John McCain (a Republican from Arizona) and Hank Brown (a Republican from Colorado), expressed similar concerns, and President Bill Clinton's top advisers feared that intervention in Bosnia might be political death for him as Vietnam had been for Lyndon Johnson. In part because of perceived lessons of Vietnam, the United States kept a discreet distance from the Bosnian conflict.

Americans expressed little opposition when President Bush sent U.S. troops on a mission of mercy to war-torn Somalia in late 1992, but when those troops in the fall of 1993 became caught in the cross fire of Somalian politics and eighteen Americans were killed, the specter of Vietnam again rose like a storm cloud over the nation. . . .The fear that Somalia might become another Vietnam forced an American pullout from that troubled nation, making it abundantly clear that the ghosts George Bush claimed to have buried still haunted the nation.

Cautionary Principles

The ongoing debate over U.S. involvement in Vietnam raises as many questions as it answers. Many of the so-called lessons are based on historical givens that can never be proved. Whether the more decisive use of military power could have brought a satisfactory conclusion to the war without causing even more disastrous consequences remains at best unprovable. Whether the adoption of a more vigorous and imaginative counterinsurgency program at an earlier stage could have wrested control of the countryside from the NLF [National Liberation Front, Communist-dominated political organization in South Vietnam] can never be known, and the ability of the United States to implement such a program in an alien political culture is at best highly questionable. That the United States exaggerated the importance of Vietnam, as liberals have suggested, seems clear. But their argument begs the question of how one determines the significance of a given area and the even more difficult question of assessing the ultimate costs of intervention at an early stage.

Each historical situation is unique, moreover, and to extract lessons from one and apply them indiscriminately to another, very different event is at best misleading. The Central American crisis of the 1980s resolved itself in a way that confounded the dire predictions, drawn from Vietnam, offered by each side in the U.S. political debate. America's military success in the Persian Gulf War reflected more the unique conditions of that conflict than the successful application of lessons drawn from Vietnam. The one valid lesson that might be drawn, therefore, is to view all historical lessons with a healthy dose of skepticism. . . .

Although it does not permit precise lessons and may seem irrelevant, Vietnam nonetheless yields enduring cautionary principles that should be kept in mind as the United States proceeds into a new and uncertain era. First is the centrality of local forces in international crisis situations. Whether the United States won the Cold War is arguable, and the role of the containment policy in that outcome will long be debated. That containment was misapplied in Vietnam, however, seems beyond debate. The United States intervened to block the apparent march of a Soviet-directed communism across Asia, enlarged its commitment to halt a presumably expansionist Communist China, and eventually made Vietnam a test of its determination to uphold world order. By wrongly attributing the conflict to external sources, the United States drastically misjudged its internal dynamics. By intervening in what was essentially a local struggle, it placed itself at the mercy of local forces, a weak client, and a determined adversary. What might have remained a local conflict with primarily local implications was elevated into a major international conflict with enormous human costs that are still being paid. Local conditions may be even more important today when the main challenge for U.S. foreign policy is not to influence relations between states but to affect events within them. These forces will vary drastically from one situation to the next, but the point is clear: we ignore them at our own peril.

Second is the limits of power. As Somalia suggests, even so-called humanitarian interventions can lead to intractable political challenges. Stopping wars requires settling the political questions over which they are fought. Ending chaos or anarchy involves guaranteeing borders or establishing government machinery where none exists. In Vietnam, such tasks ultimately proved beyond the ability of the United States. This will not necessarily be the case elsewhere, but Americans must recognize that such interventions, at the very least, will be complicated and costly. They will involve us in the "poisonous tangle of local politics." They will not lend themselves to the quick fixes we seem to prefer. Vietnam offers no easy instruction to deal with such situations. It should stand, however, as an enduring testament to the pitfalls of interventionism and the limits of power.

Coping with the Scars of War

Fred Turner

More than twenty years after the end of the Vietnam War, America still faces issues that are difficult to resolve, among them how to reconcile our brutality in Vietnam with our perception of ourselves as a force for good in the world. In the following viewpoint, author Fred Turner argues that Americans must make some sense of the conflict—perhaps by envisioning the war as a classic tragedy or betrayal—if we are to move forward. Through clarification and self-awareness, Turner maintains, we can avoid repeating past mistakes and make judicious foreign policy decisions in the future.

Turner has been a freelance reporter and critic since 1986. He has lectured at Harvard University's John F. Kennedy School of Government and at the Massachusetts Institute of Technology.

Despite the ways in which the Vietnam Veterans Memorial has encouraged us to mourn our dead soldiers and to gloss over the nature of the conflict in which they died, the war still presents Americans with an agonizing set of questions. If we accept the historical evidence that in Southeast Asia our country committed acts of self-serving aggression rather than unsuccessful acts of rescue, then we must each examine our individual relationship to those acts. Did we serve in the combat zone, at the war's ground zero? Or did we hover at the edges of protest marches, not sure quite what or even whether to shout? Our answers to these questions will determine the psychological risks we run by confronting the facts of the past. As the experiences of traumatized veterans suggest, the more entangled one became in the violence of the war and the less one did to stop it, whether on the battlefield or here at home, the more psychologically threatening an appraisal of that violence becomes today.

At the same time, if we view American actions in Southeast Asia as unwarranted and brutal, we also put at risk many of the most fundamental assumptions we hold in common, as citizens, regardless of the role we each played in the war. If Americans' motives and actions were less than benevolent in Southeast Asia, can we continue to claim that our nation is a force for good in the world? If in the future we believe that we have to take military action overseas, particularly on behalf of an ally, will we be able to take that action knowing that many of us were once convinced that we had acted on behalf of a true partner, rather than a client state, in Vietnam?

Facing the Past

The questions mount and, as they do, so too does the temptation to despair. If we accept that as citizens of the nation that sent them to war, we each bear some responsibility, however small, for the crimes our countrymen committed in Southeast Asia, then we run the risk of thinking not only that we turned away from or supported or committed evil acts, but that somehow we ourselves *are* evil. Traumatized veterans know this danger well. Varnado Simpson, for example, who killed some twenty-five people during the My Lai massacre [in 1968], sat for years in his living room in Jackson, Mississippi, the shades drawn, thinking of suicide:

> How can you forgive? I can't forgive myself for the things—even though it was something that I was told to do. But how can I forget that—or forgive? It's easy for you to say: Well, you go ahead with your life. But how can you go ahead with your life when this is holding you back? I can't put my mind to anything. . . . Yes, I'm ashamed, I'm sorry, I'm guilty. But I did it. You know. What else can I tell you? It happened.

The memories of Varnado Simpson may seem to belong to an entirely different world, to mark an entirely different order of horror, than the recollections of those who never saw combat. Yet, even today, a quarter of a century after My Lai, Americans who reach toward a full apprehension of what happened in Vietnam, who try to assign some emotional and intellectual meaning to the war, must approach precisely the knowledge that torments Simpson. They have to face the fact that millions of people who were, before Americans invaded their country, no direct threat to the United States, died needlessly.

At the same time, they cannot afford to lose hope. They cannot, as Simpson has, confine themselves to their rooms and refuse to take further action. The world has changed enormously since the start of the Vietnam War. The Soviet empire that in large part sparked American fears of a global Communist menace has crumbled. The Southeast Asian nations that presidents from Eisenhower to Nixon feared might topple like dominoes into the hands of the Communists have instead committed themselves to capitalist expansion and the pursuit of profit. Even Communist Vietnam has lately revved its economic engines. Under a government policy of *doi moi* ("renovation" or "new way") established at the end of 1986, it has loosened internal restrictions on commerce and sought out trade links with such capitalist powerhouses as Japan, Taiwan, Singapore, and even its former enemy, the United States.

Striking a Balance

This new world presents Americans with a dilemma. If, like Varnado Simpson, we absorb and dwell on the full horror of our country's behavior in Vietnam, we may become crippled. We may so fear repeating the mistakes we made twenty and thirty years ago that we fail to take necessary steps to defend our legitimate geopolitical and economic interests overseas. On the other hand, if we completely ignore the horror of the war, we may well reenact it. If we continue to imagine that, despite the war's ignoble outcome, our country entered the conflict with largely noble intentions, we may also continue to send our soldiers into conflicts that have less to do with protecting America's material security than with defending what we imagine to be our moral prominence in the world. In short, if we are to succeed in adapting to the political challenges of the future, we must somehow strike a balance between our need to ease the emotional impact of what happened in Southeast Asia.

This same struggle confronts our traumatized combat veterans every day. For these men, the knowledge of what took place during the war often remains almost unbearable. As Kurt Ocher, a former riverboat gunner, explains, "The volume of suffering [in the Vietnam War] is so massive, you really can't hold it in your mind." If they could somehow know the entirety of their histories in Vietnam at one moment, men like Ocher would likely cease to be able to function. They would lose their jobs, their marriages would dissolve, their children would drift away.

Rather than confront the totality of the violence they survived in Vietnam, men like Ocher have parceled out their recollections into several competing stories of the past. Once an active member of Vietnam Veterans Against the War (VVAW) and still a man who condemns the war as pointless and immoral, Ocher nevertheless explains that "the motion that it was for nothing is intolerable. The idea that you were scarred and your friends were butchered for just absolutely nothing is more than anyone can bear. Even me." Worse still, says Ocher, is the motion that Americans in Vietnam died while taking part in an immoral national mission. "The minute I think we were doing the wrong thing [in Vietnam], I go from being a fighting man to being a butcher," he explains. "And there is a fine line—if any— between the two in the first place."

Was Ocher a fighting man or a butcher? Did his service have meaning or did his friends die for no reason? Ocher cannot be entirely sure. It is precisely this uncertainty, however, that allows him to move forward in his life today. By breaking up his recollections, by refusing to allow them into consciousness all at once, Ocher has drastically reduced the frequency with which he is overwhelmed by his combat history. He has retained the ability to acknowledge the moral and emotional complexities of his combat roles, but he has also gained the ability to function in few and successful ways: An empathetic father and husband, Ocher in no way resembles the butcher he fears he became in Vietnam.

Tragedy and Betrayal

In the years since the Vietnam War, the fragmentation that marks Ocher's recollection of his time in combat has also come to mark our collective responses to the conflict as a whole. Like Ocher, we have asked ourselves whether Americans in Vietnam were fighting men or butchers and what, if anything, their killing and dying might have meant. And like Ocher, we have apportioned our answers to these questions, along with our suffering and our sense of shame, among a number of competing and at times overlapping narratives. We have told ourselves stories of rescue and revenge, of therapy and initiation, of mourning and recovery and over the years, these narratives have spread like a network of scars across our national discourse. Found in junior high school textbooks and presidential speeches, popular movies and private conversations, these stories have closed and partially concealed the wounds left by the war in our national self-image. Part fact, part fiction, they have allowed us to simultaneously remember and forget, and thus they have made it possible for us to move forward—however haltingly—as a nation.

Few stories have appealed to more Americans than those that recast the war as a tragedy. In the late 1980s, Harry McPherson, Special Counsel to the President from 1965 to 1969 and thus a subcontractor to the architects of the war, expressed the tragic view succinctly: Vietnam, he explained, taught us that "powerful nations may stumble, though their intentions are good, and that tragedy and failure are often the lot of humanity, even of the citizens of a great and favored nation such as ours." . . .

By framing the war as a tragedy, Americans like McPherson have accomplished several difficult psychological tasks. They have acknowledged, albeit obliquely, that what their country did in Southeast Asia caused extraordinary harm. They have also recognized the fact that, from presidents to foot soldiers, many Americans who went to Vietnam did so on behalf of what they perceived to be a noble national mission. Like the heroes of the ancient plays, many did what they thought was right, only to discover that they had committed horrible wrongs. At the same time, by assigning responsibility for their actions to forces outside their control, the tragedy theorists have managed to sidestep feelings of guilt and to reassert the validity of many of their prewar assumptions. If we do not believe that we brought about our own downfall in Vietnam, then we can continue to believe that we are a uniquely powerful nation favored by God; that we are a force for good in the world; that, though we may fail to *achieve* good, it will not be because we have not *sought* to do good. . . .

In a story line that parallels that of the tragedy narrative, many Americans have come to view the war as a noble enterprise whose successful outcome was undermined by the perfidy of politicians, the press, or antiwar protestors. To the promulgators of this betrayal theory, the leaders of South Vietnam were not puppets of the United States, but the legitimate leaders of a democratic state struggling for independence. That state had been attacked by local Communists and by its Communist "neighbor," North Vietnam, and would not survive without help from the United States. "The South Vietnamese ally was caught up in a civil war," explains [journalist] Peter Braestrup, a war "abetted by outsiders from North Vietnam." Or as G. Gordon Liddy, former Watergate conspirator and vocal proponent of the betrayal theory, explains it, the Vietnam War "was not a 'civil war.' It was aggression by one state, valid politically and having ethnically different people, against another such state." . . .

By making these claims, . . . betrayal theorists can cast themselves in the role of loyal friend and rescuer. They can maintain the assumption that American intentions abroad were then—and therefore remain—good. Like proponents of the notion that the war was a tragedy, they can assert, even in the face of historical evidence to the contrary, that their prewar assumptive world remains intact. . . .

We retain the obligation to try to get the facts of our history right. At the same time, we must find the courage to acknowledge that no matter how hard we work to recover the past, we will never entirely succeed in knowing how wrong we went in Vietnam or in reassuring ourselves that we won't go just as wrong again. The notion of healing, at least in its popular conception, often invokes hopes of self-improvement or at least a return to normalcy. But in the wake of the war in Vietnam, we have had to face the fact that our sufferings have not made us a better people and that, so far at least, we have been unable to recover the ideological coherence and sense of purpose that marked the prewar years.

Living with Scars

Like Kurt Ocher, Americans today inhabit a post-traumatic world of fragmented, conflicting narratives, each true to a degree and each in part false. Yet it is precisely their fragmentary, conflicting nature that allows us to turn toward the future. To succeed in recognizing the full horror of the Vietnam War and of America's role in it, to actually hold it in our minds, would leave us crippled individually and as a nation. If we are to take effective action in the years ahead, we must allow the psychological wounds of the past to close. At the same time, if we are to avoid repeating the mistakes of the past, we must also continue to run our fingers along the scars.

Appendix of Documents

Document 1: The Truman Doctrine

In a message to Congress in March 1947, President Harry Truman asked for economic and military aid for anti-Communist forces in Greece and Turkey and announced a policy of international resistance to Communist aggression. The Truman Doctrine led to U.S. involvement in Vietnam.

The gravity of the situation which confronts the world today necessitates my appearance before a joint session of the Congress. The foreign policy and the national security of this country are involved. . . .

The United States has received from the Greek Government an urgent appeal for financial and economic assistance. Preliminary reports from the American Economic Mission now in Greece and reports from the American Ambassador in Greece corroborate the statement of the Greek Government that assistance is imperative if Greece is to survive as a free nation. . . .

The very existence of the Greek state is today threatened by the terrorist activities of several thousand armed men, led by Communists, who defy the Government's authority at a number of points, particularly along the northern boundaries. A commission appointed by the United Nations Security Council is at present investigating disturbed conditions in Northern Greece and alleged border violations along the frontiers between Greece on the one hand and Albania, Bulgaria and Yugoslavia on the other.

Meanwhile, the Greek Government is unable to cope with the situation. The Greek Army is small and poorly equipped. It needs supplies and equipment if it is to restore the authority to the Government throughout Greek territory. . . .

I believe that it must be the policy of the United States to support free peoples who are resisting attempted subjugation by armed minorities or by outside pressures.

I believe that we must assist free peoples to work out their own destinies in their own way.

I believe that our help should be primarily through economic and financial aid which is essential to economic stability and orderly political processes. . . .

Should we fail to aid Greece and Turkey in this fateful hour, the effect will be far reaching to the west as well as to the east. We must take immediate and resolute action.

I therefore ask the Congress to provide authority for assistance to Greece and Turkey in the amount of $400,000,000 for the period ending June 30, 1948. . . .

In addition to funds, I ask the Congress to authorize the detail of American civilian and military personnel to Greece and Turkey, at the request of those countries, to assist in the tasks of reconstruction, and for the purpose of supervising the use of such financial and material assistance as may be furnished. I recommend that authority also be provided for the instruction and training of selected Greek and Turkish personnel. . . .

If further funds, or further authority, should be needed for the purposes indicated in this message, I shall not hesitate to bring the situation before the Congress. On this subject the executive and legislative branches of the Government must work together.

This is a serious course upon which we embark. I would not recommend it except that the alternative is much more serious. . . .

The seeds of totalitarian regimes are nurtured by misery and want. They spread and grow in the evil soil of poverty and strife. They reach their full growth when the hope of a people for a better life has died. We must keep that hope alive. The free peoples of the world look to us for support in maintaining their freedoms.

If we falter in our leadership, we may endanger the peace of the world—and we shall surely endanger the welfare of this nation.

Great responsibilities have been placed upon us by the swift movement of events. I am confident that the Congress will face these responsibilities squarely.

Harry Truman, "Text of President Truman's Speech on New Foreign Policy," *New York Times*, March 13, 1947, p. 1.

Document 2: Vietnam's Declaration of Independence

On September 2, 1945, Vietnamese revolutionary Ho Chi Minh believed the time was right to declare his country's independence from France. Ho intentionally borrowed heavily from America's Declaration of Independence when he created his own document.

All men are created equal; they are endowed by their Creator with certain unalienable Rights; among these are Life, Liberty, and the pursuit of Happiness.

This immortal statement was made in the Declaration of Independence of the United States of America in 1776. In a broader sense, this means: All the peoples on the earth are equal from birth, all the peoples have a right to live, to be happy and free.

The Declaration of the French Revolution made in 1791 on the Rights of Man and the Citizen also states: "All men are born free and with equal rights, and must always remain free and have equal rights."

Those are undeniable truths.

Nevertheless, for more than eighty years, the French imperialists, abusing the standard of Liberty, Equality, and Fraternity, have violated our Fatherland and oppressed our fellow citizens. They have acted contrary to the ideals of humanity and justice. . . .

We, members of the Provisional Government, representing the whole Vietnamese people, declare that from now on we break off all relations of a colonial character with France; we repeal all the international obligation that France has so far subscribed to on behalf of Viet-Nam, and we abolish all the special rights the French have unlawfully acquired in our Fatherland.

The whole Vietnamese people, animated by a common purpose, are determined to fight to the bitter end against any attempt by the French colonialists to reconquer their country.

We are convinced that the Allied nations, which at Teheran and San Francisco have acknowledged the principles of self-determination and equality of nations, will not refuse to acknowledge the independence of Viet-Nam.

A people who have courageously opposed French domination for more than eighty years, a people who have fought side by side with the Allies against the fascists during these last years, such a people must be free and independent.

For these reasons, we, members of the Provisional Government of the Democratic Republic of Viet-Nam, solemnly declare to the world that Viet-Nam has the right to be a free and independent country—and in fact it is so already. The entire Vietnamese people are determined to mobilize all their physical and mental strength, to sacrifice their lives and property in order to safeguard their independence and liberty.

Bernard B. Fall, ed., *Ho Chi Minh on Revolution: Selected Writings, 1920–66*. New York: Frederick A. Praeger, 1967, pp. 143–45.

Document 3: French Appeal for Support at Dien Bien Phu

In April 1954, French forces in Vietnam teetered on the brink of defeat at Dien Bien Phu. On April 5, at the request of the French government, U.S. ambassador to France Douglas Dillon cabled Secretary of State

John Foster Dulles for U.S. air intervention in a desperate attempt to save the battle and France's dominion in Vietnam.

URGENT. I was called at 11 o'clock Sunday night and asked to come immediately to Matignon where a restricted Cabinet meeting was in progress. On arrival [French foreign minister Georges] Bidault received me in Laniel's office and was joined in a few minutes by [French premier Joseph] Laniel. They said that immediate armed intervention of U.S. carrier aircraft at Dien Bien Phu is now necessary to save the situation.

[Commanding general Henri] Navarre reports situation there now in state of precarious equilibrium and that both sides are doing best to reinforce—Viet Minh are bringing up last available reinforcements which will way outnumber any reinforcing French can do by parachute drops. Renewal of assault by reinforced Viet Minh probable by middle or end of week. Without help by then fate of Dien Bien Phu will probably be sealed.

[French general Paul] Ely brought back report from Washington that [Chief of Staff Admiral Arthur] Radford gave him his personal (repeat personal) assurance that if situation at Dien Bien Phu required U.S. naval air support he would do his best to obtain such help from U.S. Government. Because of this information from Radford as reported by Ely, French Government now asking for U.S. carrier aircraft support at Dien Bien Phu. Navarre feels that a relatively minor U.S. effort could turn the tide but naturally hopes for as much help as possible. . . .

Bidault said that French Chief of Air Staff wished U.S. be informed that U.S. air intervention at Dien Bien Phu could lead to Chinese Communist air attack on delta airfields. Nevertheless, government was making request for aid.

Bidault closed by saying that for good or evil the fate of Southeast Asia now rested on Dien Bien Phu. He said that Geneva would be won or lost depending on outcome at Dien Bien Phu. This was reason for French request for this very serious action on our part.

Douglas Dillon, "Dillon Cable to Dulles on Appeal for Air Support at Dienbienphu," *The Pentagon Papers*. New York: Bantam Books, 1971, pp. 38–39.

Document 4: The Geneva Accords
THE 'FINAL DECLARATION'

Final declaration, dated the 21st July, 1954, of the Geneva Conference on the problem of restoring peace in Indo-China, in which the representatives of Cambodia, the Democratic

Republic of Viet-Nam, France, Laos, the People's Republic of China, the State of Viet-Nam, the Union of Soviet Socialist Republics, the United Kingdom, and the United States of America took part.

1. The Conference takes note of the agreements ending hostilities in Cambodia, Laos and Viet-Nam and organizing international control and the supervision of the execution of the provisions of these agreements.

2. The Conference expresses satisfaction at the ending of hostilities in Cambodia, Laos and Viet-Nam. . . .

3. The Conference takes note of the declarations made by the Governments of Cambodia and of Laos of their intention to adopt measures permitting all citizens to take their place in the national community. . . .

4. The Conference takes note of the clauses in the agreement on the cessation of hostilities in Viet-Nam prohibiting the introduction into Viet-Nam of foreign troops and military personnel as well as of all kinds of arms and munitions. . . .

5. The Conference takes note of the clauses in the agreement on the cessation of hostilities in Viet-Nam to the effect that no military based under the control of a foreign State may be established in the regrouping zones of the two parties. . . .

6. The Conference recognizes that the essential purpose of the agreement relating to Viet-Nam is to settle military questions with a view to ending hostilities and that the military demarcation line is provisional and should not in any way be interpreted as constituting a political or territorial boundary. . . .

7. The Conference declares that, so far as Viet-Nam is concerned, the settlement of political problems, effected on the basis of respect for the principles of independence, unity and territorial integrity, shall permit the Viet-Namese people to enjoy the fundamental freedoms, guaranteed by democratic institutions established as a result of free general elections by secret ballot. In order to ensure that sufficient progress in the restoration of peace has been made, and that all the necessary conditions obtain for free expression of the national will, general elections shall be held in July 1956, under the supervision of an international commission composed of representatives of the Member States of the International Supervisory Commission, referred to in the agreement on the cessation of hostilities. . . .

8. The provisions of the agreements on the cessation of hostilities intended to ensure the protection of individuals and of property

must be most strictly applied and must, in particular, allow everyone in Viet-Nam to decide freely in which zone he wishes to live.

9. The competent representative authorities of the Northern and Southern zones of Viet-Nam, as well as the authorities of Laos and Cambodia, must not permit any individual or collective reprisals against persons who have collaborated in any way with one of the parties during the war, or against members of such person's families.

10. The Conference takes note of the declaration of the Government of the French Republic to the effect that it is ready to withdraw its troops from the territory of Cambodia, Laos and Viet-Nam. . . .

11. The Conference takes note of the declaration of the French Government to the effect that for the settlement of all the problems connected with the re-establishment and consolidation of peace in Cambodia, Laos and Viet-Nam, the French Government will proceed from the principle of respect for the independence and sovereignty, unity, and territorial integrity of Cambodia, Laos and Viet-Nam.

12. In their relations with Cambodia, Laos and Viet-Nam, each member of the Geneva Conference undertakes to respect the sovereignty, the independence, the unity and the territorial integrity of the above-mentioned states, and to refrain from any interference in their internal affairs.

13. The members of the Conference agree to consult one another on any question which may be referred to them by the International Supervisory Commission, in order to study such measures as may prove necessary to ensure that the agreement on the cessation of hostilities in Cambodia, Laos and Viet-Nam are respected.

" 'Final Declaration' at Geneva Conference," *The Pentagon Papers*. New York: Bantam Books, 1971, pp. 49–52.

Document 5: Proposals for Action in Vietnam

In 1961, the Kennedy administration was supportive of newly elected President Ngo Dinh Diem's fight against Communist aggression in South Vietnam. A memo from Deputy Assistant for National Security Walt Rostow to Kennedy on April 12, 1961, indicates the administration's intention to become more involved in Vietnamese politics.

Now that the Viet-Nam election is over, I believe we must turn to gearing up the whole Viet-Nam operation. Among the possible lines of action that might be considered at an early high level meeting are the following: . . .

1. The briefing of our new Ambassador, Fritz Nolting, including sufficient talk with yourself so that he fully understands the priority you attach to the Viet-Nam problem.

2. A possible visit to Viet-Nam in the near future by the Vice President.

3. A possible visit to the United States of Mr. Thuan, acting Defense Minister, and one of the few men around Diem with operational capacity and vigor.

4. The sending to Viet-Nam of a research and development and military hardware team which would explore with General McGarr which of the various techniques and gadgets now available or being explored might be relevant and useful in the Viet-Nam operation.

5. The raising of the MAAG [Military Assistance Advisory Group] ceiling, which involves some diplomacy, unless we can find an alternative way of introducing into Viet-Nam operation a substantial number of Special Forces types. . . .

6. Sending the question of the extra funds for Diem.

7. The tactics of persuading Diem to move more rapidly to broaden the base of his government, as well as to decrease its centralization and improve its efficiency.

Against the background of decisions we should urgently take on these matters, you may wish to prepare a letter to Diem which would not only congratulate him, reaffirm our support, and specify new initiatives we are prepared to take, but would make clear to him the urgency you attach to a more effective political and morale setting for his military operation, now that the elections are successfully behind him.

Walt W. Rostow, "Memo from Rostow to Kennedy with Nine Proposals for Action," *The Pentagon Papers*. New York: Bantam Books, 1971, p. 119.

Document 6: Defense Secretary's Conclusions on Vietnam

Even before the United States committed itself to fighting a war in Vietnam, policymakers were aware that the cost of their involvement would be high. In a memorandum to President Kennedy dated November 8, 1961, Secretary of Defense Robert McNamara recommends that the United States fully commit to saving South Vietnam from communism despite the cost.

The basic issue . . . is whether the U. S. shall:

a. Commit itself to the clear objective of preventing the fall of South Vietnam to Communism, and

   b. Support this commitment by necessary immediate military actions and preparations for possible later actions.

   The Joint Chiefs, Mr. [Roswell] Gilpatric [deputy secretary of defense] and I have reached the following conclusions:

   1. The fall of South Vietnam to Communism would lead to the fairly rapid extension of Communist control, or complete accommodation to Communism, in the rest of mainland Southeast Asia and in Indonesia. The strategic implications worldwide, particularly in the Orient, would be extremely serious.

   2. The chances are against, probably sharply against, preventing that fall by any measures short of the introduction of U.S. forces on a substantial scale. . . .

   3. The introduction of a U.S. force of the magnitude of an initial 8,000 men in a flood relief context will be of great help to Diem. . . .

   4. The other side can be convinced we mean business only if we accompany the initial force introduction by a clear commitment to the full objective stated above, accompanied by a warning through some channel to Hanoi that continued support of the Viet Cong will lead to punitive retaliation against North Vietnam.

   5. If we act in this way, the ultimate possible extent of our military commitment must be faced. The struggle may be prolonged and Hanoi and Peiping [Peking] may intervene overtly. In view of the logistic difficulties faced by the other side, I believe we can assume that the maximum U.S. forces required on the ground in Southeast Asia will not exceed 6 divisions, or about 205,000 men. . . .

   6. To accept the stated objective is of course a most serious decision. Military force is not the only element of what must be a most carefully coordinated set of actions. Success will depend on factors many of which are not within our control—notably the conduct of Diem himself and other leaders in the area. . . . The domestic political implications of accepting the objective are also grave, although it is our feeling that the country will respond better to a firm initial position than to courses of action that lead us in only gradually, and that in the meantime are sure to involve casualties. . . .

   7. In sum:

   a. We do not believe major units of U.S. forces should be introduced in South Vietnam unless we are willing to make an affirmative decision on the issue stated at the start of this memorandum.

   b. We are inclined to recommend that we do commit the U.S. to the clear objective of preventing the fall of South Vietnam to

Communism and that we support this commitment by the necessary military actions.

Robert McNamara, "Conclusions of McNamara on Report by General Taylor," *The Pentagon Papers*. New York: Bantam Books, 1971, pp. 148–50.

Document 7: Kennedy Position on Coup Plot

The Kennedy administration grew increasingly critical of South Vietnamese president Ngo Dinh Diem's regime as time passed, but on receiving an advisory that a coup d'etat was planned against Diem, they chose a safe, middle-of-the-road response. The administration's position is expressed in a top-secret cablegram from the White House to Ambassador to Vietnam Henry Cabot Lodge on October 5, 1963.

President today approved recommendation that no initiative should now be taken to give any active covert encouragement to a coup. There should, however, be urgent covert effort with closest security, under broad guidance of Ambassador to identify and build contacts with possible alternative leadership as and when it appears. Essential that this effort be totally secure and fully deniable and separated entirely from normal political analysis and reporting and other activities of country team. We repeat that this effort is not repeat not to be aimed at active promotion of coup but only at surveillance and readiness. In order to provide plausibility to denial suggest you and no one else in Embassy issue these instructions orally to Acting Station Chief and hold him responsible to you alone for making appropriate contacts and reporting to you alone.

"Kennedy Position on Coup Plots," *The Pentagon Papers*. New York: Bantam Books, 1971, pp. 215–16.

Document 8: Tonkin Gulf Resolution

On August 7, 1964, Congress passed a joint resolution that allowed President Lyndon Johnson to respond to a North Vietnamese attack on U.S. warships in the Tonkin Gulf. The wording of the resolution allowed Johnson to expand and fight the war in Vietnam for an indefinite period of time.

Resolved by the Senate and House of Representatives of the United States of America in Congress assembled, That the Congress approves and supports the determination of the President, as Commander in Chief, to take all necessary measures to repel any armed attack against the forces of the United States and to prevent further aggression.

Sec. 2. The United States regards as vital to its national interest and to world peace the maintenance of international peace and security in southeast Asia. Consonant with the Constitution of the United States and the Charter of the United Nations and in accordance with its obligations under the Southeast Asia Collective Defense Treaty, the United States is, therefore, prepared, as the President determines, to take all necessary steps, including the use of armed force, to assist any member or protocol state of the Southeast Asia Collective Defense Treaty requesting assistance in defense of its freedom.

Sec. 3. This resolution shall expire when the President shall determine that the peace and security of the area is reasonably assured by international conditions created by action of the United Nations or otherwise, except that it may be terminated earlier by concurrent resolution of the Congress.

H.J. Resolution 1145, *Congressional Record; Proceedings and Debates of the 88th Congress, vol. 110, pt. 14.* Washington, DC: U.S. Government Printing Office, 1964, p. 18,471.

Document 9: Limited Approach to War

In 1964, the Johnson administration considered expanding the war by sending U.S. ground forces into Vietnam. In a letter to Secretary of Defense McNamara, State Department policymaker Walt W. Rostow outlines an approach that rests on the premise of limited warfare and the threat of escalation of force to intimidate the enemy. Johnson favored such an approach throughout his term of office.

1. I am convinced that we should not go forward into the next stage without a U.S. ground force commitment of some kind:

a. The withdrawal of those ground forces could be a critically important part of our diplomatic bargaining position. Ground forces can sit during a conference more easily than we can maintain a series of mounting air and naval pressures.

b. We must make clear that counter escalation by the Communists will run directly into U.S. strength on the ground. . . .

2. The first critical military action against North Vietnam should be designed merely to install the principle that they will from the present forward, be vulnerable to retaliatory attack in the north for continued violations. . . . In other words, we would signal a shift from the principle involved in the Tonkin Gulf response. This means that the initial use of force in the north should be as limited and as unsanguinary [bloodless] as possible. It is the installation of the principle that we are initially interested in, not tit for tat.

3. But our force dispositions to accompany an initial retaliatory move directly against the north should send three further signals lucidly:

a. that we are putting in place a capacity subsequently to step up direct and naval pressure on the north, if that should be required;

b. that we are prepared to face down any form of escalation North Vietnam might mount on the ground; and

c. that we are putting forces into place to exact retaliation directly against Communist China, if Peiping [Peiking] should join in an escalatory response from Hanoi. The latter could take the form of increased aircraft on Formosa [Taiwan] plus, perhaps, a carrier force sitting off China distinguished from the force in the South China Sea.

4. The launching of this track, almost certainly, will require the President to explain to our own people and to the world our intentions and objectives. This will also be perhaps the most persuasive form of communication with Ho [Chi Minh] and Mao [Tse Tung]. . . . They should feel they now confront an LBJ who has made up his mind.

Walt W. Rostow, "Letter from Rostow Favoring Commitment of Troops by U.S.," *The Pentagon Papers*. New York: Bantam Books, 1971, pp. 418–19.

Document 10: Johnson's Address—"Peace Without Conquest"

On April 7, 1965, President Johnson gives an address at Johns Hopkins University entitled "Peace Without Conquest." In it, he emphasized two diametrically opposite foreign policy goals: a commitment to fighting communism in Vietnam and a dream of peace in Southeast Asia and throughout the world.

Why are we in South Viet-Nam?

We are there because we have a promise to keep. Since 1954 every American President has offered support to the people of South Viet-Nam. We have helped to build, and we have helped to defend. Thus, over many years, we have made a national pledge to help South Viet-Nam defend its independence.

And I intend to keep that promise.

To dishonor that pledge, to abandon this small and brave nation to its enemies, and to the terror that must follow, would be an unforgivable wrong.

We are also there to strengthen world order. Around the globe, from Berlin to Thailand, are people whose well-being rests, in part, on the belief that they can count on us if they are attacked. To leave Viet-Nam to its fate would shake the confidence of all these people in the value of an American commitment and in the value of America's word. The result would be increased unrest and instability, and even wider war.

We are also there because there are great stakes in the balance. Let no one think for a moment that retreat from Viet-Nam would bring an end to conflict. The battle would be renewed in one country and then another. The central lesson of our time is that the appetite of aggression is never satisfied. To withdraw from one battlefield means only to prepare for the next. We must say in southeast Asia—as we did in Europe—in the words of the Bible: "Hitherto shalt thou come, but no further." . . .

In recent months attacks on South Viet-Nam were stepped up. Thus, it became necessary for us to increase our response and to make attacks by air. This is not a change of purpose. It is a change in what we believe that purpose requires.

We do this in order to slow down aggression.

We do this to increase the confidence of the brave people of South Viet-Nam who have bravely borne this brutal battle for so many years with so many casualties.

And we do this to convince the leaders of North Viet-Nam—and all who seek to share their conquest—of a very simple fact:

We will not be defeated.

We will not grow tired.

We will not withdraw, either openly or under the cloak of a meaningless agreement. . . .

Our generation has a dream. It is a very old dream. But we have the power and now we have the opportunity to make that dream come true.

For centuries nations have struggled among each other. But we dream of a world where disputes are settled by law and reason. And we will try to make it so.

For most of history men have hated and killed one another in battle. But we dream of an end to war. And we will try to make it so.

For all existence most men have lived in poverty, threatened by hunger. But we dream of a world where all are fed and charged with hope. And we will help to make it so. . . .

This generation of the world must choose to destroy or build, kill or aid, hate or understand.

We can do all these things on a scale never dreamed of before.

Well, we will choose life. In so doing we will prevail over the enemies within man, and over the natural enemies of all mankind.

Lyndon Johnson, "Address at Johns Hopkins University: 'Peace Without Conquest.' April 7, 1965," *Public Papers of the Presidents of the United States*. Washington, DC: U.S. Government Printing Office, 1966, pp. 394–99.

Document 11: On Sending Ground Troops to Vietnam

After escalating the war in early 1965, Johnson expressed his personal feelings about sending combat troops to Vietnam in a July news confer-ence. The president had hoped to concentrate on domestic affairs during his term in office, but the Vietnam War consumed much of his time and energy.

I have today ordered to Viet-Nam the Air Mobile Division and certain other forces which will raise our fighting strength from 75,000 to 125,000 men almost immediately. Additional forces will be needed later, and they will be sent as requested.

This will make it necessary to increase our active fighting forces by raising the monthly draft call from 17,000 over a period of time to 35,000 per month, and for us to step up our campaign for vol-untary enlistments.

After this past week of deliberations, I have concluded that it is not essential to order Reserve units into service now. If that neces-sity should later be indicated, I will give the matter most careful consideration and I will give the country—you—an adequate no-tice before taking such action, but only after full preparations. . . .

I do not find it easy to send the flower of our youth, our finest young men, into battle. I have spoken to you today of the divisions and the forces and the battalions and the units, but I know them all, every one. I have seen them in a thousand streets, of a hundred towns, in every State in this Union—working and laughing and building, and filled with hope and life. I think I know, too, how their mothers weep and how their families sorrow. . . .

But I also know, as a realistic public servant, that as long as there are men who hate and destroy, we must have the courage to resist, or we will see it all, all that we have built, all that we hope to build, all of our dreams for freedom—all, *all* will be swept away on the flood of conquest.

So, too, this shall not happen. We will stand in Viet-Nam.

Lyndon Johnson, "The President's News Conference of July 28, 1965," *Public Papers of the Presidents of the United States*. Washington, DC: U.S. Government Printing Office, 1966, pp. 794–98.

Document 12: The Tet Offensive

One month after the Tet Offensive broke on January 30, 1968, Chairman of the Joint Chiefs of Staff general Earle Wheeler reports to Johnson on military conditions in Vietnam. Wheeler's observations bring an objective perspective to an emotional incident in the war.

—The current situation in Vietnam is still developing and is fraught with opportunities as well as dangers.

—There is no question in the mind of MACV that the enemy went all out for a general offensive and general uprising and apparently believed that he would succeed in bringing the war to an early successful conclusion.

—The enemy failed to achieve his initial objective but is continuing his effort. Although many of his units were badly hurt, the judgement is that he has the will and the capability to continue.

—Enemy losses have been heavy; he has failed to achieve his prime objectives of mass uprisings and capture of a large number of the capital cities and towns. Morale in enemy units which were badly mauled or where the men were oversold the idea of a decisive victory at TET probably has suffered severely. However, with replacements, his indoctrination system would seem capable of maintaining morale at a generally adequate level. His determination appears to be unshaken.

—The enemy is operating with relative freedom in the countryside, probably recruiting heavily and no doubt infiltrating NVA units and personnel. His recovery is likely to be rapid; his supplies are adequate; and he is trying to maintain the momentum of his winter-spring offensive. . . .

—The RVNAF [Republic of Vietnam Air Force] held up against the initial assault with gratifying, and in a way, surprising strength and fortitude. However, RVNAF is now in a defensive posture around towns and cities and there is concern about how well they will bear up under sustained pressure.

—The initial attack nearly succeeded in a dozen places, and defeat in those places was only averted by the timely reaction of U.S. forces. In short, it was a very near thing. . . .

—RVNAF was not badly hurt physically—they should recover strength and equipment rather quickly (equipment in 2–3 months—strength in 3–6 months). Their problems are more psychological than physical.

—U.S. forces have lost none of their pre-TET capability.

Earle Wheeler, "Wheeler's '68 Report to Johnson After the Tet Offensive," *The Pentagon Papers*. New York: Bantam Books, 1971, pp. 615–16.

Document 13: Johnson De-escalates the War

Antiwar feeling in America heightened after the Tet Offensive, and Johnson responded by altering his war policies. On March 31, 1968, he revealed in a television address that he was taking the first steps to deescalate the war. Johnson also announced that he would not seek reelection as president.

Good evening, my fellow Americans:

Tonight I want to speak to you of peace in Vietnam and Southeast Asia.

No other question so preoccupies our people. No other dream so absorbs the 250 million human beings who live in that part of the world. No other goal motivates American policy in Southeast Asia. . . .

Tonight, I renew the offer I made last August—to stop the bombardment of North Vietnam. We ask that talks begin promptly, that they be serious talks on the substance of peace. We assume that during those talks Hanoi will not take advantage of our restraint.

We are prepared to move immediately toward peace through negotiations.

So, tonight, in the hope that this action will lead to early talks, I am taking the first step to deescalate the conflict. We are reducing—substantially reducing—the present level of hostilities.

And we are doing so unilaterally, and at once. . . .

I believe that a peaceful Asia is far nearer to reality because of what America has done in Vietnam. I believe that the men who endure the dangers of battle—fighting there for us tonight—are helping the entire world avoid far greater conflicts, far wider wars, far more destruction, than this one.

The peace that will bring them home someday will come. Tonight I have offered the first in what I hope will be a series of mutual moves toward peace.

I pray that it will not be rejected by the leaders of North Vietnam. I pray that they will accept it as a means by which the sacrifices of their own people may be ended. And I ask your help and your support, my fellow citizens, for this effort to reach across the battlefield toward an early peace.

Finally, my fellow Americans, let me say this: . . .

In these times as in times before, it is true that a house divided against itself by the spirit of faction, of party, of region, of religion, of race, is a house that cannot stand.

There is division in the American house now. There is divisiveness among us all tonight. And holding the trust that is mine, as

President of all the people, I cannot disregard the peril to the progress of the American people and the hope and the prospect of peace for all peoples.

So, I would ask all Americans, whatever their personal interests or concern, to guard against divisiveness and all its ugly consequences.

Fifty-two months and 10 days ago, in a moment of tragedy and trauma, the duties of this office fell upon me. I asked then for your help and God's, that we might continue America on its course, binding up our wounds, healing our history, moving forward in new unity, to clear the American agenda and to keep the American commitment for all of our people.

United we have kept that commitment. United we have enlarged that commitment.

Through all time to come, I think America will be a stronger nation, a more just society, and a land of greater opportunity and fulfillment because of what we have all done together in these years of unparalleled achievement.

Our reward will come in the life of freedom, peace, and hope that our children will enjoy through ages ahead.

What we won when all of our people united just must not now be lost in suspicion, distrust, selfishness, and politics among any of our people.

Believing this as I do, I have concluded that I should not permit the Presidency to become involved in the partisan divisions that are developing in this political year.

With America's sons in the fields far away, with America's future under challenge right here at home, with our hopes and the world's hopes for peace in the balance every day, I do not believe that I should devote an hour or a day of my time to any personal partisan causes or to any duties other than the awesome duties of this office—the Presidency of your country.

Accordingly, I shall not seek, and I will not accept, the nomination of my party for another term as your President.

But let men everywhere know, however, that a strong, a confident, and a vigilant America stands ready tonight to seek an honorable peace—and stands ready tonight to defend an honored cause—whatever the price, whatever the burden, whatever the sacrifice that duty may require.

Thank you for listening.

Good night and God bless all of you.

Lyndon Johnson, "The President's Address to the Nation Announcing Steps to Limit the War in Vietnam and Reporting His Decision Not to Seek Reelection. March 31, 1968," *Public Papers of the Presidents of the United States*. Washington, DC: U. S. Government Printing Office, 1970, pp. 469–76.

Document 14: Nixon's "Silent Majority" Speech

Shortly after taking office, Richard Nixon announces his plan to negotiate an end to the highly unpopular war. In a television address on November 3, 1969, he addresses his remarks to the "silent majority" of Americans who he feels support his efforts to find an honorable peace in Vietnam.

Good evening, my fellow Americans:

Tonight I want to talk to you on a subject of deep concern to all Americans and to many people in all parts of the world—the war in Vietnam. . . .

Three American Presidents have recognized the great stakes involved in Vietnam and understood what had to be done.

In 1963, President Kennedy, with his characteristic eloquence and clarity, said: ". . . we want to see a stable government there, carrying on a struggle to maintain its national independence.

"We believe strongly in that. We are not going to withdraw from that effort. In my opinion, for us to withdraw from that effort would mean a collapse not only of South Viet-Nam, but Southeast Asia. So we are going to stay there."

President Eisenhower and President Johnson expressed the same conclusion during their terms of office.

For the future of peace, precipitate withdrawal would thus be a disaster of immense magnitude.

—A nation cannot remain great if it betrays its allies and lets down its friends.

—Our defeat and humiliation in South Vietnam without question would promote recklessness in the councils of those great powers who have not yet abandoned their goals of world conquest.

—This would spark violence wherever our commitments help maintain the peace—in the Middle East, in Berlin, eventually even in the Western Hemisphere. . . .

In speaking of the consequences of a precipitate withdrawal, I mentioned that our allies would lose confidence in America.

Far more dangerous, we would lose confidence in ourselves. Oh, the immediate reaction would be a sense of relief that our men were coming home. But as we saw the consequences of what we had done, inevitable remorse and divisive recrimination would scar our spirit as a people. . . .

Two hundred years ago this Nation was weak and poor. But even then, America was the hope of millions in the world. Today we have become the strongest and richest nation in the world. And the wheel of destiny has turned so that any hope the world has for the survival of peace and freedom will be determined by whether the American people have the moral stamina and the courage to meet the challenge of free world leadership.

Let historians not record that when America was the most powerful nation in the world we passed on the other side of the road and allowed the last hopes for peace and freedom of millions of people to be suffocated by the forces of totalitarianism.

And so tonight—to you, the great silent majority of my fellow Americans—I ask for your support.

I pledged in my campaign for the Presidency to end the war in a way that we could win the peace. I have initiated a plan of action which will enable me to keep that pledge.

The more support I can have from the American people, the sooner that pledge can be redeemed; for the more divided we are at home, the less likely the enemy is to negotiate at Paris.

Let us be united for peace. Let us also be united against defeat. Because let us understand: North Vietnam cannot defeat or humiliate the United States. Only Americans can do that. . . .

Thank you and goodnight.

Richard Nixon, "Address to the Nation on the War in Vietnam. November 3, 1969," *Public Papers of the Presidents of the United States.* Washington, DC: U. S. Government Printing Office, 1971, pp. 901–909.

Document 15: Veterans Oppose the War

On April 23, 1971, John Kerry, veteran and spokesman for Vietnam Veterans Against the War, made a statement before the Senate Committee on Foreign Relations urging an end to the war. Many veterans such as Kerry felt they had been used by their government to fight an immoral war in Vietnam.

I am here as one member of the group of 1,000, which is a small representation of a very much larger group of veterans in this country, and were it possible for all of them to sit at this table they would be here and have the same kind of testimony. . . .

We are asking here in Washington for some action; action from the Congress of the United States of America which has the power to raise and maintain armies, and which by the Constitution also has the power to declare war.

We have come here, not to the President, because we believe that this body can be responsive to the will of the people, and we believe that the will of the people says that we should be out of Vietnam now.

We are here in Washington also to say that the problem of this war is not just a question of war and diplomacy. It is part and parcel of everything that we are trying as human beings to communicate to people in this country—the question of racism, which is rampant in the military, and so many other questions such as the use of weapons; the hypocrisy in our taking umbrage in the Geneva Conventions and using that as justification for a continuation of this war when we are more guilty than any other body of violations of those Geneva Conventions; in the use of free fire zones, harassment interdiction fire, search and destroy missions, the bombings, the torture of prisoners, the killing of prisoners, all accepted policy by many units in South Vietnam. That is what we are trying to say. It is part and parcel of everything.

An American Indian friend of mine who lives in the Indian Nation of Alcatraz put it to me very succinctly. He told me how as a boy on an Indian reservation he had watched television and he used to cheer the cowboys when they came in and shot the Indians, and then suddenly one day he stopped in Vietnam and he said "my God, I am doing to these people the very same thing that was done to my people," and he stopped. And that is what we are trying to say, that we think this thing has to end.

We are also here to ask, and we are here to ask vehemently, where are the leaders of our country? Where is the leadership? We are here to ask where are McNamara, Rostow, Bundy, Gilpatric and so many others? Where are they now that we, the men whom they sent off to war, have returned? These are commanders who have deserted their troops, and there is no more serious crime in the law of war. The Army says they never leave their wounded. The Marines say they never leave even their dead. These men have left all the casualties and retreated behind a pious shield of public rectitude. They have left the real stuff of their reputations bleaching behind them in the sun in this country.

Finally, this administration has done us the ultimate dishonor. They have attempted to disown us and the sacrifices we made for this country. In their blindness and fear they have tried to deny that we are veterans or that we served in Nam. We do not need their testimony. Our own scars and stumps of limbs are witness enough for others and for ourselves.

We wish that a merciful God could wipe away our own memories of that service as easily as this administration has wiped away their memories of us. But all that they have done and all that they can do by this denial is to make more clear than ever our own determination to undertake one last mission—to search out and destroy the last vestige of this barbaric war, to pacify our own hearts, to conquer the hate and the fear that have driven this country these last ten years and more, so when 30 years from now our brothers go down the street without a leg, without an arm, or a face, and small boys ask why, we will be able to say "Vietnam" and not mean a desert, not a filthy obscene memory, but mean instead the place where America finally turned and where soldiers like us helped it in the turning.

Thank you.

John Kerry, "Vietnam Veterans Against the War," *Congressional Record: Proceedings and Debates of the 92nd Congress, vol. 117, pt. 9.* Washington, DC: U.S. Government Printing Office, 1971, pp. 11,738–39.

Document 16: Nixon Announces Peace

On the day all parties in Paris acceded to peace terms, Richard Nixon gave a national address to announce the event. The Paris agreement brought an official end to America's role in the Vietnam War, but did not stop the fighting.

Good evening. I have asked for this radio and television time tonight for the purpose of announcing that we today have concluded an agreement to end the war and bring peace with honor in Vietnam and Southeast Asia.

The following statement is being issued at this moment in Washington and Hanoi:

"At 12:30 Paris time today, Jan. 23, 1973, the agreement on ending the war and restoring peace in Vietnam was initialed by Dr. Henry Kissinger on behalf of the United States and Special Adviser Le Duc Tho on behalf of the Democratic Republic of Vietnam.

"The agreement will be formally signed by the parties participating in the Paris Conference on Vietnam on Jan. 27, 1973, at the International Conference Center in Paris. The cease-fire will take effect at 2400 Greenwich mean time, Jan. 27, 1973. The United States and the Democratic Republic of Vietnam express the hope that this agreement will insure stable peace in Vietnam and contribute to the preservation of lasting peace in Indochina and Southeast Asia." . . .

As this long and very difficult war ends I would like to address a few special words to each of those who have been parties in the conflict.

First, to the people and Government of South Vietnam. By your courage, by your sacrifice, you have won the precious right to determine your own future and you have developed the strength to defend that right.

We look forward to working with you in the future, friends in peace as we have been allies in war.

To the leaders of North Vietnam: As we have ended the war through negotiations, let us now build a peace of reconciliation.

For our part, we are prepared to make a major effort to help achieve that goal. But just as reciprocity was needed to end the war, so too will it be needed to build and strengthen the peace.

To the other major powers that have been involved, even indirectly: Now is the time for mutual restraint so that the peace we have achieved can last.

And finally, to all of you who are listening, the American people: Your steadfastness in supporting our insistence on peace with honor has made peace with honor possible. . . .

Now that we have achieved an honorable agreement let us be proud that America did not settle for a peace that would have betrayed our allies, that would have abandoned our prisoners of war or that would have ended the war for us but would have continued the war for the 50 million people of Indochina.

Let us be proud of the two and a half million young Americans who served in Vietnam, who served with honor and distinction in one of the most selfless enterprises in the history of nations.

And let us be proud of those who sacrificed, who gave their lives, so that the people of South Vietnam might live in freedom, and so that the world might live in peace.

Richard Nixon, "Transcript of the Speech by President on Vietnam," *New York Times*, January 24, 1973, pp. 1, 16.

Document 17: The Paris Peace Accords

The text of the Paris Peace Accords was published in the New York Times *on January 25, 1973. Because the South Vietnamese government was unwilling to recognize the Viet Cong's Provisional Revolutionary Government, the accords were drafted in two versions, one of which is signed only by the United States and North Vietnam.*

Chapter I
The Vietnamese People's Fundamental National Rights

ARTICLE 1
The United States and all other countries respect the independence, sovereignty, unity and territorial integrity of Vietnam as recognized by the 1954 Geneva Agreements on Vietnam.

Chapter II
Cessation of Hostilities, Withdrawal of Troops

ARTICLE 2

A cease-fire shall be observed throughout South Vietnam as of 2400 hours G.M.T., on Jan. 27, 1973.

At the same hour, the United States will stop all its military activities against the territory of the Democratic Republic of Vietnam by ground, air and naval forces, wherever they may be based, and end the mining of the territorial waters, ports, harbors and waterways of the Democratic Republic of Vietnam. The United States will remove, permanently deactivate or destroy all the mines in the territorial waters, ports, harbors and waterways of North Vietnam as soon as this agreement goes into effect.

The complete cessation of hostilities mentioned in this article shall be durable and without limit of time.

ARTICLE 3

The parties undertake to maintain the cease-fire and to insure a lasting and stable peace.

As soon as the cease-fire goes into effect:

(a) The United States forces and those of the other foreign countries allied with the United States and the Republic of Vietnam shall remain in place pending the implementation of the plan of troop withdrawal. . . .

(b) The armed forces of the two South Vietnamese parties shall remain in place. . . .

(c) The regular forces of all services and arms and the irregular forces of the parties in South Vietnam shall stop all offensive activities against each other and shall strictly abide by the following stipulations:

All acts of force on the ground, in the air and on the sea shall be prohibited.

All hostile acts, terrorism and reprisals by both sides will be banned.

ARTICLE 4

The United States will not continue its military involvement or intervene in the internal affairs of South Vietnam.

ARTICLE 5

Within 60 days of the signing of this agreement, there will be a total withdrawal from South Vietnam of troops, military personnel, including technical military personnel and military personnel associated with the pacification program, armaments, munitions and war material of the United States and those of the other foreign countries mentioned in Article 3 (a). . . .

ARTICLE 6

The dismantlement of all military bases in South Vietnam of the United States and of the other foreign countries mentioned in Article 3 (a) shall be completed within 60 days of the signing of this agreement.

ARTICLE 7

From the enforcement of the cease-fire to the formation of the government provided for in Article 9 (b) . . . of this agreement, the two South Vietnamese parties shall not accept the introduction of troops, military advisers and military personnel, including technical military personnel, armaments, munitions and war material into South Vietnam.

The two South Vietnamese parties shall be permitted to make periodic replacement of armaments, munitions and war material which have been destroyed, damaged, worn out or used up after the cease-fire, on the basis of piece-for-piece, of the same characteristics and properties, under the supervision of the Joint Military Commission of Control and Supervision.

Chapter III
The Return of Captured Military Personnel and Foreign Civilians, and Captured and Detained Vietnamese Civilian Personnel

ARTICLE 8

The return of captured military personnel and foreign civilians of the parties shall be carried out simultaneously with and completed not later than the same day as the troop withdrawal mentioned in Article 5. The parties shall exchange complete lists of the above-mentioned captured military personnel and foreign civilians on the day of the signing of this agreement. . . .

Chapter IV
The Exercise of the South Vietnamese People's Right to Self-Determination

ARTICLE 9

(a) The South Vietnamese people's right to self-determination is sacred, inalienable and shall be respected by all countries.

(b) The South Vietnamese people shall decide themselves the political future of south Vietnam through genuinely free and democratic general elections under international supervision.

(c) Foreign countries shall not impose any political tendency or personality on the South Vietnamese people.

ARTICLE 10

The two South Vietnamese parties undertake to respect the cease-fire and maintain peace in South Vietnam, settle all matters of contention through negotiations and avoid all armed conflict.

ARTICLE 11

Immediately after the cease-fire, the two South Vietnamese parties will:

Achieve national reconciliation and concord, end hatred and enmity, prohibit all acts of reprisal and discrimination against individuals or organizations that have collaborated with one side or the other.

Insure the democratic liberties of the people: personal freedom, freedom of speech, freedom of the press, freedom of meeting, freedom of organization, freedom of political activities, freedom of belief, freedom of movement, freedom of residence, freedom of work, right to property ownership and right to free enterprise. . . .

Chapter V
The Reunification of Vietnam and the Relationship
Between North and South Vietnam

ARTICLE 15

The reunification of Vietnam shall be carried out step by step through peaceful means on the basis of discussions and agreements between North and South Vietnam, without coercion or annexation by either party, and without foreign interference. The time for reunification will be agreed upon by North and South Vietnam.

"The Vietnam Agreement and Protocols," *New York Times*, January 25, 1973, p. 15.

Document 18: Reagan Acknowledges Vietnam

In his inaugural address on January 20, 1981, Ronald Reagan makes one of the first public references to the Vietnam War. Reagan's wholehearted patriotism helped Americans reassess the conflict and prompted greater acceptance of Vietnam veterans.

To a few of us here today, this is a solemn and most momentous occasion; and yet, in the history of our Nation, it is a commonplace occurrence. The orderly transfer of authority as called for in the Constitution routinely takes place as it has for almost two centuries and few of us stop to think how unique we really are. In the eyes of many in the world, this every-4-year ceremony we accept as normal is nothing less than a miracle. . . .

I am told that tens of thousands of prayer meetings are being held on this day, and for that I am deeply grateful. We are a nation under God, and I believe God intended for us to be free. It would be fitting and good, I think, if on each Inauguration Day in future years it should be declared a day of prayer.

This is the first time in history that this ceremony has been held, as you have been told, on this West Front of the Capitol. Standing here, one faces a magnificent vista, opening up on this city's special beauty and history. At the end of this open mall are those shrines to the giants on whose shoulders we stand.

Directly in front of me, the monument to a monumental man: George Washington, Father of our country. A man of humility who came to greatness reluctantly. He led America out of revolutionary victory into infant nationhood. Off to one side, the stately memorial to Thomas Jefferson. The Declaration of Independence flames with his eloquence.

And then beyond the Reflecting Pool the dignified columns of the Lincoln Memorial. Whoever would understand in his heart the meaning of America will find it in the life of Abraham Lincoln.

Beyond those monuments to heroism is the Potomac River, and on the far shore the sloping hills of Arlington National Cemetery with its row on row of simple white markers bearing crosses or Stars of David. They add up to only a tiny fraction of the price that has been paid for our freedom.

Each one of those markers is a monument to the kinds of hero I spoke of earlier. Their lives ended in places called Belleau Wood, The Argonne, Omaha Beach, Salerno and halfway around the world on Guadalcanal, Tarawa, Pork Chop Hill, the Chosin Reservoir, and in a hundred rice paddies and jungles of a place called Vietnam.

Under one such marker lies a young man—Martin Treptow—who left his job in a small town barber shop in 1917 to go to France with the famed Rainbow Division. There, on the western front, he was killed trying to carry a message between battalions under heavy artillery fire.

We are told that on his body was found a diary. On the flyleaf under the heading, "My Pledge," he had written these words:

"America must win this war. Therefore, I will work, I will save, I will sacrifice, I will endure, I will fight cheerfully and do my utmost, as if the issue of the whole struggle depended on me alone."

The crisis [of inflation and unemployment] we are facing today does not require of us the kind of sacrifice that Martin Treptow and so many thousands of others were called upon to make. It does require, however, our best effort, and our willingness to believe in ourselves and to believe in our capacity to perform great deeds; to believe that together, with God's help, we can and will resolve the problems which now confront us.

And, after all, why shouldn't we believe that? We are Americans. God bless you, and thank you.

Ronald Reagan, "First Inaugural Address, Tuesday, January 20, 1981," *Inaugural Addresses of the Presidents of the United States from George Washington 1789 to George Bush 1989*. Washington, DC: U.S. Government Printing Office, 1989, pp. 331, 336–37.

Glossary

Annam A historical region and former kingdom of east-central Vietnam.

ARVN Abbreviation for Army of the Republic of Vietnam; the regular forces of the South Vietnamese military.

Beijing Capital of Communist China; also known as Peking.

Cochin China A historical region of Indonesia, now most of southern Vietnam.

Cold War State of political tension and military rivalry between nations that stops short of full-scale war.

containment Policy of restraining the expansion of a hostile power or ideology.

Council of National Reconciliation and Concord As provided in the Paris Peace Accords of 1973, a three-party organization intended to organize and help supervise free elections in South Vietnam.

counterinsurgency Political and military strategy intended to oppose and suppress rebellion.

Da Nang Second largest city in South Vietnam and site of the landing of the first U.S. combat troops in 1965.

demilitarized zone (DMZ) Dividing line between North and South Vietnam.

detente Relaxing of tension between nations.

domino theory Theory that if one nation comes under Communist control, then neighboring nations will also come under Communist control.

dove Term applied to persons who vocally opposed the war.

DRV Abbreviation for Democratic Republic of Vietnam, the official name of North Vietnam.

gradualism Lyndon Johnson's policy of slowly escalating the war to intimidate the enemy and motivate him to sue for peace.

Great Society Lyndon Johnson's domestic policy for war on poverty, improving the educational system, providing for elder citizens, and aiding urban areas.

guerrilla Member of an irregular military force operating in small bands in occupied territory to harass and undermine the enemy.

hawk Term applied to those who vocally supported the war.

Hanoi Capital of Vietnam; during the Vietnam War, the capital city of North Vietnam.

Hue Major city and ancient imperial capital of central Vietnam.

Indochina Former French colonial empire in Southeast Asia, which included Vietnam, Cambodia, and Laos.

International Commission for Control and Supervision (ICCS) Supervisory body formed in 1973 to oversee the cease-fire, the withdrawal of U.S. forces, the dismantling of U.S. bases in Vietnam, and the return of POWs.

Joint Chiefs of Staff Military advisory group to the president and secretary of defense; the Joint Chiefs include the army and air force chiefs of staff, the navy's chief of naval operations, and the commandant of the marine corps.

MACV Military Assistance Command/Vietnam; the American military command unit that had responsibility for and authority over all U.S. military activities in Vietnam.

nationalism Devotion to the interests or culture of a particular nation; also aspirations for national independence.

New Left Loosely organized political movement of the 1960s, based on the belief that problems such as economic inequality, racism, and widespread political apathy could be solved if all Americans, not just their elected representatives, decided major economic, political, and social questions.

NLF National Liberation Front; political organization of the Communist-dominated guerrilla forces in South Vietnam.

NVA North Vietnamese Army; officially called the People's Army of Vietnam (PAVN).

Pentagon Headquarters of the Department of Defense; also applied to the Department of Defense itself.

politburo The chief political and executive committee of a Communist party.

RVN Republic of Vietnam. South Vietnam.

Saigon Also known as Ho Chi Minh City; during the Vietnam War, the capital of South Vietnam.

Students for a Democratic Society (SDS) Student organization of the 1960s that fought for racial and economic equality, greater student freedom, and an end to the Vietnam War.

Tet Vietnamese holiday celebrating the lunar new year; a multiday celebration with a focus on family visits and homage to ancestors.

Tonkin A historical region of Southeast Asia, now most of northern Vietnam.

Viet Cong Derogatory name given to South Vietnamese Communist forces supported by North Vietnam.

Viet Minh Contraction of Viet Nam Doc Lap Dong Minh Hoi (League for the Independence of Viet Nam); founded by Ho Chi Minh in 1941, it provided leadership and troops in the struggle against Japanese and French rule in Vietnam.

Vietnamization Term used by Richard M. Nixon to describe the withdrawal of American combat troops and the reliance on South Vietnamese military forces to fight the war.

Wise Men A group of former government officials whom Lyndon Johnson called upon for guidance during his term as president.

Chronology

1862–1893
France gains control over Vietnam, Cambodia, and Laos, creating French Indochina.

1890
May—Ho Chi Minh is born.

1930
October—Ho Chi Minh and other nationalists create the Indochinese Communist Party.

1940
September—Japan occupies French Indochina during World War II.

1941
May—Ho Chi Minh establishes "Viet Nam Doc Lap Dong Minh Hoi" or "Viet Minh" (League for Vietnamese Independence).

1945
September 2—Ho Chi Minh declares Vietnamese independence from France, creating the Democratic Republic of Vietnam (DRV).

1946
November–December—War between the French and the Viet Minh begins in Vietnam.

1947
March—President Harry Truman asks for U.S. aid to Greece and Turkey to combat Communist insurgency; his request is the basis for the Truman Doctrine that guarantees American aid to all countries combating communism.

1950
January—Communist China begins sending military advisers and modern weapons to the Viet Minh including automatic weapons, mortars, howitzers, and trucks; with advisers and equipment,

North Vietnamese general Vo Nguyen Giap transforms his guerrilla fighters into a conventional army.

July—American involvement in Vietnam begins as Truman authorizes $15 million in military aid to the French; in the next four years the United States spends $3 billion and provides 80 percent of the war supplies used by the French.

1953
January 20—Dwight D. Eisenhower is sworn in as the thirty-fourth president of the United States.

1954
May—The French are defeated at the Battle of Dien Bien Phu; France begins to withdraw from Indochina.

June—The Geneva Accords officially end war in Indochina; Vietnam is temporarily divided at the 17th Parallel.

September—The Southeast Asia Treaty Organization (SEATO) is formed by the United States, Great Britain, France, Australia, New Zealand, Pakistan, Thailand, and the Philippines; it is intended to prevent the spread of communism in Southeast Asia and the South Pacific.

1955
October—The Republic of Vietnam (RVN) is established, headed by President Ngo Dinh Diem; Eisenhower pledges to support Diem and offers military aid.

1957
October—Viet Minh guerrillas begin terrorist activities in South Vietnam including bombings and assassinations; by the end of the year, over four hundred South Vietnamese officials have been killed.

1959
May—North Vietnam begins sending men and weapons into South Vietnam via the Ho Chi Minh Trail.

1960
December—The National Liberation Front (NLF), a Communist-sponsored political organization that trains Viet Cong guerrillas, is established in South Vietnam.

1961

January 20—John F. Kennedy is inaugurated as thirty-fifth president of the United States.

May—Vice President Lyndon Johnson visits President Diem in South Vietnam and hails the leader as the "Winston Churchill of Asia."

October—President John F. Kennedy increases military assistance to Diem, including more American advisers and helicopter units to transport and direct South Vietnamese troops in battle; by December, the cost of U.S. involvement in Vietnam has risen to $1 million a day.

1962

February—The Military Assistance Command for Vietnam (MACV) is formed.

1963

November—Ngo Dinh Diem is assassinated on November 2 during a military coup; John F. Kennedy is assassinated on November 22; Lyndon B. Johnson becomes the thirty-sixth president.

1964

August—On August 2, North Vietnam patrol boats attack the *Mattox*, an American destroyer, in the Gulf of Tonkin, leading to retaliatory U.S. air strikes. On August 7, Congress passes the Gulf of Tonkin Resolution giving Johnson the equivalent of war-making powers in Vietnam.

December—Twenty-three thousand American advisers are present in Vietnam.

December 1964–February 1965—Viet Cong launch attacks against American installations in South Vietnam; Johnson orders sustained bombing attacks against North Vietnam, code-named "Rolling Thunder"; scheduled to last eight weeks, it goes on for three years.

1965

March—Thirty-five hundred marines, the first U.S. combat troops, arrive in South Vietnam.

March–May—Antiwar teach-ins occur at several American universities.

July—Johnson announces during a press conference that he is sending forty-four additional combat battalions to South Vietnam.

December—American troop strength in South Vietnam stands at almost two hundred thousand.

1966
December—American troop strength in South Vietnam stands at almost 400,000 with over 5,000 combat deaths and 30,000 wounded.

1967
April—Antiwar demonstrations in San Francisco and New York involve nearly two hundred thousand people; Reverend Martin Luther King Jr. declares that the war is undermining President Johnson's Great Society social reform programs.

November 29—Secretary of Defense Robert McNamara announces his resignation due to disagreements over Johnson's war policies.

December—American troop strength in South Vietnam approaches five hundred thousand.

1968
January–February—South Vietnamese guerrillas and North Vietnamese troops attack one hundred cities and towns throughout South Vietnam in the Tet Offensive.

February—General William Westmoreland requests two hundred thousand additional American troops; his request is denied.

March 16—Hundreds of Vietnamese civilians are killed by American soldiers in the hamlet of My Lai.

March 31—In a message to the nation, Johnson suspends Rolling Thunder, offers to begin peace talks with North Vietnam, and announces that he will not run for a second term as president.

May—Peace talks between the United States and North Vietnam begin in Paris.

July—MACV head General Westmoreland is replaced with General Creighton Abrams.

December—American troop strength in South Vietnam stands at 540,000.

1969

January 20—Richard Nixon is inaugurated as the thirty-seventh president of the United States.

June—Nixon announces the first withdrawal of twenty-five thousand American troops from Vietnam and affirms strategy of Vietnamization.

September 3—Ho Chi Minh dies in Hanoi at the age of seventy-nine.

October 15—The Moratorium peace demonstrations take place nationwide.

November 15—The Mobilization peace demonstration draws 250,000 in Washington and becomes the largest antiwar protest in U.S. history.

November 16—The My Lai massacre, which took place in 1968, is revealed.

December—American troop strength in South Vietnam has been reduced by over fifty thousand; over forty thousand Americans have been killed in the war.

1970

February—U.S. National security adviser Henry Kissinger begins secret negotiations with North Vietnamese representative Le Duc Tho.

April 30—Nixon announces that American and South Vietnamese attacks will take place on enemy sanctuaries in Cambodia; major antiwar protests occur in the United States.

May 4—Ohio National Guard troops kill four student protesters at Kent State University.

June—The Senate repeals the Gulf of Tonkin Resolution; U.S. troops withdraw from Cambodia.

December—Congress passes the Cooper-Church bill, which forbids the use of U.S. ground forces in Laos or Cambodia; American troop strength in South Vietnam stands at 280,000.

1971

June 13—The *New York Times* begins publication of the Pentagon Papers, secret defense documents that reveal previous White

House administration's decisions regarding the Vietnam War.

December—American troop strength in South Vietnam stands at about 150,000.

1972
March—The Easter Offensive against South Vietnam begins; President Nixon orders the mining of North Vietnamese harbors and authorizes a massive bombing campaign in retaliation for the attacks.

December—Peace talks in Paris break down; Nixon again orders massive bombing of North Vietnam; American troop strength in South Vietnam stands at about twenty-four thousand.

1973
January 27—Paris Peace Accords are signed, ending official U.S. involvement in the war.

March 29—The last American combat troops withdraw from Vietnam.

April 30—The Watergate scandal results in the resignations of top Nixon aides H.R. Haldeman and John Erhlichman.

1974
July—House Judiciary Committee votes to recommend three articles of impeachment against Nixon for his role in Watergate.

August 9—Richard Nixon resigns the presidency as a result of Watergate. Vice President Gerald Ford is sworn in as the thirty-eighth president of the United States.

1975
March—North Vietnam launches a long-planned offensive against South Vietnam.

April 30—Saigon falls to the Communists; South Vietnamese president Duong Van Minh broadcasts a message of unconditional surrender; the war is over.

1982
November—Vietnam Veterans Memorial is dedicated in Washington, D.C.

For Further Research

Books

Joseph A. Amter, *Vietnam Verdict: A Citizen's History*. New York: Continuum 1982.

David L. Anderson, *Facing My Lai: Moving Beyond the Massacre*. Lawrence: University Press of Kansas, 1998.

Christian G. Appy, *Working-Class War: American Combat Soldiers and Vietnam*. Chapel Hill: University of North Carolina Press, 1993.

Larry Berman, *Lyndon Johnson's War: The Road to Stalemate in Vietnam*. New York: W.W. Norton, 1989.

Joseph Buttinger, *Vietnam: The Unforgettable Tragedy*. New York: Horizon, 1977.

Phillip B. Davidson, *Vietnam at War: The History 1946–1975*. Novato, CA: Presidio, 1988.

Bernard B. Fall, ed., *Ho Chi Minh on Revolution: Selected Writings, 1920–66*. New York: Frederick A. Praeger, 1967.

David Halberstam, *Ho*. New York: Random House, 1971.

———, *The Making of a Quagmire*. New York: Random House, 1965.

William M. Hammond, *Reporting Vietnam: Media and Military at War*. Lawrence: University Press of Kansas, 1998.

James P. Harrison, *The Endless War: Vietnam's Struggle for Independence*. New York: Columbia University Press, 1989.

George C. Herring, *America's Longest War: The United States and Vietnam, 1950–1975*. New York: McGraw-Hill, 1996.

———, *LBJ and Vietnam: A Different Kind of War*. Austin: University of Texas Press, 1994.

Seymour M. Hersh, *My Lai 4*. New York: Random House, 1970.

Michael H. Hunt, *Lyndon Johnson's War: America's Cold War Crusade in Vietnam, 1945–1968*. New York: Hill and Wang, 1996.

Arnold R. Isaacs, *Vietnam Shadows: The War, Its Ghosts, and Its Legacy*. Baltimore: Johns Hopkins University Press, 1997.

Stanley Karnow, *Vietnam, a History: The First Complete Account of Vietnam at War.* New York: Viking, 1983.

Gabriel Kolko, *Anatomy of a War: Vietnam, the United States, and the Modern Historical Experience.* New York: Pantheon, 1985.

Myra MacPherson, *Long Time Passing: Vietnam and the Haunted Generation.* New York: Doubleday, 1984.

Robert S. McNamara, *In Retrospect.* New York: Random House, 1995.

Wilbur H. Morrison, *The Elephant and the Tiger: The Full Story of the Vietnam War.* New York: Hippocrene, 1990.

Richard Nixon, *No More Vietnams.* New York: Arbor House, 1985.

Don Oberdorfer, *Tet!* New York: Plenum, 1971.

James S. Olson and Randy Roberts, *Where the Domino Fell: America and Vietnam, 1945–1990.* New York: St. Martin's, 1991.

Laura Palmer, *Shrapnel in the Heart: Letters and Remembrances from the Vietnam Veterans Memorial.* New York: Random House, 1987.

Jeffrey Record, *Reporting Vietnam, volume 1 and 2.* New York: Literary Classics of the United States, 1998.

———, *The Wrong War: Why We Lost in Vietnam.* Annapolis, MD: Naval Institute Press, 1998.

Dean Rusk, *As I Saw It.* New York: W.W. Norton, 1990.

Al Santoli, *Everything We Had: An Oral History of the Vietnam War by Thirty-Three American Soldiers Who Fought It.* New York: Ballantine, 1981.

Robert D. Schulzinger, *A Time for War: The United States and Vietnam, 1941–1975.* New York: Oxford University Press, 1997.

D. Michael Shafer, ed., *The Legacy: The Vietnam War in the American Imagination.* Boston: Beacon, 1990.

Neil Sheehan, *A Bright Shining Lie: John Paul Vann and America in Vietnam.* New York: Random House, 1988.

———, *The Pentagon Papers.* New York: Bantam, 1971.

Melvin Small, *Johnson, Nixon, and the Doves.* New Brunswick, NJ: Rutgers University Press, 1988.

Fred Turner, *Echoes of Combat: The Vietnam War in American Memory.* New York: Doubleday, 1996.

William Appleman Williams, ed., *America in Vietnam*. New York: Doubleday, 1985.

Marilyn B. Young, *The Vietnam Wars, 1945–1990*. New York: HarperCollins, 1991.

Periodicals

Philip Caputo, "Running Again—The Last Retreat," *Chicago Tribune*, April 28, 1975.

Peter Goldman, "What Vietnam Did to Us," *Newsweek*, December 14, 1981.

Peter Marin, "Coming to Terms with Vietnam," *Harper's*, December 1980.

Wendell S. Merick, "A Combat General Tells What Vietnam War Is Like," *U.S. News & World Report*, May 22, 1967.

Richard J. Newman, "Vietnam's Forgotten Lessons," *U.S. News & World Report*, May 1, 2000.

Newsweek, "How Solid a Peace?" January 29, 1973.

———, "The Tet Offensive: How They Did It," March 11, 1968.

New York Times, "Dienbienphu Is Lost After 55 Days; No Word of DeCastries and His Men; Dulles Says Unity Can Check Reds," May 8, 1954.

Robert Shaplen, "The Enigma of Ho Chi Minh," *Reporter*, January 27, 1955.

James C. Thomson Jr., "How Could Vietnam Happen?" *Atlantic Monthly*, April 1968.

U.S. News & World Report, "Bigger War for the U.S. in Asia?" August 17, 1964.

———, "Good Times—But People Are Unhappy," May 22, 1967.

———, "Opening a New Front in Vietnam," August 17, 1964.

———, "Why No Declaration of War?" May 22, 1967.

James N. Wallace, "Why U.S. Isn't Winning a 'Little' War," *U.S. News & World Report*, April 1, 1968.

Ronald Yates, "A Time to Wait for Next Rocket," *Chicago Tribune*, April 28, 1975.

Index